ORDERS
TO
KILL

ALSO BY AMY KNIGHT

The KGB: Police and Politics in the Soviet Union

Beria: Stalin's First Lieutenant

Spies Without Cloaks: The KGB's Successors

Who Killed Kirov?: The Kremlin's Greatest Mystery

*How the Cold War Began: The Igor Gouzenko Affair
and the Hunt for Soviet Spies*

ORDERS
TO
KILL

THE PUTIN REGIME AND POLITICAL MURDER

AMY KNIGHT

THOMAS DUNNE BOOKS

ST. MARTIN'S PRESS.

THOMAS DUNNE BOOKS.

An imprint of St. Martin's Press.

ORDERS TO KILL. Copyright © 2017 by Amy Knight. All rights reserved. Printed in the United States of America. For information, address St. Martin's Press, 175 Fifth Avenue, New York, N.Y. 10010.

www.thomasdunnebooks.com

www.stmartins.com

Designed by Omar Chapa

The Library of Congress Cataloging-in-Publication Data is available upon request.

ISBN 978-1-250-11934-6 (hardcover)

ISBN 978-1-250-11935-3 (ebook)

Our books may be purchased in bulk for promotional, educational, or business use. Please contact your local bookseller or the Macmillan Corporate and Premium Sales Department at 1-800-221-7945, extension 5442, or by email at MacmillanSpecialMarkets@macmillan.com.

First Edition: September 2017

10 9 8 7 6 5 4 3 2 1

To Marina Litvinenko, a woman of extraordinary
courage and perseverance

CONTENTS

CONTENTS

Nobody has proven that he's killed anyone. . . . He's always denied it. . . . It has not been proven that he's killed reporters.

—DONALD TRUMP,

speaking about Russian president Vladimir Putin,

December 2015

A dog senses when somebody is afraid of it, and bites. . . . If you become jittery, they will think that they are stronger. Only one thing works in such circumstances—to go on the offensive. You must hit first, and hit so hard that your opponent will not rise to his feet.

—VLADIMIR PUTIN,

First Person: An Astonishingly Frank Self-Portrait

ORDERS
TO
KILL

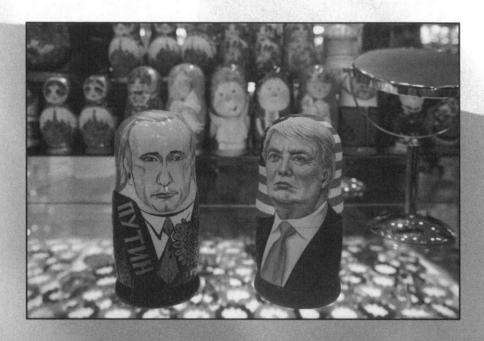

Our two leaders of the Western World.

(Photograph courtesy of Mikhail Pochuyev/TASS)

INTRODUCTION

On February 28, 2015, shortly after I had returned from London, where I attended hearings of the British High Court into the 2006 murder there of ex-KGB officer Alexander Litvinenko, I woke up to terrible news. Late on the previous night, Boris Nemtsov, Russia's leading democratic oppositionist, had been gunned down while walking with his girlfriend on a bridge just minutes from the Kremlin. I'd never met Nemtsov in person, but had had several conversations with him by phone in the spring of 2008, when I was writing an article for *The New York Review of Books* about a groundbreaking report Nemtsov had just published, together with his colleague Vladimir Milov, on the vast corruption of the Putin regime.[1] Nemtsov, who continued to meticulously document claims against Putin in further reports, and traveled to Washington to urge the U.S. Congress to broaden the list of Putin's cronies who were on the U.S. sanctions list because of their human-rights violations and the invasion of Crimea, was my hero and a hero to many others in both Russia and the West. Now he was no more.

When I heard about Nemtsov's murder, I recalled, with a shiver, a visit I'd had with Milov in Moscow in March 2008, when Nemtsov was traveling abroad. Milov explained to me why it was so important for him and Nemtsov to publish their scathing indictment of the Putin regime. They were trying, against seemingly insurmountable odds, to get the truth out about Putin and his allies so that their democratic movement would gain momentum. Milov, a former official in the Russian government, told me that he had heard that their report had created a "hysterical" reaction in the Kremlin and led to urgent high-level meetings. I asked him if he was not worried that he and Nemtsov were in danger. He just laughed and said that if anything happened to them, it would be a huge advertisement for their report. Something did happen. Seven years later, the Kremlin finally got its revenge.

Nemtsov's murder sent shock waves throughout Russia and beyond. U.S. President Barack Obama, who had met Nemtsov in Moscow in 2009, condemned the killing and praised Nemtsov for his defense of human rights and his "courageous dedication to the struggle against corruption in Russia." But Obama unfortunately avoided the fact that Nemtsov's revelations about Russian corruption were directed specifically at Putin and his close cronies, which was probably why he was killed. Obama said that "we call upon the Russian government to conduct a prompt, impartial, and transparent investigation into the circumstances of his murder and ensure that those responsible for this vicious killing are brought to justice." Did he not realize, after more than six years of dealing with the Kremlin, that a transparent investigation of the case was virtually impossible in Putin's Russia?

Many Russia experts, myself included, had already expressed the view that Putin and his colleagues were behind earlier killings of Russian oppositionists and independent journalists who criticized the regime. But the murder of Putin's most outspoken foe on the doorstep of the Kremlin took his galling vengeance against his critics to a whole new level. The Bol'shoi Moskvoretskii Bridge, where Nemtsov was riddled with bullets from a Makarov pistol, was under the extensive surveillance (both by cameras and manned patrols) of Putin's Federal Protective Service (FSO) because of its proximity to the Kremlin. Yet, strangely, the cameras were not working that fateful night and there were no patrols in sight. The killers, Chechens, were rounded up within a few days, but the person who orchestrated the murder has never been identified.

In looking at the Nemtsov killing after decades of studying the Soviet Union and Russia, I was struck by how scary and unpredictable Russia has become, even in comparison with the post-Stalin years, when Khrushchev and then Brezhnev were running the show. Yes, of course the Soviets had a massive nuclear-weapons arsenal (which the Russians still have) and there were dangerous confrontations between the Soviets and the West, most notably over Cuba in 1962 and later in the Middle East in 1967. Using the KGB, the Kremlin was ruthless in its persecution of political critics, throwing them in labor camps after mock trials or in psychiatric institutions. As a student in the Soviet Union in the summer of 1967, I was myself arrested by the KGB for consorting with dissidents and interrogated throughout the night, only to be released the next day after bribing my KGB questioners with Marlboro cigarettes. But Stalin's successors did not, with a few exceptions, resort to killing dissidents; they did not need to.

Things are different now, in many ways. When I was arrested in Kiev, Ukraine was still part of the Soviet Union, and the Kremlin was in control of a vast territory. Now Ukraine has forged its own way as an independent state, along with countries in the Baltic region and states in the Caucasus and Central Asia. The Putin regime does everything it can to maintain Russia's sway over its former empire, but is increasingly threatened by the rise of democracy outside its borders. Indeed, the Kremlin greatly fears the spillover effect from people's revolutions in Georgia and Ukraine. So its modus operandi against opposition in Russia has become a murderous game: make an example of critics by killing them.

The new U.S. president, Donald Trump, has voiced admiration for his Russian counterpart, Vladimir Putin, because, in Trump's view, Putin rules with a strong hand at home and does not hesitate to boldly assert his country's global interests. There is no doubt that Putin wields tremendous political power and that Russia's military assertiveness abroad—in Ukraine, Syria, and elsewhere—has made his country a major player in the global arena after its decline during the Yeltsin era. (This is not to mention Russia's recent use of sophisticated cyberwarfare and disinformation to influence American and European electoral processes, which adds to the picture of Russia's strength as a nation.)

But if one looks below the surface, one sees a different picture. Because of lower oil prices and Western sanctions, Russia's economy is stagnating badly, with real incomes falling and its national debt growing significantly. Corruption, rampant among the Kremlin elite, has resulted in highly publicized scandals, and it may be only a matter of time before ordinary Russians will express resentment over the huge discrepancy between their modest incomes, many below the poverty line, and the vast wealth of Putin and his cronies.

It is important to remember that, unlike Boris Yeltsin, Putin did not achieve the presidency in 2000 on the basis of truly democratic elections. Yeltsin and his inner circle designated Putin as Yeltsin's successor because, as head of the FSB, the Russian Federal Security Service, he was in a position to protect them from charges of corruption once Yeltsin left office. A huge government propaganda machine was put in place, with the help of Russian oligarch Boris Berezovsky and others, to ensure that Putin would become president in elections where no other meaningful candidate was offered.

Thanks to the Kremlin's control of Russia's three main television stations, which is where the majority of the population still gets

its news, Russians continue to be fed a steady stream of anti-Western propaganda, coupled, of course, with constant glorification of Putin. All this has maintained Putin's apparent popularity. But it is far from clear that these efforts will keep simmering discontent from rising to the surface, as it did in 2011–2012, and again in the spring of 2017, when there were mass protests against the Putin regime. The Kremlin wants to avoid a repetition of these events at all costs.

However much Trump admires Putin, the Russian president's hold on power has always been more illusory than real because it is based on the mechanisms that all dictators use to ensure their rule: control of the media, military forays abroad to focus the population away from domestic concerns, elections that exclude democratic challengers, and suppression of internal political opposition. Lacking democratic legitimacy, regimes such as that of Putin are inherently weak and unstable. Nowhere is this weakness more clear than in the Kremlin's use of political murder and terrorism as instruments to maintain its power, which is a subject I have followed closely for many years and is the topic of this book.

Nemtsov's killing was the latest in a long string of political murders that have occurred under Putin. The victims include Kremlin critic and liberal Duma member Galina Starovoitova, shot to death in 1998 (just after Putin became head of the Russian FSB); Paul Klebnikov, the American editor of *Forbes Russia*, assassinated in Moscow in 2004; the courageous journalist Anna Politkovskaya, gunned down in 2006; ex-KGB officer Alexander Litvinenko, poisoned in London a month after Politkovskaya; and numerous other Russian journalists and political activists. (Nemtsov's colleague Vladimir Kara-Murza came close to being on the list of such deaths. He was poisoned in Moscow not long after Nemtsov's murder and barely survived, only to be poisoned yet again in February 2017.)

This is not to mention those who perished in the 1999 apartment

bombings in Russia, which are widely assumed to have been the work of the FSB. Then there is the March 2013 death in London of Russian oligarch Boris Berezovsky, Putin's long-time enemy, which many view as suspicious, and finally the FSB's mysterious behind-the-scenes role in the 2013 Boston Marathon bombings. The unexplained 2012 death in London of Aleksandr Perepilichnyi, a Russian businessman and whistleblower against the Kremlin, may well also be attributed to murder, once the inquest in Britain is completed.

As this book demonstrates, there is a distinct thread that ties these many cases together: the political motives of the Putin government that hover over the killings, and the vast amount of circumstantial evidence that points to Kremlin involvement. I do not claim to have definitive proof of the complicity of Putin and his allies in these crimes. That would be impossible, given that they control the investigations and that there would be no written orders. But the evidence leads us well beyond the premise of some Western observers—that Putin has only "created an environment for the violence" but may not be personally involved. One suspicious murder might be dismissed as coincidence, but these many crimes form a familiar pattern, which has been repeated over and over since Putin arrived in the Kremlin.

The late Harvard historian Franklin Ford observed in his book *Political Murder: From Tyrannicide to Terrorism* that historical truth "is not determined by the institutional requirement that it be announced, flatly, at a given point in time. Instead it is truly the 'daughter of time,' in the sense that it is subject forever to possible revisions in light of new evidence. . . . There may be a temptation to say that because we don't know everything, we really don't know anything— we shall have to wait. That, however, seems irresponsible. . . ."[2] Many of the cases I discuss in this book are ongoing, in the sense that new details are continually emerging. In ten or twenty years, more will be known, but it would indeed be irresponsible not to present the evidence against the Putin regime that is available now and let the reader

judge. There is simply too much at stake—for the families of victims, the Russian people, and the West—to do otherwise.

Some have argued that Putin would not be so reckless as to order these killings, because he has his image to protect. But it has become clear to me that Putin's need to eliminate critics outweighs this consideration, particularly since he always has plausible deniability and the power to have key facts covered up. Also, as I argue in this book, it seems that at some level Putin wants people to suspect Kremlin involvement in these murders as a way to intimidate those who oppose him.

My conclusions lead to larger questions, which are important for the West. What do the political murders tell us about the nature of the Putin regime and its likely future course? Will the killings continue unabated? Or will the Putin regime self-destruct, given its costly military forays abroad, the steep decline in the Russian economy, and the continued revelations of high-level corruption, touching even Putin's closest comrades?

The Pentagon has been sounding the alarm about the Kremlin for several years now, warning that Russia, with its vast nuclear arsenal and its continued aggression beyond its borders, has become a huge threat to the United States and its allies. But state-sponsored political murder is a topic that Western governments have largely chosen to avoid because it raises uncomfortable truths whose implications the West is not ready to confront. How could such killings happen in what the Kremlin calls a "managed democracy," where people are free to engage in private enterprise, travel internationally, and use the Internet? The West badly needs Russia's cooperation in dealing with the Syrian conflict, Ukraine, and Iran. Can Western governments afford to shut Russia out because of its secret, or not-so-secret, political killings?

Writing in the *Wall Street Journal* in January 2017, political commentator Holman Jenkins postulated that "the CIA may . . . be able to tell us more than we already know about many convenient murders and suspicious deaths that greased Mr. Putin's rise and protected him from inopportune disclosures." But, he adds, "Let us stop kidding ourselves. . . . Western governments have kept silent even on the polonium murder in London of dissident Alexander Litvinenko, an act of international nuclear terrorism. Why? Because they are unwilling to press hard on the Putin regime, fearing either blowback or his replacement by the devil they don't know."[3]

Jenkins is all too right. Jenkins is all too right. According to one unnamed U.S. intelligence officer: "The Kremlin has aggressively stepped up its efforts to eliminate and silence its enemies abroad over the past couple of years."[4] Yet, as this book will stress, the White House and its European counterparts have largely turned a blind eye to the evidence of Kremlin complicity in these acts of murder and terrorism, for reasons of expediency. With this thesis in mind, my narrative will follow three interwoven threads: the courageous struggle of Russian independent journalists and politicians to expose the malfeasance of Putin's regime; the Kremlin's largely successful efforts to destroy this opposition through political killings, and to persuade the West that the real threat to Russia is terrorism, which they assert all nations face together; and the continued weak response among Western governments to the evidence that Putin has killed his own people and spread violence to the West. (Despite the overwhelming conclusions of a British High Court in January 2016 that Litvinenko was killed most probably on Kremlin orders, even the British government had a half-hearted reaction to the court's findings. For Russia, there were no consequences.)

The Trump administration is unlikely to change this narrative. Indeed, Trump has stated clearly that he does not believe that Putin commits political murder and has even questioned the Russian role in cyber attacks against the United States. (It is significant that, while members of both the Democratic and Republican parties in Congress voiced outrage about Russian hacking in the 2016 presidential campaign, only a very few, including senators John McCain and Patrick

Leahy, have expressed similar concern about the far more sinister aspect of Putin's rule, political murder.)

Of course, Russia's cyberwarfare, and its efforts to sway Western public opinion with propaganda and false news on the Internet, constitute a threat that needs to be met head-on. But the Kremlin's use of murder against its own people—and its cynical role in terrorist attacks, including the Boston bombings—also has important implications for the West in its dealings with Russia. In short, as this book will demonstrate, Western governments are facing in Russia a truly criminal regime. Acknowledging this publicly and insisting that the Kremlin must stop its use of covert violence should form the basis of all interactions that the U.S. and the rest of the West pursue with Russia.

It should be added that such acknowledgment may give hope to the embattled oppositionists and independent journalists in Russia who continue to make their voices heard. Recall that Western support for dissidents during the late Brezhnev and early Gorbachev years gave Russian democrats huge momentum to dismantle the corrupt and dictatorial Soviet system. Yes, Yeltsin turned out to be an erratic and ineffectual leader, whose commitment to democracy was half-hearted at best. And his political reforms were completely reversed under Putin. But that should not be reason to dismiss the current efforts of Russians who want to transform their government into a democracy.

For the purpose of my narrative, I should clarify what I mean by political murder. Franklin Ford defines the term as "homicide related to the body politic and its governance," including "everything from the most narrowly targeted assassination to random killings designed to intimidate opponents, while calling attention to a given cause."[5] This seems appropriate for the term as I use it here, although I would point out that in the cases of the 1999 attacks in Russia and the Boston Marathon bombings, where victims were killed or injured en masse, the term "political murder," as opposed to "assassination," is synonymous with state-sponsored terrorism.

Trotsky eliminated.

(Photograph courtesy of Eduardo Barraza)

1

COVERT VIOLENCE AS A KREMLIN TRADITION

Maybe all this is just what follows when you keep putting it about that cruelty is a virtue. To be rewarded like any other virtue—with preferment and power. . . . The appetite for death is truly Aztec. Saturnian.

—**Martin Amis, *The Zone of Interest***

Political murder is far from a recent phenomenon in Russia. The brutal killings we have seen under Putin's watch are not at all unique in Russia's long history. This is not to say that Russians are more bloodthirsty than other members of our international community, just that its rulers have for centuries often settled scores with political opponents through violence. In her seminal book *The Russian Syndrome: One Thousand Years of Political Murder,* Hélène Carrère d'Encausse observed: "Eleven centuries of a history notable for its murders make Russia unlike any other country."[1] Carrère d'Encausse goes back to the origins of the Russian state in ninth-century Kievan Rus to demonstrate the relationship between politics and murder that formed a continuous pattern up through the Soviet period. She argues

...t unique historical circumstances, especially the
...r Mongol invasion, resulted in political violence on a
...ssia very different from countries in the West.

...g under the Tsars

Russia's historical destiny was determined to a large extent by the
vastness of its territory and the difficulty its leaders faced in defend-
ing their country's frontiers. The two and a half centuries of Mongol occupation meant that Russia lagged far behind the West in its
political and social development. The systematic use of murder became an essential means through which the tsars maintained their
power. One need only think of the terror and violence that Ivan IV,
known as Ivan the Terrible, imposed on his subjects in the sixteenth
century. And, although Peter the Great is famous for his policies of
modernizing and Westernizing Russia, his reign was also stained with
blood. In 1718, Peter's only son and heir, Aleksei, died under mysterious circumstances while in prison in the Peter and Paul Fortress on
charges of treason. Aleksei, who had temporarily fled Russia to escape his father's tyranny, had reportedly consorted with Peter's enemies both within and outside Russia. As historian James Cracraft
observed: "Peter had proved to be the implacable monarch rather than
a merciful father, determined to brook no threat to his plans nor opposition to his rule, even if it came from his own son. Opponents of
his regime, whether at home or abroad, were given clear warning."[2]
Political opposition was a continuous feature of Peter's regime, and
the tsar used torture and execution to quell revolts. In short, Peter's
reputation for severity was well earned.

It is noteworthy that the two long reigns that followed Peter the
Great—that of Catherine the Great and Alexander I—were the result of regicide. Peter III, husband of Catherine, had only been tsar for
six months before he was murdered in July 1762 and his widow became the empress. The official story was that he died of a "hemor-

rhoidal colic aggravated by a stroke," but rumors abounded that Peter III was the victim of a murder orchestrated by his wife. Even Voltaire, who became Catherine's ardent admirer, acknowledged this: "I know that she has been accused of some little misdemeanors a propos of her husband, but these are family matters that are none of my concern. Besides, it is no bad thing if one has a fault to amend. It causes one to make great efforts to win the public's esteem."[3]

After a long and successful reign, Catherine died in 1796 and her son Paul became tsar. But his rule was short-lived. Paul was brutally murdered in his palace bedchamber by a group of noblemen who objected to the tsar's inconsistent and erratic policies, particularly those relating to international issues. Paul's son Alexander I would face suspicion about his involvement in the murder throughout his reign, with good cause, given that he knew of plans to force his father to abdicate and that violence would be used because Paul would not accede to the demands of his opponents.

It was not until the mid-nineteenth century, with the advent of Alexander II to the throne, that Russia cast off absolutism and the sovereign no longer exercised the power of life and death over his people. Alexander II emancipated the serfs in 1861 and introduced other significant political reforms in 1864 that changed the relationship between ruler and ruled. The political violence during the period of Alexander II and after would come "from below." In 1881, Alexander II was assassinated by members of a terrorist group, the Socialist Revolutionaries. Thirty years later, Pyotr Stolypin, prime minister under Tsar Nicholas II and a forceful advocate of agricultural reform, was shot to death at the Kiev Opera House by a revolutionary anarchist.

In the meantime, a peasant and mystic faith healer named Grigorii Rasputin had ensconced himself in the court and developed a close relationship with the tsar and tsarina. Rasputin was accused in court circles of using his position to influence political decisions and was thought to have actually been planning a conspiracy to get the increasingly weak and ineffective tsar to abdicate in favor of his wife. This set into motion the dramatic murder of Rasputin, who was poisoned and then shot by a group of noblemen in late 1916, the last political murder during the Russian monarchy.

The Bolsheviks Take Over

As it turned out, this brief period where ordinary people could have a say in government, however modest, would not continue. The Bolshevik seizure of power in 1917 resulted in a return to a system in which leaders, first Lenin and then Stalin, subjugated their people brutally. In Carrère d'Encausse's words: "The Soviet leaders gave this violence a dimension that no one could have foreseen, even in science fiction."[4]

Lenin created the notorious Cheka, the secret police, who killed thousands of those who opposed the Bolsheviks, after murdering Tsar Nicholas II and his family. But Stalin, as we know, far surpassed Lenin in ruthlessness toward his countrymen. When we contemplate Stalin's rule, we think of the highly publicized show trials in the late 1930s, executions for "political crimes" in the basement of Lubyanka, the NKVD prison, and mass arrests. Yet Stalin also engaged in covert violence against his perceived enemies—killings by hired assassins, staged automobile accidents, and poisonings. Such murders were useful, not only to get rid of opponents, but also to instill a sense of fear and dread in the ruling elite, who Stalin always felt threatened by.

Sergei Kirov

The first high-profile political murder under Stalin was that of Leningrad party chief Sergei Kirov on December 1, 1934, which historian Robert Conquest called "the murder of the century," because Stalin used Kirov's death as a pretext for launching his Great Terror, the infamous purges that decimated the country's elite. Kirov was shot to death by a lone assassin as he walked down the hall to his office in Leningrad's Smolny Institute. The killer, Leonid Nikolaev, was subsequently executed for the crime.

The Kirov murder has been a subject of controversy among historians ever since Khrushchev, in his speech to the Twenty-second Communist Party Congress in 1961, raised the possibility that Stalin had ordered the crime. He suggested that, after the murder, Kirov's personal bodyguard, Mikhail Borisov, had been "liquidated" while on his way to be interrogated by Stalin as part of a cover-up. (The official story was that Borisov's car had been involved in an accident.) Khrushchev noted that there was "much to be revealed" about the case. In fact, a series of party commissions was created by post-Stalin leaders, including Gorbachev, to look into the Kirov assassination, but they were all inconclusive.

In my book on the Kirov murder, I argue that there is a convincing case against Stalin for several reasons.[5] First, Stalin had clear motives to get rid of Kirov, who was a highly popular leader both in Leningrad and among party stalwarts. At the Seventeenth Communist Party Congress in early 1934, Kirov received a standing ovation for a rousing speech he made, while the applause after Stalin spoke was much less enthusiastic. There was reportedly talk behind the scenes at the congress that it was time for Stalin to step down, and Kirov's name came up as a possible successor.

In the ensuing months, as Russian archives have revealed, there was increasing tension between Stalin and Kirov, who was apparently having doubts about Stalin's harsh domestic policies. And then of course there is the fact that Stalin seized on the murder to initiate his purges, declaring, without an investigation, that the crime was part of a terrorist conspiracy, and arresting two prominent Bolsheviks, Grigorii Zinoviev and Lev Kamenev, for supposedly plotting the murder.

As for the assassin, Nikolaev, he allegedly had personal motives for wanting Kirov dead, and was mentally imbalanced. But it was never explained how he gained access to the heavily guarded Smolny Institute that day, or why Kirov's bodyguard had not been by Kirov's side at the time of the shooting. Suspicions that the NKVD had orchestrated the murder surfaced right away, and NKVD chief Genrikh Yagoda was subsequently accused of ordering the murder, and executed. But it is inconceivable that he would have acted without approval from Stalin, who by 1934 had absolute control over his secret police.

The last party commission to investigate the Kirov murder was established in 1989 under Politburo member Alexander Yakovlev. The commission, which included officials from the office of the Procurator (prosecutor), the KGB, and various archival administrations, concluded after two years that "no materials objectively support Stalin's participation or NKVD participation in the organization and carrying out of Kirov's murder." But Yakovlev dissented. Writing in *Pravda* in December 1990, Yakovlev pointed out that there were many questions left unanswered by the commission's report, including the disappearance of correspondence between Kirov and Stalin before Kirov's death and the unexplained admittance of the killer, Nikolaev, to the Smolny Institute without a special pass. Clearly, members of the commission wanted to whitewash Stalin because the idea that he had ordered the murder would bring into question the entire Soviet past. No one in the party elite was ready for that, even so late in the history of the Soviet state, a short time before its dissolution.

Several observers have pointed out the parallels between the murder of Kirov and that of Boris Nemtsov. As Russia expert Karen Dawisha observed: "In the death of Nemtsov, irrespective of who is ultimately found responsible, we once again have the assassination of a person who could have become the leader of the country."[6] And Russian historian Mikhail Iampolskii raised concerns about how Nemtsov's death might be used by the Kremlin to crackdown on critics: "One cannot exclude the possibility that the execution of

Nemtsov could become for Russia something like the murder of Kirov."[7] While of course the current Putin regime is very different from that of Stalin, one can indeed see eerie echoes of the past in the Nemtsov case, in particular the fact that Putin, like Stalin with Kirov, took direct control of the murder investigation.

Maxim Gorky

There has long been speculation about the death of Maxim Gorky in June 1936. One of Russia's best-known fiction writers, Gorky had initially supported the Bolsheviks in their revolution against the Tsar. But then he became critical of Lenin for his ruthless suppression of opposition. During most of the 1920s Gorky lived in Italy, only returning to stay permanently in Russia in 1932, following a personal invitation from Stalin. Gorky henceforth became an apologist for the Soviet regime, publishing in Russian journals and newspapers article after article filled with sycophantic praise for Stalin and his politics. He played a crucial role in the Kremlin's extensive propaganda machine and, in exchange, was given a mansion in Moscow and a large dacha in the suburbs.

After Kirov's murder, Gorky's relationship with Stalin became increasingly strained. To be sure, Gorky followed the party line on the murder, writing a dutiful article for *Pravda* the day after the killing: "A wonderful person has been killed, one of the best leaders of the Party. . . . The success of the enemy speaks not only to its abomination, but also to the inadequacy of our vigilance."[8] But the subsequent arrests of Zinoviev and Kamenev were troubling to Gorky, because it took Stalin's campaign against "counterrevolutionaries" to a new level. Both men wrote letters appealing to Gorky from prison in the hope that he would intercede with Stalin on their behalf. Gorky never received their letters, but he did pay a visit to Stalin in March 1935, apparently to discuss Kamenev, to whom Gorky was personally close. By this time Gorky himself was being publicly attacked in the press, accused of publishing counterrevolutionary literature (Dostoyevsky) and supporting the "class enemy." In response, Gorky bent over backwards to demonstrate his revolutionary zeal to Stalin in his writings.

But Stalin did not trust Gorky, particularly since Gorky and the prominent Bolshevik Nikolai Bukharin had been touting the idea of a second party, a "union of intellectuals" to participate in politics as a sort of adjunct to the ruling Communist Party. Also, by 1936 Stalin was about to have Zinoviev and Kamenev executed and he could not be sure of what Gorky's reaction would be. In the words of the writer Aleksei Tolstoy, who was a part of Gorky's inner circle: "There was no way to force him to remain silent. To arrest or exile, not to mention shoot him, would have been even less likely. The idea of hastening the liquidation of the sickly Gorky 'without bloodshed' through [NKVD chief] Yagoda had to have been viewed by the host in the Kremlin as the only way out."[9]

Indeed, this is the scenario that Russian historian Arkady Vaksberg, who draws upon archival sources released after the collapse of the Soviet Union, endorses. Gorky reportedly came down with pneumonia after he returned to Moscow from a stay in Crimea in late May 1936, and died on June 18, surrounded by Kremlin doctors who had been trying to save him for days. Vaksberg suggests that Gorky could have recovered had his food not been poisoned by a substance manufactured at a special NKVD laboratory in Moscow.

The Bolsheviks had started to develop poison for the elimination of political enemies at a Moscow toxicological laboratory as far back as 1921 or 1922. In the early 1930s, the laboratory was placed under the supervision of Yagoda and his secret police. Biochemists experimented with poisons on Soviet prisoners in order to devise a substance that could not be detected, even after the victim died.[10] During one of the Moscow purge trials two years after Gorky's death, it was alleged that Yagoda had ordered his killing. Yagoda had been close to both Gorky and his widowed daughter-in-law and almost a daily presence at Gorky's Moscow home, of course reporting back to Stalin. So he was well positioned to orchestrate the poisoning on Stalin's behalf. (As was so often the case, accusations at the infamous purge trials that followed inevitably reflected partial truths.)

As Vaksberg notes, the Kremlin's treatment of Gorky's legacy was a significant sign that he had suffered Stalin's displeasure. Immediately after his death, the Kremlin let it be known that Gorky's memory was not sacrosanct. The three literary journals that had been published under his auspices were shut down and their editorial employees arrested. There were also vendettas against many of the writers who Gorky had supported.

Further Violent Reprisals

Poisoning was part of the initial plan to kill Stalin's archenemy Leon Trotsky, though in the end he was stabbed to death with an ice pick in 1940 at his home in Mexico by a hired assassin named Ramon Mercader. This was an early example of Stalin using his secret police to pursue opponents outside his country's borders. Trotsky, a leading Bolshevik and founder of the Red Army, had been removed from power in 1927 after forming the so-called Left Opposition against Stalin. He was expelled from the Soviet Union in 1929 and ended up in Mexico City, where he continued to write and speak out, as an orthodox Marxist, against Stalinism. Although it was generally assumed that Stalin had ordered the Trotsky murder—Mercader was given a "hero of the Soviet Union" title upon his return to the Soviet Union in 1960 after twenty years in a Mexican jail—it was not until the mid-1990s that this was confirmed by a former NKVD official, Pavel Sudoplatov.[11]

After World War II ended, Stalin let up on his purges, but the knowledge that he could order political murders at will kept his fellow politburo members in constant terror. They knew full well that he resorted to covert methods when he wanted someone eliminated without a fuss. Even Stalin's daughter, Svetlana, was aware of this. She recalled in her memoirs *Only One Year* overhearing a conversation in 1948 in which her father ordered the murder of the prominent Jewish theater director Solomon Mikhoels by staging a traffic accident.[12] (Stalin, who had become a fierce anti-Semite, was later to launch an extensive purge of Jews, starting with doctors accused of medical murder, that only ended because of his death in March 1953.)

Mikhoels was not a political threat to Stalin, but his prominence as a theater figure and his travels abroad, including to the United States, left him vulnerable to Stalin's paranoia about "cosmopolitanism," the dreaded accusation that came to be applied to Jews in the period before Stalin died. In his 2016 novel *The Yid*, Paul Goldberg brilliantly portrays the dark and sinister atmosphere of this time: "At night Moscow is the czardom of black cats and Black Marias [the transport vehicles of the secret police]. The former dart between snow banks in search of mice and companionship. The latter emerge from the improbably tall, castle-like gates of Lubyanka, to return laden with enemies of the people."[13]

Goldberg's imagined story is about a plot to kill Stalin carried out by a small group of Jews, "Yids," who are earmarked for arrest, together with a black American living in the Soviet Union. The group, which includes a former theater actor associated with the director Mikhoels and a Jewish doctor, is able to kill Stalin at his dacha, Kuntsevo, and get away with murdering several police operatives and thugs who stand in their way, because of the lawlessness and fear that permeated the entire system. No one, including those who witnessed crimes, was safe from reprisals by the secret police. So everyone kept quiet, except for covert denunciations of their neighbors and work comrades. And the fact that political murders were covered up by a morass of misinformation makes the author's fictional premise—that Stalin actually died from a lethal injection, not a stroke, as the official version went—seem entirely plausible.

The Post-Stalin Leadership

Stalin's successors for the most part eschewed such violence. The post-Stalin regime was a collective leadership by men who were not inclined to live with the kind of fear that existed under Stalin. They had seen many of their colleagues disappear or be charged with crimes and executed and they wanted a semblance, at least, of security. Yes, they had first to get rid of the dreaded former police chief and fellow politburo member, Lavrenty Beria, who was executed in late 1953 after a faux trial for crimes against the state. After that, however, things settled down.[14] Even Khrushchev, at the end of a bitter power struggle in 1964, was allowed to live peacefully at his dacha to the end of his days.

The conventional wisdom in the West was that conflicts within the Kremlin had disappeared with the advent of Brezhnev, whose regime reflected outwardly a collective leadership that was always in consensus. Kremlinology, the science of deciphering what was really going on in the Soviet leadership, went out of fashion, and when there were signs of differing points of view reflected in the tightly controlled press, they were interpreted by Western analysts as simple policy disagreements. But the Soviet system had no accepted procedure for resolving such disputes and, given the complete absence of democratic elections, no means of deciding who would prevail when it came to appointments in the top leadership other than the machinations among this small, isolated group of men, who ruled from above.

When two Politburo members, Fyodor Kulakov and Pyotr Masherov, died suddenly, some Western experts, myself included, suspected foul play. Kulakov, Central Committee secretary for agriculture (a hugely important portfolio), and a full Politburo member, was sixty when he died of an officially reported heart attack at his home in July 1978. Kulakov was widely thought of as a possible successor to Brezhnev and was a mentor of Mikhail Gorbachev, who was from Kulakov's home region of Stavropol. Given the unusual circumstances that surrounded Kulakov's death—there had been no indications that he was in ill health—rumors that he had either committed suicide or was murdered began to surface.

In fact, there had been numerous signs that Kulakov was in disfavor with the Brezhnev leadership. At a Central Committee plenum earlier that same month, party agricultural policy came under heavy criticism, but Kulakov, as the main party spokesman for agriculture, was absent, although he appeared afterward at other party functions. Amazingly, although protocol dictated that all Politburo members attend Kulakov's funeral and interment in the Kremlin wall, several, including Brezhnev, failed to show up. Perhaps Kulakov's heart attack was a result of the pressure he was under. But his sudden death came at a convenient time for the Soviet leadership, given that Kulakov's political future was already under a cloud.

The circumstances of Masherov's death in a car accident in October 1980 gave observers even more reason to suspect foul play.[15] Masherov, sixty-two at the time, was Communist Party chief in the Belarus Republic and viewed as a promising political leader. He was a candidate (provisional) member of the Politburo and highly popular in Belarus. But his mentor, the former Belarus party chief Kirill Mazurov, had been unceremoniously dismissed from his post as a full member of the Politburo two years earlier after carefully orchestrated criticisms in the press. And many of Mazurov's and Masherov's protégés in the Belarus party apparatus had been replaced by Brezhnev favorites, a sure sign of Masherov's declining influence. Significantly, the long-time head of the KGB in Belarus was suddenly dismissed in August 1980, and the new security chief was an outsider from Moscow.

By the time of his death, Masherov's leadership of Belarus was under heavy criticism in the party press for alleged economic failures as well as for "local patriotism" (too much independence from Moscow). But Masherov fought back, giving a startling interview to

Pravda in June 1980, in which he made a thinly veiled jab at Brezhnev's personality cult: "What is it that sometimes happens? People meet and sit around, but in fact one person speaks and makes decisions. The others merely agree with him. The result is imaginary collective leadership."[16] Masherov's outspoken remarks doubtless incurred Brezhnev's displeasure, to say the least, especially since he had made similar comments in recent speeches to party officials in Belarus.

Masherov's car was allegedly hit by a truck when he was traveling in the countryside outside of the Belarus capital, Minsk, which meant there were no witnesses to confirm the official report. (There was no public mention of what happened to Masherov's driver.) In a surprising break with precedent, not a single member, or candidate member, of the Politburo attended Masherov's funeral and no condolences were printed in *Pravda*, as would have been expected. Had Masherov not conveniently died, it was all but certain that he would have been forced out of his post.

The KGB's Hidden Hand Abroad

There were also assassinations or attempted killings by the KGB beyond Soviet borders. Nikolai Khokhlov was a KGB officer who defected to the United States in 1954 and testified before the U.S. House Un-American Activities Committee about the operations of the KGB. While in Frankfurt, Germany for a speaking engagement in 1957, Khokhlov was poisoned by radioactive thallium, the same substance that would be suspected at first in the 2006 murder in London of former KGB/FSB officer Alexander Litvinenko. Khokhlov became violently ill and almost died, but he survived after being transferred to a U.S. military hospital. Khokhlov later wrote: "I . . . was an exhibit of the achievements of Soviet science. Totally bald, so disfigured by scars and spots that those who had known me did not at first recognize me. . . . I was nevertheless also living proof that Soviet science, the science of killing, is not omnipotent."[17] The Kremlin's message was

simple: defectors from the KGB were traitors and thus subject to retribution no matter where they were.

The KGB also had a role in the killing of Bulgarian dissident and
writer Georgii Markov, an employee of the BBC and a contributor to
Radio Liberty, who was stabbed with a poison-tipped umbrella at a
bus stop near London's Waterloo Bridge in 1978. Markov's critical
reporting on the Bulgarian Communist Party and its leader Todor
Zhivkov made him an enemy of the Bulgarian regime. A letter sent
from the Bulgarian secret services to the KGB in 1975 complained
that he mocked the Communist Party in Bulgaria and encouraged
dissidence in the country. And declassified documents from the Bulgarian secret service files show that its representatives visited Moscow before the murder to discuss the case with technical experts from
the KGB poison laboratory.[18] While the actual perpetrator of the
crime was apparently working for the Bulgarians, the KGB supplied
the poison, ricin, that was injected into Markov. The Soviets controlled all of Eastern Europe, including Bulgaria, at this time, and they
had a strong motive in preventing any dissidence that threatened
their puppet regimes.

After the Soviet Collapse

The post-1991 period, with the dissolution of the Soviet Union and
the presidency of Boris Yeltsin, a self-proclaimed democrat, issued in
a new era, one of political and economic freedom and the hoped-for
rule of law. But Yeltsin, whatever his goals, was not able to make a
smooth transformation from the Soviet system of state control. Yes, he
outlawed the Communist Party and disbanded, with much fanfare,
the KGB. But the remnants of these institutions did not disappear:
they re-emerged in a different guise. And meanwhile, a struggle en-
sued among the newly born capitalists for the spoils of the Soviet
regime. "Mafia" gangs began to appear, along with consequent blood-
letting. Entrepreneurs like Boris Berezovsky and Mikhail Khodor-

kovsky had to hire around-the-clock bodyguards. In fact, Vladimir Gusinsky, head of Most Bank and NTV, reportedly had a private security service that numbered a thousand men, many of whom were former KGB officers. Moscow and other cities in Russia became a free-for-all, with constant reports of murders or assassination attempts. Berezovsky himself was seriously wounded in June 1994 when a bomb was detonated in Moscow as his car drove by. (His driver was decapitated.) But these were not political murders. They were crimes that aimed at settling financial scores, although former or current employees of the security police were usually involved.

In October 1994, a journalist named Dmitry Kholodov opened a booby-trapped briefcase in his office at the newspaper *Moskovskii komsomolets* and was blown up. Kholodov had been working on a story about corruption at high levels in the Russian armed forces, touching even the Minister of Defense, Pavel Grachev, and was due to testify about the allegations before the Russian parliament. His editors at the paper suspected that Grachev was behind the murder, but, despite two trials, no one was ever convicted.

Then in March 1995 a murder occurred that shook Russia to its core: Vladislav Listev, one of Russia's most popular television commentators, was gunned down in the stairway of his Moscow apartment building. Listev had just been made director general of the Russian television channel ORT and had announced a general moratorium on advertising, which meant cutting out middlemen from this lucrative business. These men included Boris Berezovsky, a major shareholder. Berezovsky was one of the initial suspects in the killing, and he came close to being arrested. But he managed, in a desperate gambit, to gather political supporters and convince Yeltsin of his innocence, sending the president a long videotaped message in his defense.

In the end, as Paul Klebnikov noted in his 2000 book about Berezovsky, *Godfather of the Kremlin*, the investigation of Listev's murder was a farce. The killers were never found.[19] (As mentioned, Klebnikov himself became the tragic victim of an assassination in Moscow in 2004.) This was to mark the beginning of a pattern of unsolved murders. Russian authorities had the formidable power of a massive and sophisticated system of law enforcement. But the Kremlin had no will to pursue these cases, and in some cases actually had reasons to obstruct investigations. Yeltsin says in passing in his memoirs *Midnight Diaries*: "I was concerned that year in and year out these murders remained unsolved."[20] In fact, he was concerned mostly with enriching himself financially and staying in power.

Enter Vladimir Putin

The murders formed a backdrop for Vladimir Putin's emergence as an important figure in Moscow's power hierarchy. At the time of the Listev affair, Putin, a former KGB officer, was a deputy to St. Petersburg mayor Anatoly Sobchak and chairman of the Committee for Foreign Liaison, which governed the city's foreign trade. According to Karen Dawisha, author of *Putin's Kleptocracy*, Putin used his position for his personal financial gain, as did Sobchak and Putin's friends from the KGB. He routinely engaged in bribe taking, money laundering, and kickbacks for contracts awarded non-competitively. Both he and Sobchak were subjects of investigations by prosecutorial bodies in St. Petersburg and Moscow.[21]

After Sobchak was defeated in the May 1996 mayoral election by Vladimir Yakovlev, Putin needed to get out of St. Petersburg fast. Having made entreaties to people he knew in Moscow, he managed to obtain a position in the Kremlin as deputy head of the Presidential Property Management Department. In this capacity, Putin was responsible for Kremlin property abroad, which had earlier belonged to the Soviet Communist Party and was worth billions. In Dawisha's words: "property abroad was very thoroughly plucked before the state got its hands on it. And it was [Putin] who did the plucking."[22]

Putin had a keen sense of where he needed to be to get ahead in the tumultuous Yeltsin years and was skilled at self-promotion. In 1997, he moved to the Kremlin's Main Control Directorate, responsible for the implementation of federal laws and executive orders and also the use of budget resources by various Russian regional governments. This meant that he was in charge of the files of those in St. Petersburg who had been investigating his and Sobchak's earlier illegal activities in the city. Just as Sobchak was about to be arrested, Putin used his position to fly him out of the country secretly.

After a brief stint as first deputy chief of staff under Yeltsin in the spring of 1998, Putin received a further promotion. He was appointed chief of the FSB in July, replacing Nikolai Kovalev, who reportedly was dismissed because of the operations of the FSB's Directorate for Combating the Activities of Organized Criminal Groups (URPO). This directorate had been implicated in graft and in extrajudicial killings.

It is not clear why Putin was chosen for the FSB leadership, given that his KGB career had been undistinguished. According to two Russian historians, Yuri Felshtinsky and Vladimir Pribylovsky, his appointment did not go down well with staff employees: "He was merely a lieutenant colonel. In a military organization, where people took such things seriously, Putin's military rank could not be mentioned without either amusement or resentment. The nature of Putin's former work at the KGB was also cause for derision. Putin had worked in East Germany, where foreign intelligence employed its flunkies."[23]

Boris Nemtsov, a member of Yeltsin's government at the time, recalled: "No one knew who Putin was. He was so unremarkable that no one reacted to him, even my secretary." When Putin called Nemtsov's office on one occasion, his secretary kept Putin waiting on the line and told Nemtsov: "Someone named Putin is calling. He says he is the chief of the FSB. What should I do with him?"[24]

It was apparently because Putin was not well connected to the central FSB leadership that Yeltsin's inner circle chose him for the job. He would be loyal to Yeltsin, not to Lubyanka (FSB headquarters). Putin set about immediately to purge many of the higher FSB command and to replace them with his old KGB colleagues from St. Petersburg. He also engineered the ouster of Procurator-General Iurii Skuratov, who was cooperating with Swiss authorities in a criminal investigation of the Presidential Property Management Department, which had siphoned off millions of dollars in the making of contracts to renovate the Kremlin and deposited the money in bank accounts for Yeltsin and his family in Switzerland. Putin's agents videotaped Skuratov (or someone resembling him) engaged in sex with two call girls, and then Putin, on behalf of Yeltsin, demanded Skuratov's resignation. After Skuratov refused, the video was shown on Russian television. He was forced to resign, and the corruption investigation involving Yeltsin was called off.

Meanwhile, by the summer of 1999, Yeltsin's presidency was under siege. The Duma, led by the Communists, was preparing impeachment proceedings against him, and his public approval rating—thanks to the botched 1994–96 war in Chechnya, Russia's 1998 economic crisis, and Yeltsin's increasingly capricious style of governance—had plummeted. Yeltsin's abrupt dismissal of his popular prime minister, Evgenii Primakov, in May 1999 raised a further outcry against him.

Putin became more and more essential to Yeltsin and the "family" of supporters that surrounded him in the Kremlin. Yeltsin had unexpectedly appointed Putin head of the Security Council at the end of March and was entrusting him with the volatile situation in the North Caucasus, where bombings and kidnappings were occurring with increasing frequency. The Yeltsin team was even considering emergency rule in order to stave off an electoral defeat of his political party, Unity, by the Fatherland-All-Russia party, which Primakov led, along with Moscow mayor Iurii Luzhkov. It was in these crisis circumstances that, on August 9, 1999, Yeltsin appointed Putin prime minister and thus his designated successor as president. In a televised speech, Yeltsin had words of praise for Putin: "I have decided to now to name the person who is, in my opinion, able to consolidate society and, drawing support from broadest political forces, to ensure the continuation of reforms in Russia. . . . I have confidence in him."[25]

It is sadly ironic that Paul Klebnikov had a similarly favorable impression of Putin when the latter became Yeltsin's heir apparent. In response to suggestions that Putin was behind the September 1999 bombings in Russia, Klebnikov observed: "There is nothing in the man's past to indicate that he would commit such a monstrous crime to gain power. On the contrary, Putin's past career betrays an unusual dedication to a fixed code of conduct (albeit an authoritarian one); there is nothing to suggest the bottomless cynicism necessary to massacre one's own people to promote one's career."[26] If Klebnikov had lived to witness the next decade of Putin's rule, he would perhaps have taken back those words.

Putin and FSB Chief Bortnikov.

(Photograph courtesy of Yuri Kadobnov/AFP/Getty Images)

2

HOW THE SYSTEM WORKS: PUTIN AND HIS SECURITY SERVICES

Our best colleagues, the honor and pride of the FSB, don't do their work for the money . . . there is one very special characteristic that unites all these people, and it is a very important quality: it is their sense of service. They are, if you like, our new nobility.

—FSB Chief Nikolai Patrushev, in a speech to his agency, December 2000.

There's no super-repressive regime. There are no mythical Cheka agents that we need to be scared of. It's just a bunch of crooks.

—Russian anti-corruption blogger Aleksei Navalny, 2011

Russia under Putin has been variously described as a "managed democracy" (early on in Putin's tenure as president), an "authoritarian state" (somewhat later), and, more recently, a "kleptocracy." But the most accurate term for today's Russia is "police state." American political scientist Brian Taylor observed in his book *State Building in*

Putin's Russia: "the term 'police state' resonates because state power, as the sociologist Max Weber recognized, ultimately rests on the ability to coerce. The behavior of its coercive organizations, such as the military, the police and the secret police, tells us much about the character of a state. . . . "[1] Russia is run by police and security officials who are above the law and report only to President Vladimir Putin, himself a former secret police officer. (The Russian military tends, by tradition, to stay out of politics.) These officials have, for the most part, not reached their positions because of objective qualifications, such as education and experience, but because of personal and family connections—Putin's version of what was in Soviet days called a patronage network. As journalist Masha Lipman expressed it back in 2002, Putin "staffed his government structures with numerous mediocrities, people with no record of achievement and no vision of the task that had suddenly befallen them. Their only 'merit' was their loyalty and their origin in Putin's home base, St. Petersburg."[2]

After the Soviet Union collapsed in 1991, Russian President Boris Yeltsin had the KGB dismantled and created several separate agencies to replace it, with the idea that the powers of the security police would be diminished and democratic freedoms protected. But that is far from how things worked out. Early on in his tenure as president, Yeltsin, an impulsive, erratic leader, whose commitment to democracy was half-hearted, faced popular opposition and thus needed the police and security organs to keep him in power. So he systemically rebuilt these agencies and gave them more and more authority and resources.[3] By the time Vladimir Putin became Russian president in 2000, the security services had become every bit as powerful as the former KGB.

The *Siloviki*

Putin's so-called *siloviki*, the men who run the "power ministries," in particular the police and security agencies, share core beliefs and values. They are no longer motivated by Communist ideology, although most are former members of the Communist Party. But they believe in economic nationalism, a centralized, authoritarian government, and the restoration of the supposed greatness of the Soviet Union. They share a common nostalgia, with Putin, for the Soviet era, when the Russian empire encompassed the republics of Central Asia, the Caucasus, Ukraine, and the Baltics, and Moscow had firm control over the countries of Eastern Europe. Like Putin, the siloviki have a deep fear of democratic movements near their borders, such as in Ukraine, where they see events there as inspired by the West in order to undermine the Russian government. And they are wary of the Internet, which is now accessible to over seventy percent of the adult Russian population. Putin said famously at a media forum in April 2014: "You do know that it all began initially, when the Internet first appeared, as a special CIA project. And this is the way it is developing."[4]

But the siloviki are not immune to the attractions of Western capitalism, even though, unlike the high-profile Russian oligarchs, they are civil servants. They all engage in business on the side—timber, steel, gas and oil, airlines, or banking—enriching themselves bountifully from privileged, non-competitive state contracts, and using family members as repositories for illicit income that often comes from government coffers. (The security services also make vast sums of money offering protection—a so-called *krysha*, or "cover"—on the side, to Russian businesses.)

Before Western sanctions against many of the siloviki went into place in 2014, they skied in Switzerland, sunbathed on the Spanish and French Rivieras, and built lavish villas in Greece. They sent their children to exclusive schools in the West for their education. (The current Russian Foreign Minister, Sergei Lavrov, not a siloviki per se but part of its cult, and a virulent critic of Western values, sent his daughter to study at the London School of Economics.)[5] Sanctions imposed since the invasion of Crimea have made a dent in the lifestyles of the siloviki, but they still have their mansions in the Moscow sub-urbs. And, although they can no longer enjoy cheeses from the European continent (banned by Russia), they can still savor their cherished French wines, albeit at very high prices, given the huge decline in the value of the ruble.

The siloviki play by their own rules, which include lying about their academic credentials. Aside from loyalty to Putin, a key to success in gaining a high government post in the Russian legal and security field is to obtain a doctorate, as Putin did. In the words of Russian blogger Sergei Parkhomenko, "there is a general rule: if you want to be the head of something—get a candidate or doctors' [de-gree]." Parkhomenko, part of a group of online activists called "disser-net," did a painstaking study of dissertations of the chieftains of Russian law enforcement and found that most had been, like Putin's, blatantly plagiarized. In the case of MVD chief Vladimir Kolokoltsev and for-mer drug czar Viktor Ivanov, there was even "cross-dissemination": the two copied extensively from each others' dissertations, which were already plagiarized![6]

To be sure, there has been infighting among the siloviki, with clans emerging, as so often happens in mafia-style politics. The fac-tions center around the different security and intelligence services, state-owned corporations, and family ties. (There is a remarkable amount of intermarriage among adult children of the siloviki, remi-niscent of the Stalin era.) But for the most part the siloviki present a united front to the public. They cannot afford to do otherwise, if they want to maintain their wealth and their powerful positions. They are all complicit in the unsavory business of political murder, either as perpetrators of these crimes on Putin's behalf, or as the os-tensible investigators. Who are these men and what are the institutions they represent?

The FSB

The *Federal'naia sluzhba bezopasnosti* (Federal Security Service), the most powerful of Russia's security agencies, was established in 1995, after various reorganizations of the old KGB. Although the foreign intelligence service and the government guard agency are not under the FSB, as was the case with the KGB, the FSB is by law authorized to conduct its own intelligence operations both at home and abroad, which has opened up a whole range of opportunities. It is a formidable organization, numbering an estimated 350,000 employees. Its functions include counterintelligence, counterterrorism, combating economic crimes, guarding the borders, protecting government communications, and ensuring the security of nuclear materials and installations. In the words of Russian security experts Andrei Soldatov and Irina Borogan: "Rather than a revival of the Soviet KGB, the FSB had evolved into something more powerful and more frightening, an agency whose scope, under the aegis of a veteran KGB officer, extended well beyond the bounds of its predecessor."[7] In Soviet days, the KGB was controlled by the Politburo and did not take important initiatives without the concurrence of this Communist Party leadership body. Now there are no formal mechanisms of control over the FSB, except Putin and his closest allies.

The FSB has extensive powers of surveillance, including that of the Internet, that far surpass those of similar agencies in the West. According to Soldatov and Borogan, the FSB, through a special system called SORM, monitors "emails, Internet usage, Skype, cell phone calls, text messages and social networks. It [SORM] is one of the world's most intrusive listening devices."[8] In 2014, the Russian parliament passed a law requiring social media websites to keep their servers in Russia and hold data on users for six months. Security authorities also use a broad interpretation of the "anti-extremism" laws to block websites at their will. This became especially noticeable after democratic opposition protests erupted in Russia in 2011–12.

More recently, in November 2016, Russian authorities blocked the professional networking site Linkedin, because it did not transfer user data to servers in Russia. And in April 2017, apparently partly in response to the widespread street protests at this time, the Kremlin shut down Zello, an app with 400,000 followers that has been instrumental in organizing Russia's truckers. The FSB is also proposing changes to the Russian Criminal Code that would introduce harsh sentences for "causing damage to or threatening the critical information infrastructure of the Russian Federation," i.e. the internet. This new law would be another weapon in the FSB's arsenal as it tries to rein in the internet.[9]

Nikolai Patrushev

A prominent member of Putin's patronage network is Nikolai Patrushev, the president's closest ally, aside perhaps from Igor Sechin—who is a former deputy prime minister and now the CEO of Rosneft, the Russian state petroleum company—and Viktor Zolotov, the head of the recently created National Guard. Patrushev was FSB chief from 1999 to 2008 and since then has been head of the president's Security Council. Putin consults him on all key issues, and Patrushev has a loyal deputy, Aleksandr Bortnikov, in charge of the FSB, so we can assume he still has considerable control over the agency.

The ties between Patrushev and Putin go back to their days together in the St. Petersburg (then Leningrad) KGB during the 1970s. Putin himself acknowledged their deep friendship in his autobiographical book, *First Person*, noting that "Kolya" [diminutive for Nikolai] was one of the people whom he especially trusted. On December 31, 1999, just after Yeltsin announced his resignation and the appointment of Putin to be temporary president, Putin and Patrushev, who had replaced Putin as FSB chief in August of that year, flew by helicopter with their wives on a surprise visit to Chechnya, where a war against the republic was being waged. Putin's now ex-wife, Ly-

udmila, recalled that they celebrated together en route by drinking champagne straight from the bottle.[10] It was a defining moment, marking the beginning of Putin's and Patrushev's collaborative effort to make Putin the undisputed leader of Russia for years to come. There would be obstacles along the way, but they would be surmounted.

Patrushev was born in Leningrad in 1951, the son of a captain in the Russian navy. He graduated from the Leningrad Shipbuilding Institute in 1974 and worked briefly as an engineer before joining the Leningrad branch of the KGB that same year, working in counterintelligence along with Putin. Patrushev's immediate KGB boss during the 1980s was Oleg Kalugin, who in 1995 would defect to the United States. Kalugin described Patrushev as "energetic, purposeful, and ambitious," and they got on well. The two went hunting together, and Kalugin was impressed that Patrushev was a "modern kind of guy" who liked to read and enjoyed music. But Patrushev was ruthless when it came to dissidents, coming up with schemes for the KGB to entrap them and put them behind bars for speaking out about the failings of the Soviet regime.[11]

In 1990, after Kalugin himself started to become a "dissident" and criticized the Communist party leadership, Patrushev, as his protégé of sorts, was shunted off to the KGB in the republic of Karelia, which borders the Leningrad District. He managed to become head of the security organs there in 1992, and in the meantime promoted commercial interests between Karelia and private St. Petersburg firms owned by members of the security services. (As stated, the involvement of the KGB and its successors in business ventures, usually corrupt, has been a constant theme in post-Soviet Russia.) At some point, prosecutors in Karelia reportedly opened an investigation of Patrushev for illegal commerce involving rare Karelian birch trees, but the case was later dropped.[12]

After his stint in Karelia, Patrushev moved to Moscow in 1994, where he worked in various departments of the KGB's successor

agencies (the FSK and then the FSB). He followed in the footsteps of his friend Putin, succeeding Putin as head of the Main Control Administration of President Yeltsin in May 1998 and then becoming Putin's deputy in the FSB before taking his place as FSB chief.[13] From the moment he became FSB chief, Patrushev voiced publicly, like Putin, a deep distrust of the West, repeatedly accusing Western governments of plans to undermine Russia's political stability.

Patrushev and Terrorism

Patrushev's nine-year tenure as head of the FSB was marked by continued devastating terrorist attacks in Russia. First and foremost were the September 1999 apartment bombings. These were followed by the October 2002 attack at Moscow's Dubrovka Theater, in which 130 hostages perished; the September 2004 siege at a school in Beslan, North Ossestia, where 331 victims died, many of them children; and several other incidents. As Soldatov and Borogan observed in regard to the Dubrovka tragedy: "the operation illustrated the security services' frightening lack of preparedness for a grave hostage situation. . . . Even when armed to handle the threat of terrorism, the FSB had mounted an ill-coordinated operation and managed to bungle it."[14] Yet Patrushev was never held accountable. He received award after award from the Russian state, including, after Dubrovka, the country's highest honor—Hero of the Russian Federation.

In early 2006, when Putin ordered the creation of a new counterterrorism committee [*Natsional'nyi antiterroristicheskii komitet*, or NAK] to coordinate all federal-level antiterrorism policies and operations, he appointed Patrushev to be its chief. The committee was given sweeping powers to combat terrorism, and the FSB would run the show. Viktor Ilyukhin, a Duma deputy from the Communist Party, was among those critical of the new committee, complaining that it conferred so much power on the FSB that the security agency would become "a state within a state and a substitute for state functions and

prerogatives."[15] These words were prophetic. "Terrorism" would become the Kremlin's label for many forms of political opposition.

As part of the Kremlin's effort to strengthen anti-terrorist capabilities, a new piece of legislation was passed by the Russian parliament in February 2006 and signed into law by Putin that March. The law on anti-terrorism was a milestone in the Kremlin's efforts to fight its enemies because it authorized the FSB to hunt down and kill alleged terrorists on foreign soil. Then, in July 2006, an amendment to the existing law on "extremism" was passed, expanding the list of crimes that would fall into this category, which included acts of terrorism. As British Professor Robert Service observed: "The door was left open to brand a large swathe of opponents of Putin and his administration as extremists who needed to be eliminated. And terrorism and extremism were frequently mentioned in the same breath by Putin and his ministers. There was little attempt to make an official distinction between the two phenomena that the legislation was directed against. To that extent, there was an implicit licensing package for FSB operations abroad, as well as in Russia."[16]

Patrushev Moves On

Meanwhile, there was a slight glitch in Patrushev's otherwise successful career when he became embroiled in a conflict with another Putin crony from the St. Petersburg KGB, Viktor Cherkesov. Cherkesov had served as a first deputy director of the FSB and since 2003 had been chief of the Federal Anti-Drug Agency, known by the acronym FSNK. He was reportedly encouraging an investigation by the Procurator's office into corruption and money laundering within the upper echelons of the FSB (the so-called Three Whales scandal), which resulted in several arrests in the summer of 2006, while Patrushev was on vacation. Patrushev was later able to retaliate and have the investigation dropped, but the conflict spilled out publicly when Cherkesov, after his right-hand man in FSNK was arrested by the FSB, published an impassioned article in the Russian daily *Kommersant* in October 2007, warning that internal conflict within the security services could undermine the entire political system.[17] Cherkesov lost his job a few months later.

Perhaps because of the conflict with Cherkesov, Patrushev was transferred from his FSB post in 2008 to that of secretary of the Security Council, where he remains to this day and plays a key role in formulating both Russia's foreign and domestic policies. He also has become a very rich man, despite the fact that his income is officially that of a civil servant. The Fund Against Corruption, run by democratic activist Aleksei Navalny, reported in 2014 that the mansion owned by Patrushev and his wife in an exclusive area outside Moscow was valued at over a billion rubles.[18]

In today's Russia, children of those in political power are ensured upward career paths. Thus, in 2010, Patrushev's older son, Dmitrii, a graduate of the FSB Academy, became, at age thirty-three, the head of the state-owned Russian Agricultural Bank (*Rosselkhozbank*), the third largest bank in Russia. According to the daily *Kommersant,* the net loss for the Russian Agricultural Bank in 2015 alone was a staggering 72.6 billion rubles. The bank has had to ask for constant replenishments of its capital from the coffers of Russian reserve funds. Critics have claimed that the bank is financing loans to firms owned by members of the Patrushev family, including the senior Patrushev's nephew Aleksei.[19]

Patrushev's younger son, Andrei, after also graduating from the FSB Academy and serving in the economic security division of the FSB, became in 2006, at age twenty-five, a full-time adviser to Rosneft chairman Igor Sechin. The next year, President Putin awarded Andrei Patrushev the Order of Honor for "achievements and many years of conscientious work," although it is not clear what exactly the young Patrushev had done to earn such accolades. By 2013, Andrei's career had reached astounding heights: he became a deputy general director of the state monopoly Gazprom.[20] His father's long-time alliance with Putin has clearly paid off.

Aleksandr Bortnikov

Aleksandr Bortnikov, the current FSB chief, is another *Piterskii* (from Putin's St. Petersburg KGB clan). A year older than Putin, he joined the KGB in 1975, after graduating from the Leningrad Institute of Railway Engineers. Bortnikov is a direct protégé of Putin and Patrushev and part of the clique that includes Sechin and Viktor Ivanov, a former KGB officer who until 2016 headed the anti-drug agency. When the above-mentioned corruption scandal hit the FSB in 2006, there was a sweeping purge of officials working with Bortnikov, but he managed to emerge unscathed and replace his boss, Patrushev, two years later.

Bortnikov also escaped repercussions from another scandal. When he was head of the FSB's Department for Economic Security, he was being investigated in 2006 by the Ministry of Internal Affairs (MVD) for his part in overseeing the flow of billions of dollars that were being laundered by people close to the Kremlin's oil and gas companies through the bank MKB Diskont and sent abroad. As will be discussed later, Andrei Kozlov, first deputy chief at Russia's Central Bank, was assisting in the investigation when he was shot dead in Moscow in September 2006. The Procuracy shortly afterwards closed the investigation.[21] Meanwhile, Bortnikov maintains his connections with the banking community. His son Denis is chairman of the board of the bank VTB Severo-Zapad (VTB Bank North-West.).

In February 2015, Bortnikov visited Washington, D.C. to attend a world summit on violent extremism, and while there he stressed the need for cooperation with the American special services in the fight against terrorism. His visit came as a surprise to some, given that, as the *Washington Post* pointed out at the time, the FSB's human-rights abuses in the North Caucasus were fueling the problem of extremism: "Having Bortnikov attend the summit is like inviting the fox into the chicken coop."[22] Indeed, Bortnikov, as one of Putin's top advisers and a very hawkish one at that, should have been on the U.S. sanctions list because of the case of Sergei Magnitsky, a lawyer and whistleblower who died in a Russian prison in 2009, and for the Russian occupation of Crimea in 2014.[23] A clear purpose of Bortnikov's visit was to convince the West that Russia faces its own Muslim terrorist threat from the North Caucasus and ISIS, and thus to draw attention away from the FSB's human-rights abuses in Chechnya and elsewhere.

The MVD

The Ministry of Internal Affairs (*Ministertsvo vnutrennykh del,* MVD) is another key security agency, responsible for regular policing, organized crime, and counterterrorism. It is authorized to conduct criminal investigations and had, until recently, around 1,200,000 employees, including 200,000 internal troops, which played a key role, along with the FSB, in subduing Chechnya and other areas of the North Caucasus.[24] From 2003 to 2012, the MVD was headed by Rashid Nurgaliev, a Putin–Patrushev protégé who had served in the KGB/FSB in Karelia and was considered a Piterskii.

Nurgaliev became extremely unpopular because of his failure to stem rampant corruption and the brutal methods of his police. According to the newspaper *Moskovskii komsomolets*, during Nurgaliev's tenure as MVD chief corruption within the agency itself reached shocking proportions and involved all ranks of police officers. Nurgaliev even acknowledged this, saying "behind my very back there was bribery, abuse of authority, corruption."[25] In 2012 he was finally dismissed from his post. But, of course, as a Putin favorite, he did not go away. (Nurgaliev was sanctioned by the EU and Canada, in 2014, but not by the U.S.) Instead, he became a deputy to Patrushev in the Security Council. After Nurgaliev's departure from the MVD, *Forbes* Russia observed: "In all fairness, the chances of success for any Minister of Internal Affairs have been small. . . . The level of corruption, the practice of violence and impunity in the system is so high that national level scandals involving police have been a feature of the times."[26]

Nurgaliev's replacement, former Moscow police chief Vladimir Kolokoltsev, is not a Piterskii. Born in 1961 in the city of Perm, Kolokoltsev is a career police official, having worked mainly in the Moscow city and district offices, where he specialized in criminal investigations, including murder. Once he was appointed Minister of Internal Affairs, Kolokoltsev started an immediate purge in the upper levels of the MVD bureaucracy, firing three deputy ministers and others with connections to Nurgaliev and the FSB. But given the sheer level of corruption in the government and within the MVD itself, Kolokoltsev has not made much of an impact.

In May 2014, Putin appointed his former long-time bodyguard, Viktor Zolotov, who had moved to the MVD a year earlier, first deputy of the MVD in charge of internal troops. This assignment was a crucial one, especially because within these troops is an elite special division that is stationed in Moscow. Putin clearly wants men he trusts in place in the event of popular unrest. But then Putin upped the ante: as part of a sweeping new reform, he appointed Zolotov head of a powerful new National Guard, established in April 2016. (See below.)

The Procuracy and the Investigative Committee

The Procuracy, or Procurator-General's office, was, until 2007, a law enforcement body that rivaled the FSB. Its main responsibility was to ensure observance of the law within the government bureaucracy and to initiate and direct criminal investigations. Apparently, partly, as a result of the conflict between Pastrushev and Cherkesov, in which the then Procurator-General, Vladimir Ustinov, took sides with Cherkesov, President Putin decided that the Procuracy was too powerful. In the words of political analyst Dmitry Oreshkin: "It was too large a center of influence. It had judicial authority, police authority, and

most importantly it had the ability to reveal compromising information about the most important officials in the Russian Federation."[27]
So in 2007 Putin stripped the Procuracy of its investigative function
and created a separate investigative committee that was attached to
the Procuracy but operated independently.

The new committee took under its control sixty thousand criminal cases, including investigations of high-profile murders like those
of Anna Politkovskaya and Alexander Litvinenko. In early 2011, the
Investigative Committee (*Sledstvennyi komitet*, or SK) was officially
made an independent agency, no longer even nominally attached to
the Procuracy and reporting directly to the Russian president.[28] It has
branches in districts throughout the country. The creation of this
powerful committee was a stark and ominous reminder that Vladimir Putin wanted direct control over key criminal investigations.
Most recently, the SK has overseen the investigation of the murder of
Boris Nemtsov. The case has not been resolved to this date, according
to many observers, including the lawyer for the Nemtsov family,
because the SK is deliberately obstructing the process.

Aleksandr Bastrykin

At the head of the Investigative Committee staff of over twenty
thousand is Aleksandr Bastrykin, who had run the earlier committee. Bastrykin was a fellow law student with Putin at Leningrad State
University in the 1970s, as well as having been a local leader of the
Komsomol, the Communist youth league. He is a protégé of both Putin and his éminence grise, Igor Sechin. Following the collapse of the
Soviet Union, Bastrykin served first as rector of the St. Petersburg
Law Institute and later in various posts in the Ministry of Justice and
the MVD. In 2006, he became a deputy under the new procurator-
general, Yuri Chaika, and was instrumental in getting the president to
put him in full charge of criminal investigations, thus wresting this
powerful tool from Chaika.

In July 2008, not long after he became head of the Investigative Committee, Bastrykin was the subject of a report by Duma deputy and journalist Aleksandr Khinshtein in *Moskovskii komsomolets* claiming that he owned a private business in the Czech Republic, which is a member of NATO—this despite a law that prohibits senior Russian officials from engaging in commercial activity.[29] Bastrykin called the report a crude lie. Fours years later, Aleksei Navalny posted another damning report, based on documents from the Czech interior ministry, which confirmed that Bastrykin and his wife not only had had a business in the Czech Republic until 2009, but also a Czech residence permit.[30] Navalny suggested that this made Bastrykin vulnerable to blackmail by Western agents: "What do you think, the special services of NATO countries would not be aware that the deputy prosecutor general of Russia, a man with access to state secrets, applied to the Czech police for a residence permit?"[31]

Bastrykin showed himself to be a loose cannon when, just a month before the Navalny revelations, in June 2012, he became involved in an unseemly conflict with a reporter from *Novaia gazeta* who had written unfavorable comments about him. Bastrykin had the reporter picked up by his bodyguards and taken into a distant forest, where Bastrykin threatened him with murder and then joked that he would investigate the murder personally. When the story broke, Bastrykin was forced to apologize publicly, saying he had suffered an "emotional breakdown." Undeterred by threats, in September 2012 *Novaia gazeta* published a story showing, with documentation, that Bastrykin's wife, Olga, had owned a five-room apartment on the Spanish Riviera from 2007 to 2011. Contrary to regulations for government officials, Bastrykin had not declared the apartment in any of his statements to the authorities.[32]

All these events gave rise to speculation that Putin would have Bastrykin fired. But that did not happen. Bastrykin is privy to all information on corruption and other criminal activities—including murder—that high-level Russian officials are engaged in. It would have been risky indeed for Putin to dismiss him from his post, especially since he has the support of men like the powerful Igor Sechin.[33]

It might be added that Bastrykin is an author. In 2004, he published for a popular audience a book about the history of detective work. As it turns out, most of Bastrykin's *chef d'oeuvre* was reproduced word for word from a German book, *The Age of the Detectives*, published in Russian in 1974, and a book by American author Anthony Summers, *Empire of the FBI: the Myths, Mysteries, Intrigue*.[34] So much for the creative efforts of Putin's siloviki.

Yuri Chaika

Procurator-General Chaika, who has taken charge of the various criminal cases instigated against Putin's critics, graduated from the Sverdlovsk Institute of Law (now the Urals State Law Academy) in 1976 and then embarked on a career as a prosecutor. From 1999 to 2006, he served as Russia's Minister of Justice; then he was appointed by Putin to lead the Procuracy. Like Bastrykin, Chaika has been tainted by scandal. But it has not, thus far, damaged his career.

In December 2015, Navalny's Fund Against Corruption released a sensational 45-minute video exposing massive fraud on the part of Chaika's family, in particular his son Artem, who has vast business enterprises all over Russia as well as abroad. The video showed that Artem Chaika, together with the wife of one of Chaika's deputies, was involved in financial ventures that were linked to a Russian mafia. But the only response from the president's office was that Chaika's family was not the Kremlin's concern. The Kremlin apparently clings to the illusion that most Russians do not consult the Internet for news. In fact, Navalny's video was watched by over four million viewers in the first month after it appeared.[35]

The FSO

The FSO, *Federal'naia sluzhba okhrany* (Federal Protection Service), emerged from what was the Ninth Directorate of the KGB, the so-called guards directorate. The Ninth Directorate's role went far beyond ensuring the safety of government leaders and premises, which in itself was crucial, given that the Soviet regime was a totalitarian dictatorship. If ever there was a coup attempt against the leadership, employees of the Ninth Directorate would have been its praetorian guard. The Ninth Directorate also was responsible for the security of nuclear installations. After the KGB was disbanded in 1991, this directorate became the Main Guard Directorate (*Glavnoe upravlenie okhrany*), a separate entity numbering around eight thousand men and including an autonomous subdivision, the Presidential Security Service, headed by the infamous Aleksandr Korzhakov, who became the eyes and ears of President Yeltsin, wielding considerable political power. In 1996, Yeltsin and Korzhakov had a falling-out and Korzhakov was sacked, while at the same time the Presidential Security Service was incorporated with the GUO into what is now the FSO.

The FSO, which has twenty thousand men on its payroll, is more than just a bodyguard service. It reportedly keeps Putin informed about the other security agencies. In the words of security expert Mark Galeotti: "it has acquired a role as something of a *silovik* fact-checker, called on to stop the president from being manipulated by his briefers from the other security agencies. In information as well as physical security terms, it has become the answer to the age-old question of who watches the watchers."[36] According to journalist Yekaterina Sinelschikova: "The FSO is a powerful, multi-purpose and extremely secretive agency. There is hardly a more closed Russian security force. . . . The FSO as a special service is almost omnipotent—indeed, its people have the right to carry out operational and investigative activities, conduct wiretapping and open correspondence, detain citizens, search homes and confiscate cars."[37]

The FSO was run from early 2000 until May 2016 by a firm Putin loyalist, Evgenii Murov. His early career was in the First Directorate of the KGB, foreign intelligence, followed by work in the St. Petersburg branch of the security services from 1992 to 1998, when he moved to the FSB in Moscow. Murov and the FSO have repeatedly been linked by Russian journalists to kickbacks and bribes related to procurements in connection with the administration of the FSO's property. (Before Murov's retirement, supposedly at his own request, it was reported that he and his wife owned property in Russia that was worth over two billion rubles.[38]) In 2014, Murov was put on the U.S. sanctions list. His son Andrei is chairman of the board of directors of the state-owned Federal Grid Company, which is the main source of electricity for Russia and is listed on the London Stock Exchange.

Murov's replacement as head of the FSO is Dmitry Kochnev, who was a deputy director there and briefly head of the Presidential Security Service.[39] According to Sinelschikova: "Very little is known about the new appointee. Kochnev is a man without a biography; there is not a word about him on the Kremlin's and the FSO's websites."[40] We do know that Kochnev's entire career, since 1984, has been with the Russian security agencies, and that he has worked in the FSO since 1992. So he doubtless knows many Kremlin secrets, including that of the Nemtsov murder, which took place under the watchful eye of the FSO. He can be counted on by Putin to be loyal.

The Presidential Security Service, (*Sluzhba bezopasnosti presidenta*, or SBP), which is part of the FSO, was headed from 2000 to 2013 by Viktor Zolotov, a veteran of the security services, who met Putin when he was serving as a bodyguard for St. Petersburg mayor Sobchak. In 2013, Zolotov, as mentioned, became head of the MVD internal troops, whose job included keeping protesters against the Putin regime in check. Zolotov, reportedly a long-time judo partner of Putin's, had worked in the St. Petersburg FSB in the 1990s and had been close to Murov since the Soviet period. When Putin created his new National Guard in April 2016, Zolotov was named chief of this agency. (The SBP, which has roughly two to three thousand personnel, has been headed since June 2016 by Major General Aleksei Rubezhnoi, about whom little is known.)

Zolotov himself has an interesting background. Together with former MVD officer Roman Tsepov, Zolotov founded a private security firm, Baltik-Eskort, in St. Petersburg in 1992. The firm provided protection to family members of Putin and Sobchak, but also allegedly served as a liaison between the city government and members of the mafia, including Vladimir Kumarin, alleged head of the notorious Tambov gang. Tsepov died suddenly in 2004 from what is said to have been poisoning by a radioactive substance.[41]

According to a former SVR (foreign intelligence) officer in New York, Sergei Tretyakov, who defected to the U.S. in 2000 and who met Murov and Zolotov before his defection, they were both murderers: "[They] decided to make a list of politicians and other influential Muscovites whom they would need to assassinate to give Putin unchecked power. After the two men finished their list, Zolotov announced, 'There are too many. It's too many to kill—even for us.' "[42]

The Russian National Guard

In April 2016, President Putin issued an executive order creating a Russian National Guard (*Natsional'naia gvardiia rossii*) directly subordinate to him. With his long-time ally Zolotov at the helm, this new agency will gain jurisdiction over the MVD Internal Troops, the riot police (OMON) and Special Rapid Deployment Units (SOBR). Once the reorganization is complete, the National Guard will have an estimated 350,000 troops. The main duties of the new guard agency are stated to be fighting terrorism, extremism, and organized crime; but clearly public order will be a main component of its operations. As analyst Mark Galeotti put it:

There is no real reason for creating the NG [National Guard] out of the Interior Troops (VV) and other forces unless you have a serious worry about public unrest. Let's be clear, whatever Putin says, the militarized security forces of the VV and now NG have little real role fighting crime or terrorism; they are public security forces, riot and insurrection control and deterrence assets. . . . With Zolotov at its head, then it is even more clearly a personal, presidential Praetorian force, under a maximalist loyalist. This may not only be a force to keep the masses in check, but also the elite.[43]

The MVD, of course, comes out the big loser, since it is now deprived of its own very substantial troops.

The FSKN

The FSKN (*Federal'naia sluzhba po kontroliu za oborotom narkotikov*, or Federal Drug Control Service) was a powerful law-enforcement agency before it was disbanded by Putin in 2016. Formed in 2004, it had a staff of over forty thousand and the authority to initiate and carry out criminal investigations.[44] Viktor Cherkesov, as noted, was the first chief of FSKN, followed in 2008 by another former St. Petersburg KGB colleague of Putin, Viktor Ivanov. Ivanov had previously served as Putin's deputy chief of staff, in charge of presidential appointments and head of the board of state-owned Almaz-Antey Air Defense Concern, producers of air-defense technologies. He has been implicated by numerous Russian sources, including the murdered former KGB officer Alexander Litvinenko, in money laundering scandals.

Ivanov was put on the U.S. sanctions list in 2014. In an interview with the Russian television station RT the next year, Ivanov noted about being sanctioned: "The only ones to benefit from this were international drug traffickers, and I believe drug lords were dancing with joy at seeing the demise of such a robust counterdrug partnership."[45] Ivanov had obviously been following closely the hearings in London surrounding the Litvinenko murder, where his name was coming up a lot, because in this same interview he went to great lengths to defend himself against the allegations.

As of April 2016, FSKN was disbanded and its functions transferred to the MVD, so this meant that Ivanov would have been subordinated to Minister of Internal Affairs Kolokoltsev. He chose retirement instead. It is possible that the publicity over Ivanov's alleged corruption had something to do with what was a clear demotion for him. But also, on March 31, 2016, a Spanish court issued an arrest warrant (in absentia) for General Nikolai Aulov, a deputy director of FSKN, on charges of drug trafficking and links to an organized-crime group in Spain.[46] For his part, Ivanov was clearly caught off guard. As late as February 2016, Ivanov dismissed suggestions from the press that his agency would be disbanded: "I would like to rephrase Mark Twain: rumors about the death of my agency are greatly exaggerated."[47]

The SVR and GRU

The *Sluzhba vneshnei razvedki* (Foreign Intelligence Service, or SVR) emerged after 1991 from the First Chief Directorate of the KGB, and it continues to perform the same functions that it exercised as part of the KGB. The SVR's main responsibility is intelligence-gathering and counterterrorism abroad, along with "cooperating to support other measures necessary for state security." Those measures would include disinformation (*dezinformatsia*) and so-called "active measures," with the purpose of undermining political processes in Western democracies. Recent Russian interference in elections in both the United States and Europe is an example of such SVR operations. In 1998, a special-forces mobile unit, so-called Zaslon, consisting of some three hundred highly trained men, was established within the SVR. Its operations are shrouded in secrecy, but it seems to have been designated for special operations and could be involved with assassinations outside Russia.[48]

Recently, in September 2016, Putin appointed a new director of the SVR, Sergei Naryshkin, to replace Mikhail Fradkov, who had headed the agency since 2007 after previously serving as Russian prime minister. Naryshkin is a longtime ally of Putin, having served in the foreign intelligence service of the KGB in the 1970s and working with Putin in the St. Petersburg mayor's office in the 1990s. He served as the president's chief of staff before becoming speaker of the Duma in 2011. An economist by training, Naryshkin wrote a dissertation for a doctoral degree in economics that was exposed as fraudulent in 2015 by Dissernet. Researchers for this volunteer organization claimed that more than half of Naryshkin's text was plagiarized.[49] (No matter. Naryshkin's boss and most of those high up in the Kremlin did the same thing.) Naryshkin is on both the U.S. and European sanctions list.

Around the time of Naryshkin's appointment, there were rumors in the Russian media that the SVR would be merged with FSB to create a new supra-agency called the Ministry of State Security. But those rumors were denied by persons close to the president, including Sergei Ivanov, a veteran of the foreign intelligence service. Ivanov himself was dismissed from his post as head of the presidential administration in August 2016 but will remain a member of the Security Council. (See chapter 13.)

The *Glavnoe razvedyvatel'noe upravlenie* (Main Intelligence Administration, or GRU) is subordinate to the General Staff of the Armed Forces of the Russian Federation and gathers military intelligence through traditional espionage and technical means, including information from military space satellites. Like the SVR, it has residencies in the embassies abroad, and its agents develop their own espionage networks; but the GRU is believed to have a much larger agent network than the SVR. The GRU is also a far more secretive agency than either the SVR or FSB. It has no press office, and its organizational structure is a state secret. It is known, however, that the GRU has its own brigade of elite, highly trained special forces, which it has employed in Afghanistan and Chechnya, and doubtless in Syria. The GRU is also alleged to be the group responsible for carrying out the Russian hacking of the Democratic National Committee in the period leading up to the U.S. presidential conventions in the summer of 2016.

GRU chief Colonel-General Igor Sergun, a career GRU officer, died suddenly at age fifty-eight in January 2016 after having been in his position only three years, raising speculation in Russian media about possible foul play. Sergun was a career military intelligence officer with no obvious connections to the Putin clans. His successor is Lt. Colonel Igor Korobov, formerly a deputy of Sergun.

The Kremlin Cover

The siloviki are bound together—with Putin—in their common knowledge of each other's crimes. If the mighty edifice of the Kremlin should come crumbling down, as did the Yanukovich regime in Ukraine, they would all fall with it. This is why they maintain a unified front, despite turf wars and other internal conflicts which are kept hidden from the public as much as possible.

The FSB is probably the agency that carries out most covert assassinations, although the SVR and the GRU also engage in such efforts abroad, and Putin's Federal Protective Service does its part at home. It is crucial, of course that the investigative organs are on board as well. It is their job to make sure that the case in question is handled so that the scenarios are played out according to official plan. Sometimes, as will become clear, things do not go smoothly, particularly when evidence is challenged by journalists and families of the victims, or the law enforcement agencies inadvertently give conflicting accounts. Then, of course, there is the problem of Chechen President Ramzan Kadyrov, who is said to be deeply connected to the Chechen criminal world and is believed to have enlisted members of his elite forces to carry out killings on Putin's orders—the case of Nemtsov being the most recent example. Kadyrov has shown himself to be a loose cannon when speaking out about these murders, even though he declares himself to be Putin's obedient servant, and he reportedly has aroused the ire of the FSB.

But the Putin regime has thus far met and surmounted the challenges involved in committing political murder, including the outcry from Russian democrats and human-rights advocates. As noted when the British High Court in London reached the conclusion in early 2016 that Putin and Patrushev had "probably" ordered the killing of Alexander Litvinenko, the reaction from Western governments was muted, at best. It might even be the case that these murders are a contributing factor to the resilience of the Putin presidency thus far. They have served as a constant reminder of the consequences that befall those who challenge its rule.

Galina Starovoitova.

3

GALINA STAROVOITOVA: PUTIN'S FIRST VICTIM?

Really, something inexplicable, irrational is happening to the greatest country in the world. I am not referring to our natural resources, but to our intellectual, native talents. One can simply hope—irrationally—that our people will make a miracle . . . because it cannot be so bad in Russia that today this is what we are really reduced to.

Galina Starovoitova, interview with *Ekho Moskvy*, September 1998

"Once, our father came home from work tired and was somewhat irritated. He went to the kitchen, where he saw dirty dishes left in the sink.

"Galya, why are the dishes not washed?" He raised his voice and addressed the first person in the family he saw.

"That's not what I am meant for!" Galina said, keeping her composure.

Olga Starovoitova, sister of Galina Starovoitova

Imagine if there was a violent murder of a leading political figure in
the United States, or in any Western democracy, and the case was still
unsolved after almost twenty years, with repeated trials and thousands of pages of testimony and evidence, but no conclusion. This is
exactly what has happened in the aftermath of the murder of Duma
deputy and leader of the party Democratic Russia, Galina Starovoitova.
She was gunned down, at age fifty-two, in St. Petersburg on November
20, 1998, and we still don't know who ordered her murder.

In Russia, the wheels of justice run slowly and sometimes not at
all. This is not because Russian law-enforcement officials lack investigative tools: quite the contrary. They have all the sophisticated forensic technology that their counterparts in the West have, with the
added advantage of not being bound by the legal constraints on surveillance and searches that exist in Western countries. But the entire
Russian legal system operates under what is called telephone justice
(*telefonnoe pravo*), meaning, roughly, a call from someone higher in
rank than the judge or the prosecutor giving instructions as to how
the case should be resolved. An ordinary Russian may sometimes be
able to receive honest treatment at the hands of local law enforcement
and judicial organs. But when it comes to political cases, or the many
instances of financial malfeasance, telephone justice, accompanied often by monetary bribes, and even threats of violence, prevails.

Why is this so? Quite simply, because Russia has no tradition of a
democratic legal process. Yes, the Russian government has an impressive Code of Criminal Procedure, which is available online in English.[1] It was developed after Yeltsin became president and has been
revised several times. But the enforcement of these legal norms is left
up to those who often have their own agendas. And the Russian
parliament, which in theory has oversight over law-enforcement
bodies, is completely dominated by people who have pledged their
allegiance to the Putin government—thanks to the electoral system,
which ensures that democratic challengers are kept out. Then, of

course, the security agencies are able to dictate the entire process when they choose to.

For those Russians who greeted the 1991 Soviet collapse with optimism for the future, Galina Starovoitova's killing seven years later was a devastating blow. It was an ominous sign that sinister forces had thwarted their hopes that Russia would develop into a democracy. Boris Nemtsov, who had just left the Yeltsin government as first deputy prime minister, attended a meeting of Russian democrats on November 22 to honor Starovoitova, along with another former member of Yeltsin's economic team, Anatolii Chubais, and former prime minister Egor Gaidar. Nemtsov observed afterwards:

> This is a very, very big tragedy and disaster for Russia. I knew Galina Vasil'evna [Starovoitova] for eight years and she was a very, very smart, very honest member of the Russian parliament and she was one of the most outstanding politicians in my country. It seems to me that the reason [for her murder] is that St. Petersburg represents bandit capitalism. . . . Russia needs a very concrete program to overcome crime, including organized crime and political terrorism.

Nemtsov added pointedly that Russia needed "a lot of changes and improvements, including in the KGB [sic], internal affairs [MVD], prosecution services, and others."[2]

Nemtsov thus far had been a team player in Kremlin circles. One wonders if Starovoitova's killing marked the beginning of his awakening to the sinister aspects of what was going on at the highest levels of the government. Gaidar was no less vehement in his words. He called the crime a "political murder" and accused the government of lack of courage in taking steps to stop such killings. (Eight years later, the day after Litvinenko's death by poisoning in London, Gaidar would come close to death, falling into a coma, from a mysterious poison administered to him while he was attending a conference in Ireland.) The fears and concerns of Russian democrats were justified by all that followed—a former KGB chief as Russian president, appointments of former KGB officials to key posts in the government, and an eroding of the modest civil rights that had been earned under Yeltsin.

Why was Starovoitova singled out for murder? That is a question that has plagued Russian democrats and the independent Russian media for almost two decades. The answer involves rampant, violent corruption in Starovoitova's hometown of St. Petersburg, Starovoitova's efforts to expose this corruption, and her campaign to make former KGB officials accountable for their actions in the Soviet period. But above all, it was her charisma as a leader who could have made Russia a democracy.[3] For those who did not want Russia's path to go in that direction, she was a prime target for elimination. Starovoitova apparently did not realize this. Asked not long ago if his mother had felt threatened, her son Platon said she did, but that she had been reassured by three things: "She was very well known, very popular; she was a woman; and she was not involved with business or money. Here they killed [only] for money."[4] Unfortunately, Starovoitova's assumptions were wrong.

Who Was Starovoitova?

Galina Starovoitova was a remarkable woman in many respects. When I met her in Washington, D.C., in 1994, she was a fellow at the U.S. Institute of Peace, where she wrote an impressive study of self-determination efforts on the part of former republics of the Soviet Union.[5] I was struck by her modesty and quiet determination, combined with a distinct toughness. Born in 1946 in the Russian city of Cheliabinsk in the Ural Mountains, Starovoitova was exceptionally well educated. She was trained in Leningrad initially as an engineer, but then moved on to sociology, eventually earning a doctorate degree in social anthropology specializing in ethnic minorities. Her political awakening came in 1968, when she read Evgenia Ginzburg's memoirs of her experience in Soviet prison camps, *Into the Whirlwind*, and when Soviet troops invaded Czechoslovakia, suppressing the Prague Spring. She was one of the few Soviet citizens to sign a letter of protest against the invasion.[6]

Starovoitova earned a position as a senior researcher at the USSR Academy of Sciences Institute of Economics in the late 1970s and did field work, as an ethnic psychologist, in the southern republics of the USSR, including Armenia. When the Soviet Union held its first democratic elections in 1989, Starovoitova ran as a delegate from Armenia and was elected, with an overwhelming majority, to the USSR parliament. In 1990 she became a deputy to the Russian Republic parliament and, after the Soviet collapse, was a delegate to the Russian Federation Duma, along with being President Yeltsin's adviser on inter-ethnic relations. This was an important post, because of the significant numbers of non-Russian minorities within the new Russian Federation, but Starovoitova's forceful advocacy of their rights put her into conflict with the Yeltsin government and she was dismissed in 1992.[7]

In 1995, Starovoitova was elected to the Duma from St. Petersburg, as a delegate from a single-member constituency, rather than from a party list. But she had already formed, with Lev Ponomarev and Gleb Yakunin, a bloc called Democratic Russia. Her name was put forward, representing this bloc, as a candidate for the Russian presidency in 1996, but the Russian Central Election Commission denied her the right to be on the ballot on technical grounds. In 1998, Starovoitova became chairperson of Democratic Russia, by then registered as an official party.

During the 1990s, Starovoitova traveled widely, meeting with leading Western politicians, including Margaret Thatcher and Henry Kissinger, always impressing her interlocutors with her vast knowledge and her leadership qualities. As a strong advocate for ethnic minorities, she saw democracy through the lens of these persecuted peoples, but also understood the larger picture of how the totalitarian Soviet past affected efforts to create a true civil society in the new Russian state. The crux of the problem, in Starovoitova's view, was that the officials who had thrived in the Soviet period—in particular, members of the former KGB—were still playing a dominant role in Russian politics.

With this in mind, Starovoitova introduced a bill in the Duma in 1992 proposing "lustration" (cleansing) of individuals from the government who had been responsible in the Soviet period for violating human rights. This included persons who had worked for the Communist Party apparatus as full-time employees and former members of the KGB. The bill failed to pass, and when Starovoitova reintroduced it in 1997, it also was not adopted. Starovoitova's efforts made her the archenemy of the entrenched former Communists and KGB officers, which of course included Putin. According to Starovoitova's sister Olga, "If this law had passed, we would be living in a different country."[8] Indeed, Putin would not have become the Russian president. Starovoitova's advocacy of a complete overhaul of the laws governing the security services, with a view to enhancing civilian control of them, was an additional threat to people like Putin.[9]

Corruption in St. Petersburg

As a deputy to the Russian Duma from St. Petersburg, Starovoitova began a campaign against corruption in that city, which in the nineties was basically run by criminal gangs. City officials either turned a blind eye in return for kickbacks or actively participated in illegal ventures. We know now that Putin, as a deputy to Mayor Anatoly Sobchak, started reaping profits from these criminal operations very early on, as did the mayor. According to an investigation carried out by a commission headed by St. Petersburg politician Marina Sal'ye, Putin, as head of foreign economic relations for the city, was issuing licenses for the export of raw materials, which were to be exchanged for food imports. (St. Petersburg had a severe food shortage.) The commodities, worth hundreds of millions of dollars, were sold abroad, but no food ever appeared and the money disappeared. One of the alleged beneficiaries of this scam, aside from Putin, was Gennadii Timchenko, a founder of the oil trading company Gunvor, and a member of Putin's clique.[10]

In his job at the mayor's office, Putin also supervised the licensing of gambling casinos, which the city had a major investment in. Many of the gambling companies were run by former KGB officers, who were connected with the mafia and collected bribes or "black cash." As mentioned earlier, one agency that reportedly served as a liaison between the mayor's office and organized crime was the security firm Baltik-Escort, which was headed by Putin's crony Zolotov and Roman Tsepov. This firm was said to be closely connected to two notorious criminal groups—the Tambov gang and Malyshev gang, both of which worked with Putin.[11]

Putin became connected with the boss of the Tambov gang, Vladimir Kumarin (aka Barsukov), through the St. Petersburg Real Estate Holding Company (SPAG), where Putin sat on the advisory board. SPAG, it was later reported, was a vehicle for laundering money earned illicitly, including from a drug cartel. Kumarin, who was involved with two subsidiaries of SPAG, was known throughout St. Petersburg as the "night governor" because of his power in the city. Another figure who played an important role in SPAG was Vladimir Smirnov, who worked with Kumarin on several projects and was head of the Ozero Dacha Cooperative, where Putin was a member. Smirnov would later be appointed by Putin to head Tekhsnabeksport, the state company that supplies nuclear products to foreign governments.[12]

Putin, as we know, left St. Petersburg after the defeat of Sobchak in the 1996 mayoral elections and went to work in Moscow for the

Yeltsin administration. But he retained close ties to his native city, particularly to the security services there, through his close friend Viktor Cherkesov, head of the St. Petersburg branch of the FSB from 1992 to August 1998 and then Putin's first deputy at the FSB in Moscow. Cherkesov, whose long-time deputy Aleksandr Grigor'ev replaced him in the St. Petersburg FSB, was coincidentally on the same flight from Moscow to St. Petersburg that Starovoitova flew on the night of her murder, though he had already moved to Moscow to take up his new post.[13]

Putin, Cherkesov, and their allies from the security services cannot have been happy about Starovoitova's efforts to make corruption an issue in the upcoming St. Petersburg municipal elections. Indeed, even though Putin was no longer living and working in that city, his past connections with the mafia were sure to come out at some point if Starovoitova and her democratic allies persisted in their efforts to expose financial malfeasance on the part of the St. Petersburg government. Of course, it was not just Putin and his allies who worried about exposure. Starovoitova's sister Olga, who worked as her personal assistant in St. Petersburg, observed: "Galina Vasil'evna was one of the most prominent campaigners against corruption of the times. She was always submitting deputy's inquiries, for example about the stealing of books from the Academy of Sciences or fraud in distributing housing to soldiers. She was hated by almost half of the Duma."[14] But it was the men in the security services who had the power to destroy her and get away with it.

The Prelude: Killings in St. Petersburg

During 1997 and 1998, a series of violent murders took place in St. Petersburg, forming the backdrop for Starovoitova's killing. On August 18, 1997, Mikhail Manevich, a deputy governor of St. Petersburg who had run the city's privatization program, was gunned down as he drove to work on Nevsky Prospect. On February 27, 1998, Igor

Dubovik was fatally shot outside his home and died on the spot, with his money and documents intact. Dubovik was a lawyer for the governor of St. Petersburg, Vladimir Iakovlev, and a member of his advisory council. On September 28, 1998, Evgenii Agarev, a St. Petersburg City Hall official, was killed when a bomb exploded in the stairwell of his apartment building. Then on October 10, 1998, Dmitrii Filippov, chairman of the board of directors of Bank Menetap in St. Petersburg, was struck by a radio-controlled bomb blast as he entered his apartment. He died three days later. Five days after this, Mikhail Osherov, an aide to the vice-speaker of the Duma, Gennadii Seleznev, was shot as he was leaving his apartment. He survived following a long operation, but became an invalid.[15]

Osherov had run Seleznev's Duma election campaign and was first vice-president of the Academy of National Security (ANB), an ad hoc group of former KGB officers and Communists that Seleznev had created in St. Petersburg. The ANB was rumored to have secret aims of a right-wing takeover of the Russian government, similar to the attempt that occurred in the autumn of 1993, when Yeltsin resorted to bloodshed to defeat his opponents in the Russian parliament.[16]

Iurii Shutov, a businessman and deputy in the St. Petersburg legislature with ties to the criminal underworld, would be arrested in 1999 and accused of organizing several of the above-mentioned killings. Shutov had briefly, in 1990, worked as an adviser to Sobchak, but they had had a falling-out and Shutov had become a bitter enemy of both Sobchak and Putin, collecting and publishing evidence of their corruption and, at one point, accusing Putin of collaborating with enemy intelligence services when he served in the KGB in East Germany. In 1999, Shutov would claim that he had tapes of telephone conversations that showed FSB involvement in the Starovoitova murder at the highest levels. Clearly, Putin needed to have Shutov out of the way, and arresting him was a good solution. Shutov spent several years in pre-trial detention before being finally convicted, in 2006, of a number of contract killings. He died in a labor camp in Perm, Siberia, where he was serving a life sentence, in December 2014.[17]

Although it was convenient to attribute those contract killings to Shutov, he had actually had little motive. The men targeted were all foes of former St. Petersburg mayor Sobchak and had plenty of information on his past corrupt activities in the city. Also, in two of the murders, bombs containing hexogen were used. These are complicated devices, and hexogen is not easily available, which suggested FSB complicity. Shutov's name had been on the official list of possible killers of Starovoitova, but was later dropped from it.[18]

Starovoitova's Assassination

Starovoitova flew from Moscow to St. Petersburg early in the evening of November 20, 1998. According to testimony by an assistant who accompanied her on the trip, it was only at the very last minute that she decided to leave Moscow that night. Thus her killers would have had very short notice of her plans. She was met at the airport by her press secretary, twenty-eight-year-old Ruslan Linkov, who came with a car and driver. On the way to Starovoitova's apartment, they stopped by at her parents' home so she could take them some caviar and smoked eel as a gift from Moscow. She and her parents talked about her son, who was living in London, and her beloved grandson, on whom she doted.[19]

Linkov and Starovoitova then left for the center of the city, to Starovoitova's apartment on the Griboyedov Canal. They entered the building and started up the stairs, which were difficult to see because all the lights had been turned off except for one in the immediate entrance. As they approached the second-floor landing, where Starovoitova's apartment was, shots broke out and Starovoitova fell to the ground, fatally wounded. Linkov later recalled, during the trial of the accused killers, seeing both shooters: a man (who he eventually identified in court), and a woman standing behind the man. (As it turned out, the latter was a man dressed in women's clothing and wearing a wig.) But defense lawyers for those accused in the shootings pointed to contradictions in Linkov's testimony with earlier statements to investigators. Because there was no light on the second floor, where Starovoitova was shot, even the flash from a gun being fired would not have enabled Linkov to get more than a vague outline of the killers.[20]

Linkov was at some point also shot, but what actually happened remains unclear because it was reported in court documents and in the press that, strangely, there was an interval of several minutes between the two shootings. And despite being supposedly gravely wounded, and in and out of consciousness, Linkov managed to make a call on his mobile phone to the police to report the crime, then knocked on the door of the couple across the hall, Vladimir and Galina Andreev, and made another call to a friend at the media outlet Interfax.[21] In their later testimony, the Andreevs recalled hearing a conversation in the hallway before they opened the door to Linkov. (The guns had had silencers, so they heard no shots.) Both were doctors, and Vladimir Andreev bandaged a laceration that was near Linkov's ear.

Within a short time, Galina's sister, Olga, arrived, followed by several FSB officials, including Cherkesov, who clearly wanted to be on top of the investigation and would doubtless report directly back to his FSB boss, Putin. Linkov had already been taken away by ambulance. The killers left behind the two guns that were used to kill Starovoitova, but the gun that fired at Linkov disappeared and was reportedly found much later on a former police officer living in Latvia.[22] A key question is why the assassins did not finish Linkov off, as they did Starovoitova. They were hired professionals, and they could see that he was alive as they hastened away.

Ruslan Linkov

Olga Starovoitova has steadfastly discounted rumors that Ruslan Linkov was not badly hurt in the attack and that he may have been complicit in the killing of her sister. In a 2013 interview with *Ekho Moskvy*, she recounted how after the murder she went to the White Knights Military Academy Hospital, where Linkov was being treated. She was not able to see him, but the doctor in charge showed her the x-rays, which he said revealed that Linkov had been shot in the shoulder and neck.[23]

Olga apparently did not know that the doctor at the Military Academy Hospital, Iurii Shevchenko, was very close to Putin. He had treated Putin's wife, Lyudmila, when she was badly hurt in a 1993 car accident, and he had attended Anatoly Sobchak in 1997 when he had supposedly suffered a heart attack just as he was about to be arrested for corruption (and was then spirited out of the country from his hospital bed by a team organized by Putin).[24]

According to Olga, representatives from the FSB wanted to see Linkov right away, but Linkov told them he would not talk to them because of how badly they had treated dissidents. He demanded to see only the chief of the FSB, Putin. (So much for Linkov being unconscious for days as the press was initially told.) Olga said in her interview that Putin then paid a visit to Linkov, who discussed with him all the details of the murder.[25]

The visit from Putin to Linkov was confirmed by American journalist Andrew Meier, who interviewed Linkov extensively two years later. Meier noted that since the time of the murder, Linkov had been "an object of ridicule and suspicion" in St. Petersburg because of his strange, theatrical appearance and his soft, high-pitched voice. Linkov told him that it was a miracle that he had survived the shooting, and that he had been in the hospital for two months, guarded around the clock by the FSB. Interestingly, he confided to Meier that he had been close to Putin for several years before Starovoitova's murder. They had first met in 1990, when Linkov was twenty years old. According to Meier: "Linkov and Putin had enjoyed a long-running conversation. Linkov did not consider it protection, or providence, but the president had for years tendered a strange affection toward him. Whenever Linkov called, Putin agreed to meet."[26]

Linkov told Meier that he had been one of Putin's first visitors at his office when Putin became head of the FSB in the summer of 1998. In Linkov's words: "I don't know why, but Putin likes to think he's one of us. He's always telling me how he supported Galina Vasil'evna and our cause—from the very beginning." Later, on a visit by Putin to St. Petersburg, the two went to Starovoitova's grave together. Linkov confided in Meier that he had told Putin that he strongly suspected that St. Petersburg governor Vladimir Iakovlev and Duma deputy Gennadii Seleznev had ordered the murder of Starovoitova and that Putin promised him: "I'll look into it. I'll ask them [the FSB] to dig harder."[27]

Linkov's account to Meier appears to be either a deliberate deception or a result of brainwashing by Putin. It is hard to believe that in 1990 Putin, an aspiring member of Sobchak's entourage, would have been interested in spending time with a young man who was just twenty. (Unless Putin, as some critics claim, really is gay or a pedophile.) More to the point, why would Linkov have reason to believe that Putin was a supporter of Starovoitova's democratic causes? After all, Putin had brought Cherkesov, notorious throughout St. Petersburg as a persecutor of dissidents in the KGB days, to Moscow as his first deputy in the FSB. Starovoitova, before she died, had come to the defense of Russian naval officer Aleksandr Nikitin, who had been charged with treason by Cherkesov's St. Petersburg FSB investigators for blowing the whistle about leaky submarines. And of course another question is why Cherkesov, as head of the FSB in St. Petersburg until August 1998, was not able to solve any of the contract killings that had taken place up until his departure for Moscow. As for the Starovoitova case, despite his ubiquitous presence on the night of the murder, which in itself arouses suspicion, Cherkesov was apparently at a loss to get to the bottom of the crime.

Investigation and Trial

Immediately after the Starovoitova murder, an operative-investigative group was formed to handle the case, with representatives from the FSB, MVD, and Procuracy. President Yeltsin said he would lead the investigation, although there is little evidence that he actually did. Yeltsin was preoccupied by the financial crisis that Russia was experiencing, and his own political future was in grave doubt. A year after the killing, the deputy chief of the St. Petersburg FSB told a reporter that authorities knew who had killed the politician, but that they had to keep quiet so as not to hamper the criminal case.[28]

In the next three years, the investigative group questioned more than a thousand witnesses, conducted searches, hauled in suspects, and examined forensic evidence. Finally, in November 2002, the FSB announced that its officials had arrested six men, all employees of a St. Petersburg-based guard service, for the crime and that it was seeking two others, Mikhail Glushchenko and Viacheslav Shevchenko, both former deputies to the Russian Duma representing the LDPR (the right-wing Liberal Democratic Party of Russia) and both connected to the Tambov gang.[29]

The trial began in late December 2003 and continued, with several breaks, until June 2005. Two of the six suspects were acquitted of charges and released; another, accused of a peripheral role, was freed because he had already served the required term; and three were found guilty: Iurii Kolchin, an employee of the GRU (military intelligence) at the time of the killing, was sentenced to twenty years' imprisonment for organizing the murder and driving the get-away car, while Vitalii Akishin received twenty-three years for shooting Starovoitova, and Viacheslav Leliavin was sentenced in a separate trial the next year to eleven years as an accomplice. Oleg Fedosov, the other shooter who had dressed in women's clothes, disappeared. All the men were connected to the Tambov criminal gang. The motive was said to be that Starovoitova opposed candidates that the gang wanted to place in the city Duma. Although Akishin confessed to the shooting, Kolchin insisted on his innocence and produced several witnesses who testified that he had been home on the night of the murder.[30]

Kolchin and the others could not have acted on their own, and even Glushchenko and Shevchenko, if indeed they were involved, had no convincing motives for the murder. The question on everyone's minds was who had ordered the killing. Linkov, encouraged by Putin, continued to insist that leaders of the far right were the ultimate culprits, and that included Seleznev and Vladimir Zhirinovsky, head of the LDPR. All were well suited as villains for the purposes of Putin, who was portraying himself as a democrat in opposition to the right wing of Russian politics. The real threat, Starovoitova, was gone, and her murder could be passed off on those who seemed her most obvious opponents.

Pursuing this theory, the prosecution called Lyudmila Narusova, the widow of Sobchak—who was deeply indebted to Putin for protecting her husband—as a witness in September 2004. She told the court that Starovoitova was an archenemy of Zhirinovsky, the LDRP, and Glushchenko, and that Zhirinovsky had threatened Starovoitova with reprisals before her death. Zhirinovsky fought back, appearing at his own initiative in St. Petersburg in November to testify that, although he and Starovoitova were at odds on many issues—enemies, in fact—he had no involvement in her murder. He repeated earlier unsubstantiated claims that Starovoitova had had large sums of money with her when she returned to her home and suggested that Linkov had robbed her and had her killed. Linkov was, Zhirinovsky pointed out, the only one who knew that Starovoitova was arriving by plane to St. Petersburg on the night of her murder.[31]

The effort to connect Zhirinovsky and his allies with Starovoitova's murder did not bear fruit, but prosecutors nonetheless continued to focus on Glushchenko (alias Misha Khokhol), a key player in the entourage of criminals and politicians that dominated St. Petersburg in the nineties. When his name came up in the investigation of the Starovoitova murder in 2002 as a possible organizer of the crime, he quickly fled to Spain and laid low. Later, assured by Russian law-enforcement authorities that he could safely return to Russia, Glushchenko appeared in St. Petersburg in 2009 to renew his passport. He was promptly arrested on charges of extortion and the possible murders of three people in 2004 in Cyprus, including the abovementioned Duma deputy Shevchenko. Shevchenko, a St. Petersburg businessman with ties to the Tambov gang, supposedly wrote a letter—"discovered" by chance on the Internet by none other than Ruslan Linkov—in which he described how Glushchenko had been enlisted to carry out Starovoitova's killing by LDPR leaders in exchange for getting on a list of deputies for the upcoming 1999 Duma elections.[32]

After several years in a Siberian labor camp, Kolchin, who had been convicted of organizing the crime, broke down and confessed his guilt in 2011, telling investigators that none other than Glushchenko had ordered him to murder Starovoitova in May 1998 during a meeting at Glushchenko's dacha. Glushchenko, already serving time in a Siberian labor camp, for other murders, admitted to the killing in April 2014 and named the notorius mafia figure Kumarin as the mastermind (*zakazchik*). The motive was said to be Starovoitova's campaign to uncover the activities of criminal gangs in St. Petersburg, including those of the Tambov group, which Kumarin headed. Glushchenko apparently saw his confession as a kind of plea bargain. It is standard FSB practice to get people who are already convicted of offenses to confess to additional crimes when they are incarcerated. But his plan backfired, and in August 2015, Glushchenko was sentenced by a St. Petersburg City Court to seventeen additional years in prison.

Kumarin, meanwhile, had been persuaded by his and Putin's friend Vladimir Smirnov to return home to St. Petersburg from Germany, where he had been living in exile, in 2007. He was arrested in September of that year on charges of extortion and convicted, with a sentence of fourteen years in prison. According to a WikiLeaks document, based on a conversation between Russian Procurator-General Chaika and an informant for Stratfor, the global intelligence service, Putin himself gave the go-ahead for Kumarin's arrest.[33]

In a lengthy interview—answering written questions by Russian journalist Zoia Svetova from his prison cell in Moscow in late March 2016, Kumarin was, not surprisingly, bitter.[34] He noted that "now Chaika himself is being called a criminal, just as he labeled me." (This was in reference to the serious corruption allegations against Chaika that had recently been made by Aleksei Navalny.) Kumarin complained that, although he had already had two heart attacks and was officially classified as an invalid, the prison he was in, the notorious *Matrosskaia tishina*, had no doctors and predicted that he would probably die there. (He is now charged with the 2006 murder of a St. Petersburg businessman and his bodyguard, but not with Starovoitova's killing.)

Interestingly, Kumarin claimed that he had never known Vladimir Putin and had no business connection with him or his St. Petersburg allies, despite the overwhelming evidence to the contrary. Chaika himself acknowledged the ties between Putin and Kumarin in the above-mentioned secret conversation reproduced by WikiLeaks. And Aleksandr Litvinenko, in his book *The Gang from Lubianka,* observed: "The Tambov gang would not have lasted a day in St. Petersburg if its leader, Kumarin-Barsukov, were not friends with Patrushev and Putin. They had dachas next to each other. They fried kebobs together."[35]

Presumably Kumarin has hoped that his denials about ties with Putin would mitigate his possible prison sentence on murder charges and improve his conditions there. But perhaps he is just lucky to be alive. Russian journalist Viktor Shenderovich, who has documented the close ties between Putin and Kumarin in the nineties, had this to say about Kumarin's fate: "If I were in his place, I would worry about my life, because apparently he made an agreement to be silent in exchange for good living conditions in prison. . . . But Putin will not stay in power and new people might make a contract with Kumarin where good living conditions are exchanged for a story about his years together with Vladimir Vladimirovich. I think Putin understands this."[36] In other words, Kumarin cannot count on Putin protecting him.

Questions Remain

The Starovoitova case is officially closed. But for many, including Starovoitova's sister, her son, and others, it remains open. Glushchenko and Kumarin do not hold up credibly as those who ordered the murder, because neither had a motive to kill such a prominent figure as Starovoitova. Olga Starovoitova told an interviewer in 2016 that she did not consider Glushchenko guilty of the murder, adding that she could not help but compare it to the killing of Boris Nemtsov: "They kill those who the people listen to, who can't be bought or have their mouths shut."[37] Human-rights activist Lev Ponomarev, who was very close to Starovoitova as a fellow leader of Democratic Russia, observed in August 2015: "The special services in some way participated in the affair. And of course the head of the agency [then Putin] bears specific responsibility. All the more so since everything has dragged out for so long and we see that the mastermind is still not known. The idea that Kumarin might be the one who ordered the murder is crazy."[38]

It strains credulity that the Russian investigative organs would have had such a hard time solving this murder, where they had a witness, Linkov, the three weapons that were used, with fingerprints, plus numerous eye-witness accounts of what happened before and after the crime. Clearly, the FSB had to build a scenario that would incriminate people who were already known in the criminal world, elicit confessions, and ensure that those who had ordered the crime were protected. The Starovoitova case was the beginning of a pattern that has continued under Putin ever since. The strategy is simple: drag out the case for as long as possible so the public loses interest, and yet give the impression that investigators are doing a thorough job, supposedly leaving no stones unturned.

As FSB chief and shortly thereafter the Russian president, Putin could dictate the course of the investigation of Starovoitova's murder, with the help of his trusted friend Cherkesov. In the end, Putin achieved two goals: getting rid of his nemesis, Starovoitova, and imprisoning for life the men who knew too much about his criminal activities in St. Petersburg. It might be added that it is probably no coincidence that Starovoitova's murder came just three days after FSB officer Alexander Litvinenko, accompanied by several colleagues, appeared in a nationally televised press conference to announce that their FSB superior had ordered them to kill Boris Berezovsky, then head of the National Security Council. This dramatic announcement caused a huge uproar, leading to Litvinenko's imprisonment, exile, and subsequent murder, which is discussed in detail later in this book. But luckily for the FSB, it was soon overshadowed by news of Starovoitova's killing.

As for Linkov, by all accounts he is a strange character. Devoted to Putin and claiming that they shared a close personal relationship, he may or may not have been a collaborator in the murder. But clearly he was enlisted early on by Putin to further the official line that extreme-right politicians were the perpetrators of Starovoitova's murder and that Putin could not have been behind the crime because he had always supported her democratic efforts.[39]

Linkov, capitalizing on his fame as a victim of the 1998 crime, and portraying himself as a human-rights activist, published a book, *Zapiski nedobitska* (Notes of a Survivor) in 2007.[40] Disappointingly, for those who had hoped to learn more about Starovoitova's murder, the book had little to say in that regard. Although Linkov talked about the need for legal protection of dissidents, he carefully avoided saying anything negative about Putin. Indeed he wrote fondly that Putin, in 1990, had had his driver take him and Starovoitova to meet with voters for the Duma elections in districts of St. Petersburg. Ten years later, he said, Putin himself reminded him that he had done this. As an analyst for the Russian paper *Kommersant* observed about the book: "If Linkov is for democracy, then I am against it."[41]

There were plenty of people who wanted Starovoitova out of the picture in 1998, and the atmosphere of lawlessness and unaccountability for assassinations in St. Petersburg provided ample opportunity for would-be killers. Nonetheless, Starovoitova was such a prominent political figure that potential killers would have known that there would be a huge outcry, along with demands to find the perpetrators that far exceeded the clamors for justice in earlier murders. Thus it is difficult to imagine that whoever killed Starovoitova would have embarked on this dangerous mission without the assumption of protection by someone high up in the security services. There were three people who occupied such positions in November 1998: Vladimir Putin, head of the FSB; Viktor Cherkesov, his first deputy; and Cherkesov's replacement as FSB chief in St. Petersburg, Grigor'ev. All were well connected with the underground criminal world, and yet it took their agency, the FSB, four years to even make any arrests in the crime. And still, after close to twenty years, no credible *zakazchik* has been identified.

The September 1999 bombings.

(Photograph courtesy of STR/AFP/Getty Images)

4

TERROR IN RUSSIA: SEPTEMBER 1999

What?! Blowing up our own apartment buildings? You know, that is really . . . utter nonsense! It's totally insane. No one in the Russian special services would be capable of such a crime against his own people.

Vladimir Putin, *First Person* (2000)

Maybe I'm afraid of finding out the truth because the truth might even be worse than what happened.

Svetlana Rozhkova, who lost her mother in the bombing of a Moscow apartment house

Nineteen ninety-nine was not a good year for Russia's relations with the West, which came under increasing strain. President Bill Clinton had been a firm supporter of the Yeltsin presidency, despite the strong objections of Washington to the first war in Chechnya, launched in late 1994. Indeed, Clinton and Yeltsin met an unprecedented eighteen times during the period when both were in office. (On one of

Yeltsin's trips to Washington, he brought Nemtsov, then still first deputy prime minister, and reportedly introduced him to Clinton as his successor.)[1] Clinton had pushed strongly for a Comprehensive Test Ban Treaty with Russia, but the treaty was defeated by the U.S. Senate in October 1999 because of concerns about how it would affect the strategic balance. Meanwhile, the Kremlin leadership felt threatened by NATO's expansion of the alliance into Eastern Europe in that September to include Poland, Hungary, and the Czech Republic, and also by U.S. plans to build a national missile defense system. Then there was the war in Yugoslavia, where Russia's ally Serbia was bombed by NATO forces in an effort to stop Serbia's "ethnic cleansing" of Albanians in Kosovo. And, although Clinton had supported the IMF's granting of billions of dollars of loans to Russia, growing evidence of Russian money laundering and corruption, including a huge scandal involving the Bank of New York, had caused an uproar among Russia's Western critics.

It was against this backdrop, along with growing discontent with Yeltsin at home, that four apartment bombings occurred in Russia in September 1999. These devastating terrorist attacks were, for Russians, what 9/11 would be for Americans two years later. As Russian human-rights activist Sergei Kovalev observed, "the explosions were a crucial moment in the unfolding of our current history. After the first shock passed, it turned out that we were living in an entirely different country."[2] Indeed, the bombings changed Russia's political landscape irrevocably, in particular by catapulting Vladimir Putin into the Russian presidency and giving Russian authorities an excuse to blame almost every subsequent political murder or act of terrorism on Chechens or other ethnic minorities from Russia's North Caucasus regions. The attacks, not surprisingly, created a sense of extreme vulnerability on the part of the Russian people and made them highly receptive to the allure of a strong, no-nonsense leader (unlike the ailing and unpredictable Yeltsin). Enter Vladimir Putin.

Weak Response from Russian Authorities

It is important to note that a prelude to the September series of terrorist attacks occurred early in the evening of August 31, 1999, when a bomb exploded at an underground shopping center at Moscow's Manezh Square. One person died and dozens were injured. The Dagestan Liberation Army (Dagestan being a republic of the Russian Federation in the North Caucasus) claimed responsibility for the explosion and said that such attacks would continue until Russian troops left their territory. Two Dagestani terrorists were later convicted of the crime.

This attack should have put the Russian security services on high alert in order to prevent further terrorism. But the authorities were remarkably complacent. In fact, on September 2, *Nezavisimaia gazeta* published an interview with FSB chief Patrushev in which he was asked whether additional security measures were being taken because of the blast. Patrushev responded that heightened security was already in place due to the beginning of the school year on September 1, but that "there is no basis for a more intense regime because of the bomb at Manezh Square."[3]

The initial September bombing occurred on the fourth of that month at an apartment building in the city of Buinaksk, Dagestan, killing fifty-eight people and wounding more than a hundred others. The apartment building housed soldiers from the 136th Motor-Rifle Brigade of the Russian Ministry of Defense, along with their families. But the majority of those killed were Dagestanis, not ethnic Russians, and the region had already been rife with conflict, so the attack did not generate a great deal of reaction.

The second bombing took place on the night of September 8–9 at a nine-story apartment house on Gurianova Street in Moscow, killing one hundred people and wounding over six hundred. Prime Minister Putin went ahead with a planned trip to New Zealand, as if to demonstrate that there was no cause for panic. Then on September 13, a powerful explosive blew up at an eight-story apartment building on Kashirskoe Highway in Moscow, killing 124 and wounding seven. And finally, on September 16, a bombing took place at an apartment house in the city of Volgodonsk, Rostov District: nineteen people died and eighty-nine were wounded.

As the Russian journal *Itogi* noted on September 21, Russians did not voice indignation over the fact that their government had taken no exceptional measures until after the second Moscow blast. But looking back a decade later, Russian journalist Vladimir Vedrashko was incredulous: "Imagine that the New York twin towers had been blown up within an interval of several days. Could an American possibly imagine that after the first blast, authorities would take no action that was outside the normal?"[4] Such was the climate in Russia at that time, despite the heady years of democracy under Yeltsin. Most people were schooled in the Soviet era, when outrage over government malfeasance, if it was felt, was simply not expressed.

Historian John Dunlop, in his path-breaking study of the September bombings, reports that in fact the FSB and some members of the Security Council received a detailed warning on the day of the first Moscow attack that there would be further bombings. An officer of the GRU who had been serving in Southern Russia approached liberal Duma deputy Konstantin Borovoi with information about planned attacks, along with a list of participants. Borovoi duly passed on this warning to members of the Security Council with ties to the FSB and sent the GRU officer to speak with them, but they ignored the information and took no preventive measures.[5]

Aftermath of the Bombings

As Dunlop shows, the authorities afterward deliberately kept the circumstances around these terrorist attacks murky, with highly contradictory versions of what had happened and who was to blame. Indeed, journalist Iulia Kalinina observed in 2002: "The Americans

several months after 11 September 2001 already knew everything—
who the terrorists were and where they came from. . . . We in general know nothing."[6] The brother of Luba Morozova, who perished in the Gurianova Street blast, voiced a feeling that was probably widespread: "There are bigger fish involved. That is why it is taking so long."[7] But, aside from some courageous investigative reporters, Russians kept their doubts to themselves.

Morozova's daughters, Tatiana and Aliona, both now residing in the United States, were among the few who did everything they could to find answers as to who was responsible for the blasts. They enlisted a lawyer, Mikhail Trepashkin, a former FSB officer, to help. But Trepashkin's efforts to get crucial documents from the authorities failed. And in October 2003, shortly before the trial of two men accused in the Moscow bombings, Trepashkin was arrested for possessing an illegal weapon and sentenced to four years' imprisonment. An additional charge of divulging state secrets was later added. (Trepashkin had made himself an enemy of the FSB well before he became involved with the bombing cases. In November 1998 he had participated with Alexander Litvinenko in the now-infamous press conference where they accused the FSB of ordering the murder of Boris Berezovsky.)[8]

The Russian people grown skeptical over the years of what their government has told them about these terrorist attacks, in particular about the role of the security services. In August 2015, *Ekho Moskvy* conducted a poll asking respondents their views of the bombings, along with the October 2002 hostage-taking at a Moscow theater and the September 2004 siege at a school in Beslan. Only 35 percent said that they believed these terrorist incidents were a complete surprise to the Russian security services. Thirty-three percent thought the security services knew of the attacks beforehand but were not able to prevent them; another 11 percent said that the security services knew about preparations for these acts of terrorism and deliberately did nothing; and 4 percent thought that the security services actually enabled the attacks. In a second poll, Russians were asked whether they had a clear idea as to who perpetrated the September 1999 bombings. Over two thirds of those polled said no.[9] This was after fifteen years of investigations, trials, and official pronouncements! The poll results become even more significant when considering that some respondents would have been hesitant to express their opinions openly on such a highly sensitive topic.

Of course, it may well be that the views of Russians on the 1999 bombings are irrelevant, given that they have been powerless to do anything about what happened. The efforts of an independent commission to investigate the bombings, created in 2002 under Sergei Kovalev, were continually frustrated by the government's refusal to cooperate. The commission, which Trepashkin assisted before he was arrested, was not allowed to interview witnesses under oath and was denied access to key documents and testimony. After one of its members, Sergei Iushenkov, was shot to death and another, Iurii Shchekochikhin, died of an apparent poisoning, its work ground to a halt.

The Kremlin Pursues Its Story Line

The bombings are best understood in the context of the political intrigues that were occurring in the Kremlin at the time. Yeltsin, suffering from alcoholism and ill health, was faltering badly as the Russian president, and it was clear that he could not possibly run for another term in early 2000. Thus, as noted earlier, the group that surrounded him, known as "the family," had to come up with a successor who the Russian people would support, but who would also protect their own interests—i.e., guarantee that none of them, including Yeltsin, would be prosecuted for corruption. The family—which included Yeltsin's daughter Tatiana Dyachenko, Valentin Yumashev (a journalist and adviser to Yeltsin, who later married Tatiana),

Aleksandr Voloshin (head of the presidential administration), and oligarchs Roman Abramovich and Boris Berezovsky—settled on Putin, who Yeltsin appointed as prime minister on August 9, 1999. But Putin was virtually unknown to the Russian public: something was needed to jump-start his candidacy as Yeltsin's successor.

Russian military forces were at this time carrying out anti-terrorist operations in Dagestan, following an incursion there by Chechen militant Islamist leaders Shamil Basaev, Movladi Udugov, and Khattab (an ethnic Saudi), an attack that was apparently encouraged by Berezovsky, Putin, and others because it was used as an excuse for Russian military intervention. According to a close associate of the late Berezovsky, Alex Goldfarb, Berezovsky had been negotiating a deal with the rebels in exchange for their incursion into Dagestan:

> In the spring of 1999 on the threshold of the autumn Duma elections, there was achieved a secret agreement [*dogovorennost'*] between Basaev and Udugov, on the one hand, and the Kremlin top leadership, on the other, for a short victorious (for Russia) war in the Caucasus. To achieve this end, Udugov even flew to Moscow. It was proposed that, in response to the provocations of the Wahhabis [radical Islamists] in Dagestan, Russia would begin limited military actions which would be crowned by the return of the Upper Terek District of Chechnya [to Russia]. As a result, the [moderate] Maskhadov regime in Grozny would fall, and his place would be taken by Basaev and Udugov.[10]

Goldfarb later claimed that, while Berezovsky was in on the negotiations, he actually opposed the rebel incursion. But political commentator Andrei Pointkovsky raised the question as to why, if Berezovsky really had been against the plan, he continued to support Putin even after the September bombings:

Hundreds of people were killed and a war broke out in which tens of thousands would die. Mysterious bombings of apartment buildings took place, for which no one would claim responsibility. Was it not time, finally, to open the country's eyes, to tell the shaken society about the Kremlin's secret agreement and thereby stop the war? . . . Berezovsky believed in him [Putin] after this plan was realized before his very eyes? The person he fostered and continued to lead to the presidency?[11]

Goldfarb later acknowledged:

In retrospect, Berezovsky should have realized that Putin was not playing the limited war gambit developed by Udugov, but chose all-out war as the defining theme of his bid for the presidency. . . . He disagreed with Putin, but he had promised to steer clear of Chechnya. So he decided to leave this aside for a while. They were still part of the same team. They had an election to win, and Boris completely immersed himself in party politics.[12]

The family decided that it needed an excuse to launch a second war in Chechnya as a means of rallying the Russian people around the new, relatively unknown Putin. But the violence in Dagestan was not enough to justify the full-fledged invasion of Chechnya that began in October. Something more was needed—hence the explosions. In the words of journalist and human-rights activist Alexander Podrabinek: "There was a lull after the first Chechen campaign [1994–96]. It seemed that now there would be peace. But the situation in Russia had developed in such a way that peace was disadvantageous to people who wanted to come to power. War was their 'magic wand,' it was their trump card, which they did not fail to take advantage of."[13]

Chechens Again As Enemies

As Podrabinek noted, the authorities immediately attributed the September bombings to the Chechens, as if all had been planned beforehand: "Normally those in power—investigators and politicians—would show some restraint, at least to give the impression that they were thinking things through before making conclusions. But they did not pause. Right away they laid [the bombings] on the Chechens. It was clear that the authorities were prepared for this turn of events. The impression was that this came as no surprise. And this was confirmed by many later developments."[14]

In fact, the explosion in Buinaksk was subsequently blamed on natives of Dagestan, not Chechnya. But the alleged ringleader was Khattab, the so-called Black Arab, who was based in Chechnya and conducted training camps for rebel fighters there. In March 2001, the Supreme Court of Dagestan sentenced two men, Isa Zainutdinov and Alisultan Salikhov, to life imprisonment for carrying out the Buinaksk bombings, and four others to lesser sentences for their participation in the crime. (Although the Russian Constitution allows the death penalty, a moratorium was placed on executions in 1999, when Russia was seeking membership in the Council of Europe.) The same court, in April 2002, found Ziiavudin Ziiavudinov guilty of organizing the bombings and sentenced him to twenty-four years in prison. (Another alleged perpetrator, Magomed Salikhov, was tried separately and then, after being found not guilty, was subsequently killed in a confrontation with the FSB.)

As Dunlop points out, the trials of the accused in the Buinaksk attack were carried out with gross violations of their rights—they were tortured and blackmailed and coerced into confessing. So it is difficult to know whether all of those charged—seven in all—were actually guilty. More significantly, the fact that these men were able to enter Dagestan from Chechnya freely with large amounts of explosives—their vehicles were inspected by the local MVD and FSB—suggests that security authorities had advance knowledge of the bombing. In fact, one of the accused, in his final statement at his trial, said: "The transport of the explosives had been shadowed from the very beginning to the end by the special services."[15] It should be added that a second bombing in Buinaksk that same night was barely averted. A Zhil-130 automobile with 2,706 kilograms of explosives was discovered in a parking lot near residential buildings and was disarmed by military sappers just minutes before it would have exploded.

In May 2001, prosecutors announced that they were bringing five people to trial for the Moscow and Volgodonsk explosions. The five were all residents of the Karachay-Cherkessian Republic in the south of Russia. In the end, the accused were not found guilty of the bombings, but were convicted of a series of other terrorism-related crimes. It was not until two years later that a conviction was made in these bombings, which were said to have been carried out by members of a single terrorist group. Former traffic policeman Stanislav Liubichev was sentenced to four years in prison for accepting a bribe to allow a vehicle filled with explosives to enter into the city of Kislovodsk in the summer of 1999. The explosives were later used in the September bombings.

Meanwhile, two alleged terrorists, ethnic Karachis Iusuf Krymshamkhalov and Adam Dekkushev, were arrested in Georgia in 2002 and extradited to Russia, where they were tried and convicted in January 2004 by a Moscow court of participation in the Moscow and Volgodonsk bombings. The proceedings were carried out in secret with no members of the press allowed, and the defense lawyers claimed that prosecutors had falsified much of the evidence. While Dekkushev admitted his participation in the Volgodonsk bombing, he said that he had been given heavy narcotics. Krymshamkhalov acknowledged that he had transported explosives to Volgodonsk, but insisted he did not know that they were to be used for blowing up apartment houses. Both defendants got life sentences.

Organizers and Masterminds

The two convicted men were said to have been operating on the orders of Achemez Gochiaev, another native of Karachay-Cherkessiia. Gochiaev's name had come up early on in the investigation as the alleged organizer of the Moscow and Volgodonsk bombings. He had reportedly rented several premises in Moscow to plant explosives, including the building on Gurianova Street, and was said to be a direct subordinate of the warlord Khattab. The story of Gochiaev created much stir in the media but led to a dead end. Having disappeared, Gochiaev sent several communications to those conducting independent investigations into the bombings, in particular Aleksander Litvinenko and other members of the entourage around Berezovsky, who by this time had fled to London. He gave details about his role in the renting of storage areas in Moscow apartment buildings, but he claimed that he had not known what they were to be used for and that he had been framed. In exchange for information about the people he had dealt with in Moscow, Gochiaev, obviously aware of Berezovsky's considerable wealth, asked for money.

As Mikhail Trepashkin discovered, however, Gochiaev was not the person who had rented spaces for the explosives in Moscow. His photograph did not match the original composite photograph that had been compiled based on witnesses' descriptions. The police had apparently doctored the photograph later to make it look like Gochiaev so that the real culprit would not be identified. After painstaking research, Trepashkin was able to identify this key person in the bombings as one Vladimir Romanovich, a shadowy figure with ties both to the FSB and the Moscow criminal underworld. Immediately after Trepashkin made his discovery public, the mysterious Romanovich was killed in a car crash in Cyprus; thus, in Trepashkin's words, "the concrete trail of the *zakazchik* was broken."[16]

To sum up the paltry results of years of official investigations and prosecutions in the four bombings: seven men, Dagestanis, were convicted of organizing and carrying out the attack at Buinaksk, supposedly acting under the *zakazchik* Khattab. Two persons from the Karachay-Cherkassia, unemployed and eager to earn money, were convicted in the bombings in Moscow and Volgodonsk, but only as middlemen, not organizers. (A third individual was killed while Russian authorities were apprehending him in Georgia.) The man who organized the bombings, whether it was Romanovich or someone else, has never been apprehended and is probably dead. And the *zakazchik* again was said to be Khattab.

What is the evidence that Khattab was actually the person who ordered the 1999 bombings, rather than the FSB? Khattab was definitely a large presence in Chechnya at the time and viewed as a serious challenge by Russian authorities. Born in Saudi Arabia, he started his career as an international jihadist in Afghanistan, joining the *mujahidin* just as the Russians were withdrawing their troops from the country. He then moved to Tadzhikistan in 1994 and on to Chechnya in 1995, where he aligned himself with Chechen rebel Shamil Basaev and set up training camps for fighters against the Russians. Khattab supposedly was charismatic and able to recruit Muslims of all nationalities to the struggle against the Russians. And he apparently had his own resources and funding that could be used to recruit people to carry out terrorist missions.[17]

As several observers have pointed out, however, neither Khattab nor Basaev had any motive for bombing innocent Russian citizens. Alexander Litvinenko and Yuri Felshtinsky, authors of the book *Blowing Up Russia*, noted that "the Chechens knew it was not in their interest to carry out any terrorist attacks. Public opinion was on their side, and public opinion, both Russian and international, was more valuable to them than two or three hundred lives abruptly cut short."[18] General Aleksandr Lebed, governor of Krasnoyarsk District at the time, concurred: "Any Chechen commander who wanted revenge would have begun to blow up [Russian] generals. He would have struck at the buildings of the Ministry of Internal Affairs or the FSB, or at weapons storage areas or at atomic electric power stations. He would not have chosen as a target simple and innocent people."[19]

Khattab himself reportedly told an AP journalist around the time of the blasts that he and his rebels intended to bomb Russian cities. But he then insisted to the Interfax news agency on September 14, 1999 that he had nothing to do with the bombings: "We would not like to be akin to those who kill sleeping civilians with bombs and shells."[20] Russian authorities reportedly spent a year planning Khattab's assassination. Their intelligence agents eventually managed to infiltrate themselves into Khattab's Chechen enclave, and in March 2002 one of them handed over a letter to Khattab that was laced with poison. He died within hours.[21]

The FSB as Prime Suspect

The most persuasive evidence against the theory of Khattab as mastermind, supposedly in retaliation for the Russian incursion into Dagestan, is that the bombings could not have been planned and executed in the short time after the Russian foray there in August 1999. As journalist David Satter has pointed out, determining targets, renting spaces, and preparing and transporting explosives required several months' time.[22] And then of course there is the fact that the bombs contained hexogen (RDX), which is considered the most powerful of military explosives and is difficult to obtain. It became known, however, that a scientific research center in Moscow, Roskonversvzryvt-sentr, served as storage place for hexogen from military sources and that the director of the center was conducting illegal trade in the explosive under the watchful eyes of the FSB.[23]

Clearly, Russian law-enforcement authorities, with significant investigative tools and legal powers at their disposal, failed miserably in uncovering the real culprits in these explosions. It is thus reasonable to conclude that the Russian government never intended to unravel the secrets behind the bombings. That the authorities went through the motions in their investigations without actually producing results suggests strongly that Putin and the FSB were complicit in a cover-up. In addition, there is considerable evidence that the security services knew about the bombings before they happened.

Among such evidence is an episode that occurred in the Duma on September 13, 1999. Duma speaker Gennadii Seleznev, a Communist, announced that he had just received a report that an apartment building in Volgodonsk had been bombed the previous night. But this was three days before the bombing in that city actually took place— on September 16! LDPR leader Vladimir Zhirinovsky asked Seleznev at a Duma session on September 17 how he possibly could have informed the Duma about the explosion three days before it happened, and Seleznev avoided a direct answer. When asked several years later about his announcement, Seleznev said he could not remember what he had said, but that he had had no forehand knowledge that there would be a terrorist incident in Volgodonsk. He claimed that Zhirinovsky had simply stirred up a scandal over his statement. But of course there is a stenographic record of what was said in the Duma, so Seleznev's denials were futile.[24]

Kremlin sources offered a feeble explanation for Seleznev's September 13 announcement—that there actually had been a small explosion in Volgodonsk the evening before. According to the Volgodonsk MVD, an improvised explosive device made from a hand grenade blew up on the street at six in the evening on September 12, slightly wounding three people. But Seleznev had specifically referred to an apartment house, and this small explosion, with no casualties, would hardly have merited an announcement in the Duma. It is worth noting that Seleznev had close ties to the security services through the ad hoc Academy of National Security that he had established in St. Petersburg. It is very likely that, through these connections, Seleznev received advance information about the Volgodonsk bombing. And probable that he mistakenly referred to Volgodonsk, where a bombing was planned, instead of where a terrorist bomb actually had exploded at 5 A.M. on September 13—on Kashirskoe Highway in Moscow.

The Scandal Over Ryazan

For those who have studied the 1999 bombings, the smoking gun that pointed directly to the FSB as perpetrator of these attacks was the now-famous incident that occurred in the city of Ryazan, which is about 120 miles southeast of Moscow.[25] On the evening of September 22, six days after the Volgodonsk blast, residents of an apartment house on Novoselov Street noticed three suspicious strangers, two men and a woman, exiting the basement of the building. After the three drove off in a white Russian-made car, a Zhiguli, the residents called the local police. The police discovered three sacks of what looked like sugar in the basement, along with a timed electrical device. While the police, soon joined by FSB officers, took the sacks out of the building, residents of the seventy-seven apartments were evacuated (all but a few invalids who could not be moved).

A source of considerable controversy about whether the sacks contained explosives was the fact that when explosive experts tried to detonate the substance, nothing happened. Yet a gas analyzer got a positive reading for the presence of hexogen. One explanation for the discrepancy was that the amount tested for detonation was very small, and presumably an explosion would have taken place if all three sacks had been ignited when the electrical device went off at the time it was set for, 5:30 A.M. on September 23.[26]

Whatever the case, local authorities, both MVD and FSB, were convinced that they had averted a terrible explosion; they then scoured the city for other bombs. On the morning of September 23, the Russian media duly reported, with great sensation, that a bomb attack had been averted in Ryazan. Prime Minister Putin, in a brief public statement that morning, seemed to concur: "If the sacks which proved

to contain explosives were noticed, then there is a positive side to it."
On September 24, MVD Chief Vladimir Rushailo, who headed a special commission for combating terrorism, also spoke about the
thwarting of the terrorist attack in Ryazan and praised the local authorities for their vigilance.[27]

But in the meantime, on the evening of September 23, two of the
suspects who had planted the bags in the basement of the apartment
on Novoselov Street had been apprehended by local authorities in Ryazan. It turned out that they were employees of the FSB and thus
were released on the orders of FSB headquarters in Moscow. Now it
was time for damage control on the part of the FSB leadership. On the
morning of September 24, shortly after Rushailo spoke, FSB chief Patrushev weighed in with a surprising announcement on nationwide
television: there had never been a real bomb in the Ryazan apartment
house. The sacks contained no explosives and were placed there as
part of a "training exercise" to test the public's vigilance. The people
of Ryazan and the local enforcement agencies were outraged. And indeed, even the Ryazan FSB branch was caught off-guard, issuing a
statement that "the information about [a training exercise] was for us
completely unexpected and came just when our FSB department had
located in Ryazan the people who planted the explosives and were
detaining them."[28]

On September 27, the FSB closed its investigation into the episode of suspicious sacks in the Ryazan apartment building because of
the "absence of criminal acts." The residents of the building in question were not satisfied and wanted to press a case against the FSB in
court. They were put under heavy pressure by the local FSB to drop
their complaint, which they did.

The Russian Procuracy looked into the matter further, but without result. On March 22, 2000, four days before the presidential
elections which gave Putin a resounding victory, it pronounced its decision: "a criminal case will not be opened in relation to employees

of the Federal Security Service of the Russian Federation involved in the training exercises in Ryazan."[29] All official documents relating to the incident were sealed.

That same day, in an effort at damage control, Gennadii Zaitsev, former commander of the FSB's elite "Alpha" troops, along with a retired commander of the FSB's crack Vympel division, Dmitrii Gerasimov, elaborated on the "training exercise" in Ryazan. Gerasimov claimed that no live detonating devices had been used in the venture, and Zaitsev added that members of Vympel arrived in Ryazan and bought sacks of sugar at a market in preparation for a planned test: "It could not possibly have been an explosive. The experts [the bomb squad that arrived on the scene the night of September 22] simply ignored basic rules and used dirty instruments on which there were traces of explosives from previous analyses."[30]

Meanwhile, on March 13, an enterprising journalist from *Novaia gazeta* published an article claiming that a military arms depot just thirty kilometers from Ryazan housed a large cache of hexogen in bags marked "sugar."[31] This seemed to confirm that the three bags in the basement of the Novoselov apartments contained the same substance. Then on March 23, 2000, the television channel NTV aired a program titled "Ryazan Sugar," in which residents of the apartment house questioned three high-ranking FSB generals about what happened on the evening of September 22. The generals were unable to reply satisfactorily to any of their questions. According to David Satter: "When the program ended, the residents were more convinced than ever that they had been unwitting pawns in an FSB plot and had only through a miracle escaped with their lives."[32] Not surprisingly, in May 2000, Russian tax police stormed the headquarters of NTV, and Vladimir Gusinsky, the predominant shareholder in the station, was forced to sell out to the state-owned Gazprom as a guarantee that he would not be prosecuted.

Ryazan Reassessed

The Ryazan issue did not die down. In London, Boris Berezovsky and his supporters (the so-called BAB group) gathered their own evidence. In early 2002, Litvinenko and Yuri Felshtinsky, a historian residing in the United States who travelled often to London, published a book in Russian in which they discussed the Ryazan events in great detail, reinforcing the arguments put forward by the Russian media to show that the FSB had intended for a bomb to go off in Ryazan on September 22, 1999.[33] Then in early March 2002, a film called *Assassination of Russia* premiered in London and Moscow. The film, financed by Berezovsky, was a forceful indictment of the FSB and its behind-the-scenes role in the Ryazan affair.[34]

Apparently to rebut the arguments in the film, Rustam Arifdzhanov, the editor-in-chief of a publication called *Top Secret* (*Sovershenno sekretno*), which had close ties with the security services, addressed the Ryazan issue, claiming that he had access to secret documents. In a lengthy June 2002 article, Arifdzhanov presented a phantasmagoric picture of what had happened, replete with minute details of the special operation the group of three from the elite Vympel forces had undertaken. As John Dunlop observed, one problem with this new, officially sponsored version of the Ryazan incident was that the operatives were portrayed as having taken numerous precautions to cover their tracks and yet they returned, for some reason, to the scene of the crime that night and mingled among the residents who had been evacuated.[35]

The final word on Ryazan from Russian authorities came in May 2002, when the Russian Procuracy responded to an inquiry from a Duma deputy about the September 1999 bombings. The Procuracy's report noted that the Ryazan exercise, allegedly code-named "whirlwind-anti-terror," had been a joint undertaking by the head of the FSB and the Minister of Internal Affairs, and that the two officials had signed a directive for a plan to confirm the readiness of local authorities to respond to acts of terror by sending groups of faux terrorists to various locations.[36] The problem with this explanation was that Minister of Internal Affairs Rushailo was obviously completely in the dark when he appeared publicly on September 24, 1999 to congratulate local authorities for averting a terrorist attack in Ryazan.

And then, of course, the very idea of such an exercise made little sense. As one Russian analyst asked: "What, in the end was the supposed intention of the Ryazan exercises and what were they trying to verify? The rapid response of the militia? For that, it would have been sufficient to put the sacks of sugar in the basement, have the militia informed by the inhabitants of the building, and then, having evaluated the militia's level of responsiveness, revealed that it was just a test."[37]

To some, such as Evgenii Ikhlov, a member of the group Human Rights and no friend of the security services, the hypothesis that the FSB had intended for a bomb to detonate in Ryazan still made no sense, regardless of all the evidence. In Ikhlov's view, FSB officials had no logical reason to do so, because they had already achieved what they had intended by the earlier bombings. Russian society was completely mobilized against the Chechens, and another blast, killing hundreds, would have made the authorities look weak and incompetent. Ikhlov postulated that yes, the FSB had added some hexogen to the sugar in the bags and used a real detonator. But the intention was to have FSB officers then thwart what appeared to have been a bombing so they would look like heroes. The plan backfired when the Ryazan police unexpectedly tracked down the people who had planted the sacks of sugar. Patrushev was then compelled to say that the whole thing had been only a training exercise.[38]

But Sergei Iushenkov, a Duma deputy and member of the Kovalev Commission, argued that the FSB, and Putin, had clear aims in their plans to blow up the Ryazan apartment house on September 22, however misguided. On September 23, he noted, a group of governors demanded from President Yeltsin that he cede some of his powers to Prime Minister Putin. That same day, Yeltsin published a secret decree on initiating military actions in Chechnya, and on September 24 Putin ordered Russian military troops to invade the republic. According to Iushenkov, who would be assassinated in 2003: "These actions and steps were undertaken precisely because there had been formed in society the opinion that the apartment houses in Volgodonsk, Moscow, and, nearly, the house in Ryazan had been prepared to be blown up by Chechen rebels."[39] Iushenkov was apparently hypothesizing that, if the FSB's plan to blow up the Ryazan building had not been foiled at the last minute, Yeltsin might have been pressured to step down as president immediately, with Putin taking over.

Looking Back on September 1999

It is worth noting that the extensive reporting about the September bombings by the BAB group in London, including a film on the subject, was questioned even by fervent critics of the Putin regime in Russia. Berezovsky's record of colluding with members of Yeltsin's "family" to encourage an incursion by Chechen rebels into Dagestan in August 1999, and his promotion of Putin's candidacy as the heir to Yeltsin, understandably made democrats like Sergei Kovalev hesitant to accept all of what Berezovsky produced in London at face value.[40] And the book by Litvinenko and Felshtinsky, valuable as it was for its commentary and analysis, did not contain references to sources.

But, as journalist Dmitrii Sokolov pointed out: "The FSB and its whistleblowers were not on equal grounds. Information on the case is secret, with no access permitted. One can understand and excuse mistakes made by journalists in their investigations (if, in fact, there were mistakes), but how to justify the contradictions that issued from the authorities, who had all the information?"[41] The 1999 bombings in Russia were the regime's darkest secret. And those who attempted to get at the truth of this terrible episode in Russia's past would be eliminated, one by one.

It should come as no surprise that the Russian government not only cynically prevented information about the September 1999 bombings from emerging, but also did little to address compensation for the victims and their families. Some of the victims' families took their own initiative. Thus, in September 2007, a Civic Organization for Victims of Volga-Don (the Volgodonsk attack), with seven hundred adults and two hundred fifty children as members, was formed. (The head of the organization has insisted that this represents only a small fraction of those who suffered harm from the attack.) The group has met with nothing but indifference from officials at all levels of the government. President Putin rejected outright their appeal for a law that guarantees special compensation to those disabled by acts of terrorism.[42]

A lawyer for the victims, Igor Trunov, estimated that about three thousand people were recognized as having suffered losses as a result of the bombings in Moscow and Volgodonsk. But only a few dozen received compensation, and even that was very small—seven thousand rubles, or about two hundred dollars. As Trunov observed: "many people regarded these seven thousand rubles as a mockery of the authorities and didn't seek help, since the compensation failed even to cover their travel expenses, not to mention the loss of their beloved ones, and lost health, housing and property."[43]

How can one explain the continued support for Putin, given the government's handling of the bombing cases and the suspicions among Russians that the FSB was behind the attacks, or at least that the security services did not do their job in protecting Russian citizens? According to Sergei Kovalev, most Russians are simply indifferent: "I have met people who were convinced that the accusations [of the involvement of the security services] were true, and yet they voted for Putin with equal conviction. Their logic is simple: genuine rulers wield the kind of power that can do anything, including commit crimes."[44] One wonders how long this dynamic will hold. It is not far-fetched to suggest that, if Russians start to question the legitimacy of their leader, their thoughts will return to the violent events of September 1999.

Clinton and Putin, Japan, July 2000.

(Photograph courtesy of Pool/Getty)

Bush and Putin, St. Petersburg, June 2003.

(Photograph courtesy of REUTERS/Alamy Stock Photo)

5

SILENCING CRITICS

It isn't just one story that ends with a journalist's death; a climate of intimidation builds. If no one is punished, killers are
emboldened, and violence repeats.

Myroslava Gongadze, The Committee to Protect Journalists

Russia stands on the threshold of a new era. I am convinced we
will be witnesses of a huge revitalization of Russian society.

Paul Klebnikov, editor of the Russian edition of *Forbes*, three months

before he was murdered

The brutality of Russia's second military campaign in Chechnya—
particularly after the Kremlin, in early December 1999, gave an ulti-
matum to residents of the capital, Grozny, to leave the city or be
killed—drew harsh criticism from Western governments. (There was
even speculation about economic sanctions against Russia.) President
Bill Clinton, while acknowledging that Russia had to pursue counter-
terrorist operations in the wake of the apartment bombings, warned
that such operations could incite even more extremism.[1] Nonetheless,

in a telephone conversation in February 2000 with British Prime Minister Tony Blair, Clinton expressed optimism about the new Russian leader: "We're trying to resolve bilateral issues with Russia and kind of get this Chechnya thing resolved. Putin has enormous potential, I think . . . he's very smart and thoughtful. I think we can do a lot of good with him. . . . His intentions are generally honorable and straightforward, but he just hasn't made up his mind yet. He could get squishy on democracy."[2] President George W. Bush had a similarly favorable impression of Putin, noting famously after their first meeting in June 2001: "I looked the man in the eye. I found him to be very straightforward and trustworthy and we had a very good dialogue. I was able to get a sense of his soul."[3]

The September 11, 2001 terrorist attacks in the U.S. cemented the friendship between Bush and Putin, and they also quelled U.S. concerns about the Kremlin's military campaign in Chechnya. Putin was the first government leader to call Bush and voice his condolences over the attacks. He later said in a televised address to Russians: "Russia knows directly what terrorism means. And because of this we, more than anyone, understand the feelings of the American people. In the name of Russia, I want to say to the American people—we are with you."[4]

Indeed, the 9/11 attacks were serendipity for Putin. The atrocities being committed daily by Russian troops in Chechnya could now be justified as part of a global war against terrorism. Putin went on to offer logistic and intelligence support to the United States in its war against Al Qaeda in Afghanistan, including the use of bases in the former Soviet Union. In doing this, Putin endeared himself further to Bush, while linking Russia's fight against Chechen separatists to the overall struggle against global terrorism. As terrorism expert Elena Polakova noted in a recent book: "The triumph of Putin's position became clear when U.S. Secretary of State Colin Powell declared [in May 2002] that Russia was 'fighting terrorism in Chechnya, there is no doubt about that.'"[5] Polakova points outs that this shift in Western opinion was furthered by reports about connections of North Caucasus rebels with Al Qaeda, although in fact there was little solid evidence to link Chechen terrorists to Osama bin Laden.[6]

When Boris Berezovsky, having fled Russia, visited Washington with his aide Alex Goldfarb not long after 9/11, they were told by Thomas Graham, then a top State Department official, that Putin was now considered a U.S. ally. This news caused the two men great consternation, given that Berezovsky had become an outspoken Putin opponent. As Berezovsky said to Goldfarb after their meeting with Graham, "Volodya [Putin] is so fucking lucky. If there was no bin Laden, he should have invented him. I wonder whether the Americans understand that he is not their friend at all. He will play them and the Muslims against each other, exploring every weakness to his advantage."[7]

Addressing Domestic Criticism

Although Putin now had international opinion on his side, the Kremlin still had to suppress its own internal critics, including the courageous Russian reporters who were witnessing the devastation of Chechnya firsthand. In the year 2000 alone, five reporters covering the Chechen conflict—Aleksandr Efremov, Luisa Arzhieva, Vladimir Yatsina, Iskandar Khationi, and Adam Tepsurgaev—were killed. To be clear, Efremov, Arzhieva, and Yatsina died in war zones. But Khationi and Tepsurgaev were actually assassinated. Khationi, a correspondent for Radio Free Europe, who reported on human-rights abuses in Chechnya, was butchered with an axe outside his Moscow apartment block. Tepsurgaev, who filmed footage from Chechnya for Reuters, was shot to death by an unknown assailant in a Chechen village.[8] Clearly, someone wanted to discourage journalists from showing the outside world what was happening in that republic.

What was in fact happening? When Russians began their bombing campaign of Chechen territory in September 1999 and moved troops into Chechnya in early October, it soon became clear that their "anti-terrorist" operation was really a full-scale war against the civilian population. Grozny was bombarded daily, reducing buildings to rubble, killing scores of innocent people and causing thousands of refugees to flood out of the city. Federal forces began carrying out "cleanup" operations in areas under their control, which resulted in widespread murder, rape, and wanton violence against civilians. The Kremlin installed a puppet Chechen regime, headed by Akhmat Kadyrov, which ignored the atrocities being committed by Russian troops in exchange for monetary rewards.

Anna Politkovskaya, in her book *A Small Corner of Hell: Dispatches from Chechnya*, described the terrible suffering she witnessed in the monthly trips she had been making to Chechnya: "Torture is the norm. Executions without trial are routine. Marauding is commonplace. The kidnapping of people by Federal soldiers . . . is the stuff of everyday Chechen life." As for Putin, Politkovskaya observed: "He's in the Kremlin, enjoying the respect of the world community as an active member of the international 'antiterrorism' VIP club, the so-called coalition against terror." She went on to note: "Bush is in Moscow . . . fraternization . . . a 'historic visit' . . . but barely a word about Chechnya, as if the war did not exist."[9]

Outside of Chechnya, Russian journalists were reporting on the rampant corruption that was plaguing the Putin government at all levels. And sometimes they paid for their investigations with their lives. In addition to the five journalists mentioned above, scores of other Russian journalists were killed during Putin's first term in office.[10] These cases could not be attributed directly to the Kremlin, because they often involved reporters covering local corruption throughout the country. But the general atmosphere of lawlessness and impunity that the Kremlin did nothing to discourage was what gave rise to these crimes. And it also meant that many of the perpetrators went unpunished.

Igor Domnikov

On May 12, 2000, Igor Domnikov, a reporter for *Novaia gazeta,* was attacked in the entryway of his apartment building in southeastern Moscow by unidentified assailants. He was beaten unconscious on the head with a heavy metal object, suffering traumatic injuries. No money or documents were stolen by the killers. After being hospitalized in a coma for more than two months, Domnikov died on July 16 at age forty-two. His murder was not only devastating for his family (his parents, wife, and young son), but for his colleagues at *Novaia gazeta.* The editors there could not understand why Domnikov had been singled out for what seemed to be retribution for his writing: "Igor of course wrote critical articles, but the entire newspaper team was committed to investigating the dirty work of the authorities at all levels." As *Novaia gazeta* pointed out, Domnikov was reporting on financial malfeasance and bribery within the government of the region of Lipetsk. But, after all, the paper noted, "when are Russian officials not involved in corruption? This is the routine and only lazy reporters don't write about it."[11]

The investigation of the case dragged on for years. Finally, in 2007, five members of a notorious criminal gang headed by Eduard Tager'ianov, were convicted in the death of Domnikov, as well as in a number of other murders. (In fact, because Domnikov did not die immediately, the crime was not called murder but rather "inflicting bodily harm leading to death.") But these were only the attackers. The mastermind was still at large. It was not until December 2013 that Pavel Sopot, a member of Tager'ianov's gang, was sentenced to seven years in a labor camp for organizing the attack on Domnikov. In fact, investigators concluded that Sopot was actually acting on the orders of the former vice-governor of Lipetsk, Sergei Dobrovskii, who Domnikov had criticized in his reporting.[12] In the end, because the case dragged on for so long, Dobrovskii was able to avoid being tried because the statute of limitations ran out. In May 2015, a Moscow court declared the case closed.[13] Such is the way with Russian justice.

Sergei Iushenkov

Meanwhile, questions over the 1999 apartment bombings would not go away. Sergei Iushenkov, a liberal member of the Duma, was serving as vice-chair of the Kovalev Commission on the bombings when, in April 2003, he was shot four times in the chest as he walked from his car to the entrance of his apartment building. He died immediately. On that very day, Iushenkov's party, Liberal Russia, had officially registered to compete in the next Duma elections that December.

Iushenkov was an especially prominent parliamentarian, and his death was devastating to his colleagues in the political world. Boris Nemtsov, at the time the leader of the Duma faction Union of Right Forces, noted that Iushenkov was a key inspiration of Russia's democratic movement and that he was a person of flawless reputation. (Ironically, given his own assassination almost twelve years later, Nemtsov added that he hoped *this time* [italics added] the murderers would be found.)[14]

Iushenkov, who was fifty-three years old when he died, first entered politics in 1990, when the Soviet Union was still an entity, representing the bloc Democratic Russia as a deputy to the RSFSR Supreme Soviet (later the Supreme Soviet of the Russian Federation). He was one of those who defended Yeltsin and his supporters at the Russian White House during the coup attempt in August 1991 by organizing a chain of civilians to block a possible assault by KGB troops. Iushenkov was elected a deputy to the Russian Duma in 1993 and was at the time of his death a vice-chairman of the Duma Committee on Security. He was a rarity among politicians, in that he had no interest in reaping the rewards of the privatization of state enterprises that occurred under Yeltsin. As political analyst Leonid Radzikhovskii observed, he was among a small minority that "did not become wealthy in politics, who didn't steal, whether directly or through hidden connections," although he "had every chance, whenever he wished, to take part in the winners' feast, in the privatization of government property. . . . To him, it was repulsive."[15]

In 2000, Iushenkov founded, with Boris Berezovsky, the movement Liberal Russia, which in March 2002 became a party. The goals of the party were to promote small and medium businesses and to turn Russia into a European-style democracy. Berezovsky's presence in the party's leadership became a source of contention, however, especially since Russian authorities apparently were refusing to register the party as long as Berezovsky, living in London and now a bitter foe of Putin, was a part of its ruling body. In October 2002, Berezovsky was removed from the leadership of Liberal Russia. In the meantime, on August 21, 2002, one of Liberal Russia's leaders, Duma deputy Vladimir Golovlev, was shot dead on the street near his Moscow home while walking his dog. His killers were never found.

Iushenkov was not deterred by Golovlev's murder from pressing forward with his political agenda. At the beginning of March 2003, he flew to London and had talks with Berezovsky, with whom he reconciled despite past differences, about strategies for Liberal Russia in the months leading up to the December parliamentary elections. One plan that Iushenkov had in mind was to organize mass protests against the authoritarian measures of the Putin regime and the war in Chechnya. After Iushenkov was murdered, Liberal Russia foundered and did not gain the required votes to have its candidates participate in elections.[16]

Investigation of the Iushenkov Murder

Russian investigators acted quickly in the Iushenkov case, rounding up two suspects, including the alleged *zakazchik*, and charged them by June 2003. (Four others would later be detained.) The suspects were held in Moscow's high-security Lefortovo Prison. The investigation

was led by Procurator-General Vladimir Ustinov and deputy MVD
chief Rashid Nurgaliev, both of whom could be counted on to create
a Kremlin-inspired scenario of the murder. The alleged mastermind of the murder was Mikhail Kodanev, a leader of Liberal Russia
along with Iushenkov. Kodanev was accused of hiring his party aide,
Aleksandr Vinnik, to carry out the crime, along with four accomplices,
all of whom had criminal records. Supposedly, Kodanev's motives
were that he was being pushed out of the leadership of Liberal Russia
by Iushenkov and that he wanted the money Berezovsky had contributed to the party for himself.[17]

Berezovsky, who had met with Kodanev several times in London, insisted publicly that Kodanev could not possibly have ordered
Iushenkov's murder, because he had no motive. And Kodanev's
defense attorney, who was hired by Berezovsky, pointed out at the
trial, which began in March 2004, how sloppy the investigators had
been. The case against Kodanev rested solely on the testimony of Vinnik, which was highly contradictory. Vinnik gave conflicting accounts
of his meeting with Kodanev, who had allegedly paid him $50,000 to
kill Iushenkov. It was never made clear where the money had come
from or what Vinnik had done with it. Investigators did not bother to
follow up. Vinnik claimed that Kodanev had told him that he wanted
Iushenkov dead because the latter had made an agreement with Berezovsky that gave Kodanev a lesser role in Liberal Russia. Yet he said
that Kodanev paid him the money to kill Iushenkov in February 2003,
before the meeting between Iushenkov and Berezovsky in London
over the fate of the party took place.[18]

The jury found Kodanev guilty, along with Vinnik and two accomplices. Kodanev was sentenced to twenty years' imprisonment.
Grigorii Pasko, a journalist and environmental activist who had been
persecuted by the FSB and had become associated with Iushenkov not
long before his death, connected the Kremlin directly with the murder.
Pasko stated: "Who killed Sergei Iushenkov? I would like to remind

[you] here that FSB Major-General Alexander Mikhailov threatened Sergei Iushenkov directly on television, in the talk show *Poedinok* (Duel). Everyone saw and heard the general saying: 'Mr. Iushenkov, we will take care of you later on.' "[19]

Berezovsky maintained from London that the Kremlin was behind the murder as part of an effort to thwart challenges from democratic parties in the forthcoming Duma elections: "You have to look at the pattern: two of our party members have been killed, and I cannot enter Russia."[20] But others pointed out that Liberal Russia had so little support among the population that it did not pose an electoral threat to the Kremlin. Most probably it was a combination of factors that made Iushenkov a target for murder, especially his public contention that the FSB had organized the September 1999 bombings.

Iushenkov and the FSB

Iushenkov had flown to London in March 2002 for the world premier of *Assassination of Russia,* the above-mentioned documentary about the FSB's role in the 1999 explosions. He returned to Russia with copies of the film to be distributed all over the country, including in the Duma. The next month, Iushenkov carried his campaign to publicize the FSB's involvement in the bombings to the United States. He showed the film on Capitol Hill, at the Woodrow Wilson Center in Washington, and at Harvard and Columbia universities. According to Alex Goldfarb, who accompanied Iushenkov for much of his tour: "Invariably he made a strong impression. He was a good speaker and he projected passion and conviction."[21]

The Kremlin cannot have been happy about Iushenkov's promotion of *Assassination of Russia,* especially at a time when Putin was engaging in a charm offensive toward the West, trying to convince Western leaders that he was a reliable partner in the battle against international terrorism. Then, of course, as co-chairman of the Kovalev Commission, Iushenkov began pressuring Russian authorities to furnish information that they had refused to release on the bombings. As he told Goldfarb: "I don't have to prove anything. The government has been accused of mass murder of its own citizens, and half of the people believe it; this is enough for me. Presumption of innocence does not apply to governments; it's a device to protect people from the government. Putin has an obligation to dispel the suspicions."[22]

A further source of Kremlin ire toward Iushenkov was undoubtedly his questioning of the FSB's role in the October 2002 Moscow theater siege. In early 2003, the Kovalev Commission expanded its purview to look into the circumstances of the siege. There were several aspects of the hostage crisis that suggested the FSB had inspired the attack, not the least of which was that fifty known Chechen terrorists had gathered in Moscow with weapons and explosives under the very nose of the FSB. And once the terrorists were finally incapacitated by the poison gas that had been funneled into the theater, why had the police and the FSB reportedly executed all of them, instead of keeping them alive to provide valuable information?[23]

In fact, Chechen sources in London claimed that one of the terrorists, Khanpash Terkibaev, had in fact escaped the theater and was living in hiding in Chechnya. Terkibaev was suspected of being an agent of the FSB, and a file on him was handed over to Iushenkov by Litvinenko when Iushenkov was in London in early April 2003. Iushenkov then gave the file to Anna Politkovskaya—who, ten days after Iushenkov was shot, published a sensational article based on interviews with Terkibaev, in which she alleged that the authorities had known about the hostage seizure before it happened.[24]

Alex Goldfarb recalls that he was initially "of two minds" about who had ordered Iushenkov's murder, especially when the authorities first came up with a zakazchik, Kodanev, who seemed to have a motive: Kodanev was losing his standing in Liberal Russia after Iushenkov reconciled with Berezovsky. But Litvinenko, who Goldfarb saw often in London, convinced him that indeed the FSB had ordered the murder. The two killers, Litvinenko noted, were drug addicts who had probably been recruited by the FSB when they were in jail with promises of a reduction in their sentences for drug activity if they carried out the killing and named Vinnik as the organizer. Vinnik was apparently told he would get a lesser sentence if he in turn accused Kodanev. This was, according to Litvinenko, a classic FSB operation. There would be others.[25]

Iurii Shchekochikhin

Iurii Shchekochikhin, a member of the Kovalev Commission, a Duma deputy from the Yabloko Party and one of Russia's most respected investigative journalists, died suddenly in July 2003 at the age of fifty-three from apparent poisoning. A 1975 graduate of the journalism department of Moscow State University, Shchekochikhin had worked as a reporter for several leading Russian newspapers and since 1996 had been a journalist for *Novaia gazeta,* where he became deputy editor. He was an outspoken critic of both the first and second Chechen wars and was among the first to voice skepticism toward official versions of such incidences as the 2000 *Kursk* submarine disaster, in which the entire crew perished, and the Moscow theater hostage crisis.[26]

In addition to his work for the Kovalev Commission, Shchekochikhin had been investigating the corruption scandal involving a large Moscow furniture store called Three Whales [*Tri Kita*], whose managers were suspected of weapons-smuggling, money laundering, tax evasion, and bribery of government authorities, in particular customs officials and employees of the MVD, FSB, and Procuracy. After Shchekochikhin published a story in early 2002 noting that millions of dollars had been laundered by owners of the Three Whales, rumors abounded about the involvement of top law-enforcement officials, who were allegedly using the furniture business to funnel vast sums of money through the Bank of New York. In apparent retaliation for his revelations, Shchekochikhin was beaten up outside his home by unknown assailants, and he received death threats against himself and his family, which prompted him to hire security protection for one of his sons. He remained steadfast. In February 2003, his party Yabloko issued a defiant statement: "If the life of a journalist and his family is the price to pay for telling the truth, then there is no freedom of speech in the country."[27]

Shchekochikhin kept digging, using his Duma position to request interviews from government figures and gain access to documents. He also wrote to Putin directly, requesting that Putin intervene in the Three Whales case. Although Putin said he would, nothing ever came of it. This is hardly surprising, given that senior officials from the security services were implicated. On June 2, 2003, Shchekochikhin published yet another article in *Novaia gazeta*, providing new details of the far-reaching corruption in the case. He observed that, whereas authorities in Europe and the United States had arrested people connected to the affair, Russian law-enforcement agencies had done nothing. He concluded: "Do not tell me fairy tales about the independence of judges. Until we see a fair trial, the documents of the case will be eliminated, witnesses intimidated or killed, and investigators themselves prosecuted."[28]

Shchekochikhin, a member of both the Duma Anti-Corruption Committee and the Security Committee, was also investigating financial malfeasance on the part of former Minister of Atomic Energy Evgenii Adamov. Shchekochikhin uncovered evidence that Adamov had stolen millions of dollars that the U.S. Department of Energy had given to Russia to improve its nuclear security. In March 2003, Shchekochikhin passed on a report against Adamov to the Procuracy, but with no result. Adamov was finally arrested in Switzerland in 2005 and extradited to Russia. Despite the fact that he was found to have defrauded the Russian government of $31 million and convicted of these charges by a Moscow court in February 2008, his sentence was suspended by a higher court two months later, and he was released from prison.[29]

Shchekochikhin Meets His Fate

Shortly before his death, Shchekochikhin met in Moscow with officials from the FBI to discuss the Three Whales scandal and its
connection to the Bank of New York. He was planning on flying
to the United States in early July to testify about the case, as well
as about Adamov's defrauding of the Russian government. But he
never made the trip. In mid-June he fell ill, and was hospitalized in
grave condition on June 21.

Shchekochikhin's death, on July 3, was excruciating. He lost his
hair, his skin peeled off his body, and he suffered failure of all his major organs—kidney, liver, lung, and brain. His wife, Nadezda Azhgikhina, herself a journalist, told me that when she saw her husband's
body after he died, he was unrecognizable: "he was only fifty-three
and he looked like a man in his eighties."[30] Officially the cause of
death was toxic epidermal necrolysis, also known as Lyell's syndrome,
a very rare and often deadly affliction that is usually caused by an al-
lergic reaction to drugs. But in this case doctors could not establish
the substance that caused the reaction. Shchekochikhin did not take
any medications, and his only allergy was to honey. When Shchekochikhin's family requested his medical records so that they could learn
more about his illness, they were told that information about the di-
agnosis and treatment was a "medical secret." Later, when pressed,
the Procuracy claimed that Shchekochikhin's medical record had
been accidentally thrown out by a charwoman.[31]

The Procuracy did not initiate a criminal investigation into
Shchekochikhin's death on the grounds that the cause had been established. But in 2008, his family and former newspaper colleagues
managed to persuade the Russian Investigative Committee to open
another investigation. The process was short-lived, and the case
was soon closed again. Sergei Sokolov, Shchekochikhin's newspaper
colleague, stated in 2010 that he and his colleagues had new evidence
that they were looking into and that they would get to the bottom of

the case. But the years have passed, and still there are no answers.[32] His widow remains hopeful: "I do believe, and so does Grigory Yavlinsky [leader of the Yabloko party], that we will know the truth sooner or later. . . . We are waiting until someone will be ready to talk," she told me.[33] Shchekochikhin was hardly the only one in Russia to write about high-level corruption, but what probably sealed his fate was his giving of information to the FBI and his planned trip to the United States to present testimony. As with Iushenkov (and later Nemtsov), approaching the Americans was something that would not be tolerated by the Kremlin; Shchekochikhin had crossed a tripwire.

Paul Klebnikov

A little over a year after Shchekochikhin's death, another muckraking journalist died in Moscow, this time an American. On July 9, 2004, Paul Klebnikov, editor of the Russian-language *Forbes* magazine, was walking from his office to the subway at around 9:30 P.M. when a Zhiguli automobile drew up beside him and its tinted windows were lowered. Klebnikov was shot four times in the chest and stomach and once in the head. The editor of the Russian edition of *Newsweek*, Aleksandr Gordeev, happened to be nearby and rushed to the scene. Klebnikov was still conscious and able to tell him that he had seen the face of the killer—a dark-haired man thirty to thirty-five years old. Emergency medics came quickly and took Klebnikov to the hospital, but he died in the hospital elevator. Two unidentified persons had pushed their way into the elevator cab, despite pleas of medics that it was overloaded. The cab fell to the basement floor, where its doors were stuck for fifteen minutes as Klebnikov lay dying.[34]

The forty-one-year-old Klebnikov, who was descended from a family of prominent Russians, left behind a wife, Musa, and three small children, who lived in the United States but visited Moscow often. Klebnikov had intended only to spend a year in Russia working for *Forbes* and then to return to his family. Just the day before he was killed, he had sat with Musa at a Moscow playground, watching one of their boys play in the bright sunshine, before Musa and the children flew back home.[35]

Klebnikov's most recent piece for *Forbes* had listed the hundred wealthiest businessmen in Russia, which could hardly have endeared him to the Kremlin, given that several of these men were close to Putin. First on the list was Mikhail Khodorkovsky, with a net worth of over $15 billion. (Khodorkovsky had been arrested by Russian authorities on charges of tax evasion and fraud the year before.) Second was Roman Abramovich, with a net worth of $12.5 billion.[36] Although he was generally optimistic about Russia and its future, in an interview the morning of his murder Klebnikov had this to say: "It [the government] is meddling in absolutely everything it thinks should be meddled in. All too soon, we may begin talking of another danger. Instead of [this danger] being posed by oligarchs, it will be posed by the bureaucratic machinery applying the law as it sees fit."[37]

Russian Authorities Respond Quickly

Literally hours after Klebnikov's killing, Russian authorities claimed that Chechens were the perpetrators, thus reinforcing the Kremlin's familiar line about Chechen terrorists. Then, after an almost year-long investigation, the Procurator-General announced in June 2005 the identity of five Chechens who were involved in the killing. Three were in custody—Kazbek Dukuzov, Musa Vakhaev, and Fail Sadretdinov—but two others remained at large, including the alleged mastermind, Chechen rebel leader Khozh-Akhmed Nukhaev, who was said to have paid the killers to carry out the murder. Nukhaev, according to the Procuracy's account, was motivated by a 2003 book Klebnikov had published about him in Russia, *A Conversation with a Barbarian*, which was based on extensive interviews the journalist had conducted with Nukhaev in Baku, Azerbaijan.[38]

Those who knew Klebnikov were surprised by the Procuracy's claim that Nukhaev had ordered his killing, because Klebnikov's book did not portray Nukhaev or Chechens in a bad light. The book's publisher, Valerii Streletskii, voiced particular skepticism: "I cannot imagine what could have displeased Nukhaev about this book."[39] Journalist Anna Politkovskaya agreed: "the suggestion by the law-enforcement agencies that the perpetrators were Chechens taking revenge for a badly written book about the adventurist Khozh-Akhmed Nukhaev is nonsense."[40] Nukhaev was a well-known Chechen businessman and politician, with deep ties to the criminal world. The so-called godfather of the Chechen mafia in Moscow, he was said to be the model for the book *Icon* (later made into a film) by Frederick Forsythe. Nukhaev, who at one point had been deputy prime minister of Chechnya, had in the nineties established several businesses and organizations promoting ventures, including oil, that would both be profitable for him and at the same time help Chechen militants in their struggle against Russia.[41]

By this time, Nukhaev was implicated in numerous crimes—he had been arrested several times, but was always released—and was on the wanted list of Russian law-enforcement agencies. But he nonetheless had visited Moscow freely before he left Chechnya to live in Baku in 1997. This suggested that he had a covert arrangement with the FSB, which was using him for its own purposes. As one source observed: "The FSB pays close attention to Nukhaev's activities within and outside of Russia."[42] Aside from the lack of an obvious motive, the theory that Nukhaev was the zakazchik in the Klebnikov killing was also thrown into question by reports that Nukhaev had been killed in Chechnya in early 2004, several months before Klebnikov was murdered.[43] Whether or not those reports were true, Nukhaev completely disappeared and most probably has been dead for a very long time.

Trials in the Klebnikov Case

In May 2006, the three men charged in the Klebnikov murder were acquitted by a jury after a closed trial. Later that year, the Russian Supreme Court overturned the verdict and announced a new trial. But two of the accused Chechens who had earlier been exonerated—Vakhaev and Dukuzov—failed to show up for the retrial and the other defendant, Sadretdinov, was already in prison on other charges, so in 2007 the case was dropped. President Putin had told Klebnikov's family in September 2005 that he knew who the killers were and that they would be brought to justice. But when the journalist's wife and brother went to Moscow for a ceremony to honor him five years after his death, they saw nothing to encourage them. Klebnikov's brother Peter could only say this: "It gets whittled down. They chip away at the resolve of the family and the people who care about it. It's death by a thousand blows."[44]

The Klebnikov case was revived in 2013, with a new twist. In September of that year, former militia officer Dmitrii Pavliuchenkov, a defendant in court proceedings over the 2006 murder of Anna Politkovskaya, claimed that two of the accused in the latter case, former militia officer Sergei Khadzhikurbanov and one Loma-Ali Gaitukaev, had enlisted him to trail not only Politkovskaya, but also Klebnikov in the days before his murder.[45] The connection between the murders of Klebnikov and Politkovskaya was the prosecution's suggestion that Gaitukaev, in both cases, was acting on orders from Berezovsky. A witness had supposedly heard Gaitukaev discussing plans to murder Klebnikov with Nukhaev, but the witness said it was clear that Nukhaev was only the middleman and that the orders came from abroad (i.e., Berezovsky).[46]

It Is Easy to Blame the Dead

By this time, investigators had long been leaking to the Russian media the theory that Berezovsky had ordered the Klebnikov murder from London and had used Nukhaev as a middleman. Given that he died in March 2013, it was all the more convenient to implicate Berezovsky because he could not challenge the accusations. The main thrust of the argument implicating Berezovsky was that Klebnikov had published an article for *Forbes* in 1996 ("Godfather of the Kremlin") in which he painted Berezovsky as a crook with ties to the Chechen mafia and even suggested that he was behind the 1994 murder of journalist Vladislav Listev. Berezovsky was beside himself and in 2000 took *Forbes* to court in London for libel. (Forbes was forced to apologize for misrepresenting Berezovsky but was not subjected to fines.) Klebnikov then went on to expand his material on Berezovsky into a book with the same title as his article, which appeared in 2000.[47]

Shortly before his death, Klebnikov was supposedly looking into Berezovsky's tenure as deputy secretary of the Security Council and the Kremlin's point man on Chechnya. There were reports that Berezovsky had funneled money designated for the reconstruction of Chechnya into his own pocket, and Klebnikov had expressed to a fellow journalist his interest in the matter. One of Klebnikov's sources of information was a former vice-premier of Chechnya, Ian Sergun, but Sergun was also murdered, just two weeks before Klebnikov was killed. Berezovsky's former security guard Sergei Sokolov claimed that after Klebnikov's 1996 article appeared, Berezovsky told him in no uncertain terms that Klebnikov should be killed. (Sokolov's statements became part of the evidence in the murder case.) Klebnikov's brother Peter recalled that Klebnikov felt threatened by Berezovsky, and a business associate of Berezovsky in London told Forbes that Berezovsky had voiced to him the idea of killing Klebnikov.[48]

Musa Klebnikov and Paul's brother Peter told me when I met with them in July 2016 that there should be more investigation into the Sergun case and the relationship between Paul and Berezovsky, who they have not ruled out as the possible mastermind of Paul's murder.[49] But most of those who knew Berezovsky considered the idea that he would order the murder of Klebnikov to be far-fetched. Berezovsky was known to be passionate and often voiced feelings of revenge toward those who offended him; but Klebnikov's writings, in their view, would hardly have motivated Berezovsky to have him murdered. Klebnikov's article about Berezovsky came out seven years before his murder. His 2000 book on the same subject had mixed reviews and did not create much of a stir. Critics claimed that his book relied extensively on the disgruntled former chief of Yeltsin's security guard Aleksandr Korzhakov, who was fired by Yeltsin in 1996. More importantly, Berezovsky had been living abroad since 2000 in France and then London, where he was at the mercy of his British hosts. It was hardly in his interests (or even his ability) to organize political murders in Russia, despite his possible connections to the Chechen mafia. As one observer noted, Berezovsky was "pathologically afraid" of having Britain's security services focus on his ties with that group.[50]

Endings Dragged Out

In 2015, the chief investigator in the Klebnikov case announced on behalf of the Investigative Committee that their probe had come to an end because the three main suspects—Kazbek Dukuzov, his brother Magomed, and Khozh-Akhmed Nukhaev—were out of reach. All were on the authorities' wanted list. But in early 2016 the Procurator-General's office overturned this decision and kept the case open, on the grounds that Sergei Khadzhikurbanov, in a penal colony for the murder of Anna Politkovskaya, might provide more information on the Klebnikov murder.[51]

In the Klebnikov case, like those of many other political murders in Russia, investigators went through the motions of trying to solve the crime without really doing so. It was if they had been hired as actors in a play, where the scenario was already written. The fact that most trials in Russia are held in secret enables this process. Questions about evidence can be ignored. No one is held responsible for sloppy work, lost documentation, forced confessions, or the fact that key suspects and witnesses disappear. As Peter Klebnikov observed to me about the trial in his brother's case: "It was a farce. There were many impediments to justice. The jurors were threatened, the judges changed, the shooters were released."[52]

Peter and Musa are still hopeful that there will be a resolution of the murder case, although they told me that they are concerned about the fact that time is running out. They have not been allowed access to important evidence that they think might lead to the mastermind and are frustrated by the communications they receive from Russian investigators, who they say are deeply divided about the case. As Musa told me, "they are not doing their job because their hands are tied." She and Peter have not seen evidence of Putin's involvement in the murder, but they are convinced that the order to assassinate Paul came from the upper echelons of power. They are also certain that the Chechens who were charged did in fact commit the crime. Of course their main goal is to have the mastermind identified and prosecuted. And that, sadly, may not happen, at least as long as the current regime remains in the Kremlin.

Andrei Kozlov. *(Photograph courtesy of ITAR-TASS Photo Agency/Alamy Stock Photo)*

Anna Politkovskaya. *(Photograph courtesy of Jeremy Sutton-Hibbert/Alamy Stock Photo)*

6

MAFIA-STYLE KILLINGS IN MOSCOW: KOZLOV AND POLITKOVSKAYA

Why am I still alive? If I speak seriously about this, I would understand it as a miracle. It really is a miracle.

Anna Politkovskaya, 2005

Prelude

Relations between Russia and the United States continued to flour-
ish after their mutually declared partnership in the war on terror. In
May 2002, President Bush traveled to Moscow, where he and Putin
signed the Moscow Treaty on Strategic Offensive Reductions, in which
the United States and Russia pledged to reduce their mutual nuclear
arsenals by nearly two thirds within the next ten years. After the
signing, Bush had this to say:

> President Putin and I today ended a long chapter of confron-
> tation, and opened up an entirely new relationship between
> our countries. Mr. President, I appreciate your leadership. I
> appreciate your vision. I appreciate the fact that we've now
> laid the foundation for not only our governments, but future

governments to work in a spirit of cooperation and a spirit of trust . . . I understand full well that the people of Russia have suffered at the hands of terrorists. And so have we. And I want to thank President Putin for his understanding of the nature of the new war we face together, and his willingness to be determined and steadfast and patient as we pursue this war together.[1]

Apparently forgetting about Chechnya, a part of Russia, Bush added that "America welcomes the dramatic improvement in freedoms in Russia since Soviet days."

Bush visited Russia again at the end of May 2003, this time St. Petersburg, for the formal ratification of the Moscow Treaty on June 1. Again, he was effusive in his praise for Putin: "I'm honored to be here, Mr. President, and I'm honored to be with my good friend, Vladimir Putin. . . . President Putin and I have agreed to expand and strengthen high-level contacts and communications between our two governments. . . . In a recent address to the Russian Duma, President Putin committed to working for a sustainable democracy in Russia where human, political, and civil rights will be fully ensured. That is the vision of a strong leader.[2]

The cordial relationship between Moscow and Washington would start to sour, however, when the Kremlin's commitment to democracy was thrown into question by the high-profile arrest in October 2003 of Russian oligarch Mikhail Khodorkovsky. Khodorkovsky, CEO of the Russian oil giant Yukos, was charged with fraud and tax evasion, but it was widely assumed that the charges were spurious and that the real reason for his arrest was his involvement in politics, which Putin considered a threat to his rule. (The arrest, orchestrated behind the scenes by Igor Sechin, head of Rosneft, also enabled Rosneft to take over many of Yukos's assets.) Congress was quick to respond to the Khodorkovsky affair, with the Senate passing a resolution in December 2003, noting that his arrest raised questions about the selective application of law in Russia.[3]

Then, of course, came the killing of Paul Klebnikov the following July, which drew Washington's attention, particularly since he was an American. A few days after the murder, Virginia Congressman Frank Wolf spoke ominously about Russia's "dark side" and said the U.S. must insist on a thorough and open investigation of the case.[4] And in early 2005, Hillary Clinton, then a senator from New York, Klebnikov's home state, talked at great length about his murder in remarks she gave in the Senate.[5] She said she had urged Bush to raise the case directly with Putin, but if Bush had in fact done so, it had little effect. 2006 would witness the most shocking and audacious Russian contract killings yet.

Kozlov: A Promising Career Cut Short

Andrei Kozlov was a superstar in the Russian banking world. After graduating at age twenty-four from the prestigious Moscow Institute of Finance in 1989, Kozlov was hired straightaway by the Central Bank of what was then the USSR. In 1991, after the Soviet collapse, he became director of the Securities Department at the Bank of Russia, where he operated at the nexus of relations between the government and private banks. By 1995, at only thirty, he had been elevated to a deputy chairman—an unprecedented feat, given that the Bank of Russia was conservative by nature—and in 1997 Kozlov was promoted to first deputy chairman.[6]

Kozlov's seemingly brilliant career suffered a setback in 1998 as a result of the financial crisis in Russia that year. A decline in oil prices and a general slowdown in the world economy had left the Russian government's foreign-exchange reserves significantly depleted and caused a huge fiscal deficit. In August 1998, the government devalued the ruble, defaulted on domestic debt, and declared a moratorium on paying foreign debt. When the Central Bank allowed a floating exchange rate for the ruble in September, its value fell sharply. Kozlov had publicly urged individual investors in commercial banks to transfer their money to short-term government bonds in the state savings bank (Sberbank) in order to protect their investments. But in fact their investments lost more than half their value after the ruble was devalued and the government defaulted on its bonds.[7]

By January 1999, the government admitted that it had made a mistake. There were reports in the media (unsubstantiated) that Kozlov and his colleagues in the securities department had siphoned off money from a $22.6 billion IMF bailout and put it in secret accounts. Kozlov resigned from the Central Bank, along with its chairman, Sergei Dubinin. When Kozlov left the bank, he reportedly called his subordinates together and said with a smile, "now you will see something you have never seen." Much to their surprise, given that Kozlov never drank, he downed a glass of champagne.[8]

Kozlov, who was by all accounts forceful and self-confident, bounced back quickly, going into the private sector as chairman of the board of the newly established Russkii Standart Bank. He then moved to Aeroflot's new travel company, Mir Aeroflota, and later worked for the Washington-based Financial Services Volunteer Corps, which provided consulting services to banks. In April 2002, Sergei Ignatiev, the newly appointed chairman of the Russian Central Bank, invited Kozlov back as first deputy chairman. He soon achieved new prominence as an advocate of vigorous banking reform. But he also made a lot of enemies.

Going After Illegal Money

Kozlov's responsibility at the Central Bank was supervision and enforcement of banking regulations, particularly those designed to curb money laundering. During the Yeltsin years, organized crime had completely infiltrated the banking sector, thus enabling vast sums of illegal money to flow out of the country readily. According to one report, twenty-five of Russia's largest banks had links with organized crime by 1995. Although Putin presented himself as a law-and-order president who wanted to fight corruption, after he took office the Kremlin continued to use organized crime for its own purposes, which included using a number of smaller, low-profile banks to "wash" illegal financial gains in order to make them appear legitimate.[9]

As first deputy of the Central Bank, Kozlov initiated a deposit-insurance system that filtered out banks that were unreliable with investors' money, and he also revoked licenses of banks suspected of money laundering and other illicit practices. In the first six months of 2006, more than seventy private banks lost their licenses. Kozlov also became the "talking head" of the bank, instead of Ignatiev, who avoided publicity. In the words of one Russian journalist: "On the one hand, this suited the qualities and ambitions of Kozlov, who always took pleasure in giving interviews and 'shone' in public. On the other hand, this arrangement suited Ignatiev and other leaders of the Central Bank. After all, the loudest and most public official always gets the bad things hung on him and in such cases is sacrificed for the sake of peace and quiet."[10]

In early September 2006, Kozlov and his colleagues announced new initiatives at a Russian Banking Association conference in Sochi. One was that auditing companies would share responsibilities for financial malfeasance on the part of banks and thus would be obliged to report to the Central Bank when they came across illegalities. Second, bankers who were found guilty of financial crimes would be banned from the banking profession for life. These new, harsh measures can hardly have endeared Kozlov to the banking community.[11]

The Hit

Just days later, on the evening of September 13, 2006, Kozlov left work to play in a soccer match among Central Bank employees at the Spartak Sports Complex in Moscow. The game ended at 8:30 and, shortly before 9 P.M., Kozlov exited the indoor arena and walked to his parked Mercedes with his driver, Aleksandr Semenov. Despite his high position in the Central Bank, Kozlov did not have his own body-guard, so Semenov was the only one who accompanied him. Imme-diately after Kozlov got in the car, two men approached. One went straight to the window and shot Kozlov twice in the head. The other shot Semenov in the chest as he was still putting Kozlov's belongings in the trunk. Semenov started to run back to the sports center, but the killer shot him in the back. He died almost immediately. Kozlov was rushed to the hospital, where doctors operated on him, but they could not save his life. He died in the early hours of the morning, leaving behind a pregnant wife and three children.[12]

The killers, meanwhile, had escaped on foot through the heavily forested park that surrounded the complex, after discarding their weapons. Putin made no public statements on the murder for two days. On September 15, he called Sergei Ignatiev to his office and they talked for over an hour. Then came Aleksandr Bortnikov, at the time head of the FSB's Department for Economic Security, and MVD chief Rashid Nurgaliev. Following another talk with Ignatiev, Putin finally spoke out and called the assassination "a sign of the exacerbation of economic crime."[13]

In response to the murder, Putin created a committee under the Procurator-General's Office to fight economic crime and appointed former Labor Minister Gennadii Melikian to take Kozlov's place as bank regulator. But these were half-hearted measures. Indeed, as Swedish economist Anders Aslund observed, these moves actually suggested that Putin intended to dismantle the stringent inspec-tion system that Kozlov had introduced: "[Putin] says that we need to strengthen bank inspection, after which he demolishes bank inspec-tion, both institutionally, by setting up this committee, giving the Prosecutor-General's Office the main responsibility for fighting money laundering—that is, taking away responsibility from the very decent Central Bank—and secondly, by appointing the weakest person [Melikian] going in the Central Bank to run the bank inspection responsibilities that remain."[14]

Scandalous Revelations

As it turned out, Putin had good reason for rolling back Kozlov's ambitious reforms of the banking system and, more importantly, for wanting Kozlov out of the picture. A huge financial scandal, involving several of his cronies, including Bortnikov, had been about to erupt at the very time of Kozlov's murder. This was revealed much later, when, in May 2007, Moldovan investigative journalist Natalia Morar broke a sensational story in *New Times* magazine, a publication noted for courageous and accurate reporting. Morar reported, from sources in the MVD, that Austrian police authorities had linked Kozlov's murder to a multi-million-dollar money laundering scheme in Russia. At the time of his death, Kozlov had been assisting the MVD's Department of Economic Security in an investigation of the scheme, whereby high-level Kremlin officials had funneled large sums through Diskont Bank and the Austrian Bank Raiffeisen. Just five days before Kozlov was killed, a criminal case against certain individuals at Diskont Bank, which had already had its license revoked, was initiated by the MVD.[15]

Bank Raiffeisen was the conduit for the money laundering because it received deposits from the Russian government for the construction of the North European gas pipeline. According to an MVD source: "Under the cover of this money, a parallel flow of money from a number of high-level Russian officials and commercial enterprises controlled by the FSB Department of Economic Security went [into Bank Raiffeisen]." Among these officials were Bortnikov and Rosneft's Igor Sechin, one of Putin's closest allies.[16] Kozlov had been playing with fire.

Not surprisingly, the Procuracy's office, which had the ultimate authority, closed the MVD's case against Diskont Bank shortly after Kozlov was murdered on the grounds that the case was "insignificant." Austrian authorities sent the Russian Procuracy all the documentation they had on the money laundering case and never received an answer. Morar's article in *New Times* created a stir in the independent media when it appeared months later, but by this time public interest in the Kozlov murder, such as it was, had subsided. And Morar, following an article she wrote in December 2007 about illegal Kremlin funding of pro-Kremlin parties in the 2007 legislative elections, was banned from re-entering Russia. She was lucky, in that she escaped the Kremlin's retribution with her life. After her piece on money laundering appeared, Morar had been warned indirectly by the FSB: "There is no need to end your life with an article—someone might simply wait for you at the entrance to your apartment building, and they will not find a killer afterward."[17]

Aleksei Frenkel

As for the Kozlov murder investigation, law-enforcement authorities quickly arrested three hapless Ukrainian men in their mid-thirties— taxi drivers living on the outskirts of Moscow—who had allegedly carried out the crime. By early January 2007, the Procuracy announced the arrest of the presumed *zakazchik*, a young banker named Aleksei Frenkel, former chairman of VIP-Bank, which had been denied access to the deposit insurance system in 2005. After Frenkel appealed the denial in a court of arbitration and the court decided in his favor, the Central Bank revoked VIP-Bank's license because of money laundering. These events, according to the Procuracy, propelled Frenkel to have Kozlov killed.[18]

But many observers, particularly those close to Kozlov who understood the banking system, thought it unlikely that Frenkel was behind the murder. Between the beginning of 2006 and the time of Kozlov's murder, a total of forty-one banks had lost their licenses, so

Frenkel was hardly the only banker who suffered the ill effects of Kozlov's policies. All who knew Frenkel—and he had many friends—said that he was completely incapable of ordering a murder. Also, Frenkel was highly competent, and whoever was behind the killing displayed recklessness, hiring not professionals, but thugs, to do the job. Finally, the media for weeks before Frenkel's detention had been reporting that investigators had determined who had murdered Kozlov and had made arrests. Yet Frenkel, by all accounts, showed no signs of concern and went about his business. If he really was the culprit, why would he not have simply fled Russia, taking with him considerable sums of money?[19]

During the trial of Frenkel and the others accused, which began in March 2008, Frenkel's lawyer produced testimony that Kozlov's widow, Ekaterina Kozlova, had given investigators shortly after his death. Kozlova said that two weeks before his murder, her husband had told her about Diskont Bank losing its license and mentioned that large sums of money had been transferred out of the bank. But at the trial, Kozlova for some reason backed off from her earlier statements and said that her husband had only mentioned vaguely that Diskont Bank was having troubles. She did, however, tell the court that Kozlov had a premonition that he would be killed shortly before the murder, asking her "how will you live without me?" Although he mentioned "big crooks and thieves" in banks more than once, he never spoke about Frenkel and his bank.[20]

Kozlov's former colleague, Deputy Chairman of the Central Bank Viktor Mel'nikov, also testified that Kozlov had expressed concern about repercussions from his removal of licenses from certain banks and had mentioned that FSB generals might be after him.[21] But the defense evidence for the most part had little effect, because the court, on technical grounds, did not allow defense witnesses to testify in front of the jury. Indeed, the trial, which lasted eight months, with interruptions, was a deeply flawed process. After three initial sessions, the judge declared that the proceedings would henceforth be held in secret because Kozlov's widow had been threatened and there were concerns for her security. The jury found seven defendants, all of whom denied the charges against them, guilty. In November 2008, Frenkel was sentenced to nineteen years in prison, while his alleged accomplices received prison terms ranging from six years to life.[22] Frenkel's defense lawyer appealed the decision, but the Supreme Court dismissed the appeal in November 2009.

Anna Politkovskaya

With Kozlov gone, the way was clear for those high up in the Kremlin to pursue their corrupt financial dealings unimpeded. The Procuracy and the FSB had also silenced those few investigators in the MVD who were inclined to reveal the massive financial fraud carried out by those close to the Kremlin. But there was still the irksome problem of independent journalists who wrote about other transgressions of the Putin regime. First and foremost was Anna Politkovskaya, the crusading, world-renowned Russian reporter for *Novaia gazeta*.

Politkovskaya, also the author of several books on Putin's Russia and Chechnya, was born in 1958 in New York City, the child of Soviet diplomats assigned to the UN. (She obtained American citizenship in the 1990s, on the basis of her birth, but continued throughout her life to live in Moscow.) Politkovskaya graduated in 1980 from the department of journalism at Moscow State University, where she met her future husband, Aleksandr Politkovskii, who was five years her senior. They stayed together for over twenty years and had two children, Ilya and Vera, but they were opposites in many ways and finally split up in 2001.

Although Aleksandr was a successful television journalist in the years of Gorbachev's *perestroika*, his career faded in the nineties, just as Anna's was taking off. He later spoke about their different approaches to their profession. He was a straightforward reporter.

What Politkovskaya wrote, he said, "was not really journalism, it was part literature and part something else . . . she was a complicated person and this was reflected in her writing."[23]

In a documentary film about Politkovskaya produced after her death by Swiss film maker Eric Bergkraut, Aleksandr explained his views on his wife more clearly: "Her sense of justice was the focal point of her life. Lying was forbidden. One must always tell the truth. This was the principle she always lived by. And it was precisely what took her to Chechnya."[24]

What Aleksandr understood was that Politkovskaya could not suppress her feelings of indignation when she witnessed what was happening in Russia after Putin came to power. Indeed, she became the most vocal critic of President Putin, writing justifiably disparaging comments about both his policies and him personally. For example: "I often think: is Putin a person at all? Or a frozen iron statue? I think and the answer is not that he is a person." And: "Why do I dislike Putin? This is precisely why. I dislike him for a matter-of-factness worse than thievery, for his cynicism, for his racism, for his lies, for the gas he used in the Nord-Ost [Dubrovka theater] siege, for the massacre of innocents that went on throughout his first term."[25]

Defending the Chechen Cause

As mentioned, Politkovskaya was one of the few journalists to cover the conflict in Chechnya. She believed her mission was to report on what she called the "dirty war" that Putin had started as prime minister in 1999. By the time of her murder in October 2006, Politkovskaya had made at least fifty trips to Chechnya, despite the danger she continually faced in what was, after all, a war zone. At one point in 2001, she was arrested there by the FSB and accused of spying for Chechen rebels. The FSB kept her for several days, interrogating her repeatedly and threatening her with rape and murder. It was only because of the publicity about her plight in the Russian independent press that she was finally released. She later said that the ordeal was worth it because it enabled her to better understand what Chechen prisoners of the FSB were forced to endure.[26]

Politkovskaya wrote in unsparing detail about the pain and suffering of Chechens and the terrible human-rights abuses visited upon them by Russian forces. As a result of her reporting from Chechnya, the European Court of Human Rights in Strasbourg condemned the Russian government. (The Kremlin paid no mind.) Although she was careful not to romanticize Chechen rebels, who could be equally brutal, she was highly respected in Chechnya. When Chechen separatists took over 900 hostages at Moscow's Dubrovka Theater in October 2002, they requested that Politkovskaya be a mediator between them and Russian authorities. Her efforts were unsuccessful because the rebels were demanding that Russian forces pull out of Chechnya, which the Kremlin of course would not consider. What followed, as noted earlier, was carnage.[27]

Politkovskaya was outraged by this, raising in *Novaia gazeta* a number of questions about how the FSB had handled the crisis. First and foremost was why the FSB did not have medical help on hand to treat the victims immediately after they had funneled toxic gas into the theater to subdue the terrorists. And secondly, why did the FSB then kill the terrorists instead of keeping them alive to find out who was behind their venture? Thanks to information passed to her by Sergei Iushenkov, Politkovskaya managed to track down the one terrorist who escaped, Khanpash Terkibaev, and interview him. He told her that he had special connections with the FSB, which led Politkovskaya to conclude that the FSB had known about the terrorists' plans and that this was part of the Kremlin's strategy to demonize Chechens. Terkibaev was later killed in an automobile crash in Baku, Azerbaijan.[28]

A similar situation played out in September 2004 when Chechen rebels took more than 1,000 hostages at a school in Beslan. Again, Politkovskaya had been asked by the hostage-takers to mediate. But on the plane flight to Beslan, she fell violently ill. Here is what she later recalled: "I succeeded in getting a seat on a plane, ordered a cup of tea, and a certain time later lost consciousness. Already in the hospital [in Rostov], a doctor informed me that I had been poisoned with a powerful unidentified toxic substance. I suspect three FSB officers who were flying in business class. . . . One of them addressed the stewardess with a question and the other put a tablet in my cup. I survived by a miracle. . . . Honestly speaking, I never thought that they [the special services] would go so far."[29] This episode, as it turned out, was a harbinger of what was to come.

As with the theater-hostage crisis, authorities could not explain how a group of heavily armed terrorists had managed to enter Beslan unnoticed and again why all the terrorists except one, who escaped, were reported to have been killed. (In April 2017, the European Court for Human Rights, in a case filed by the victims' families, ruled that Russian authorities were negligent in their obligation to protect human life.)[30]

According to later accounts from Politkovskaya's friends and co-workers, her reporting had started to take a toll on her. She never fully recovered from the poisoning, and the situation in Chechnya affected her deeply. The editor-in-chief of *Novaia gazeta* had this to say: "Not that she was any less beautiful. But . . . the naïveté and cheerfulness disappeared. . . . She used to be full of laughter and good humor. But the laughter diminished with every passing year."[31]

The Contract Killing of Politkovskaya

On the afternoon of October 7, 2006, Politkovskaya stopped at the Ramstor Shopping Center in Moscow to buy groceries, including some special items for her daughter, Vera, who was expecting her first child, a girl, in a few months. Politkovskaya was excited about the upcoming birth of her granddaughter and wanted to make sure that Vera, who lived with her, was eating well. Surveillance cameras at the store later revealed that she was being followed by a man and a woman there. Politkovskaya drove home and entered her apartment building on Lesnaia Street shortly after 4 P.M. Just as she was going into the elevator with her groceries, a man wearing a baseball cap shot her in the temple, chest, cheek, and thigh, threw the Izh pistol—which had a silencer—down, and left in a green Lada, visible on CCTV. Politkovskaya died immediately.[32]

Politkovskaya had a premonition that she might be killed. She had told her son Ilya two or three days before the murder that she had encountered strange people in the stairwell of her apartment. (Her killers had been following her for several days.) But, according to her colleague at *Novaia gazeta* Sergei Sokolov, she had been preoccupied with personal concerns: "Anna was a very careful person. She always was acutely aware of any danger. She was not suicidal, but loved life, her family, her children and future grandchildren, who she did not live to see. But at the same time, when this terrible thing happened in October 2006, everything had come over her—her mother's illness, her father's [recent] death, and her daughter's pregnancy. . . . Anna lost vigilance and they caught her when she was defenseless."[33]

Months passed, until finally, in August 2007, Procurator-General Chaika announced that ten persons had been arrested in connection with the Politkovskaya case and that they included a former employee of the MVD and a former FSB officer. The organizers of the crime, Chaika said, were part of a criminal group from Chechnya, and the person who had ordered the crime was living abroad. The zakazchik's motive was to "destabilize the political situation in Russia" and "discredit the leadership of the country." Clearly, Chaika was pointing the finger at Berezovsky in London, although he did not mention him by name and only said that Russia was seeking extradition of the individual. Shortly thereafter, the case was removed from the Procurator's office and handed over to the newly formed Investigative Committee under Bastrykin.[34] This change was apparently the result of the above-mentioned power struggle among the siloviki that had erupted in 2006.

Trials and More Trials

By the time the case went to trial in October 2008, there were only three defendants: two Chechen brothers, Dzhabrail and Ibragim Makhmudov, who were accused of driving the getaway car, and former MVD officer Sergei Khadzhikurbanov, said to have organized the murder. As previously mentioned, Khadzhikurbanov had also been implicated in the murder of Klebnikov. The alleged triggerman was the third brother of the Chechens, Rustam Makhmudov, who was reported by Bastrykin to have escaped abroad—a familiar story.

As for the former FSB officer whose name had come up repeatedly in the case, Pavel Riaguzov, he was reported by the prosecutor's office as having passed on information about Politkovskaya, including her home address, to a third person in the criminal world. He also met with Khadzhikurbanov and spoke several times on the telephone with one of the Makhmudov brothers before the murder. Riaguzov was arrested, released, and re-arrested several times and eventually cleared of charges in the Politkovskaya murder, but he was accused of abuse of office and extortion. Clearly, there was confusion among prosecutors as to what to do with Riaguzov, whose appearance with the others as a defendant in the murder case would have pointed to FSB involvement.[35]

The trial, as usual, was held in secret, in a Moscow military court; but there was a jury, which found all three defendants innocent. According to a Russian human-rights activist: "Because evidence had been handled so carelessly, the [defense] lawyer Murad Musaev was able to convince the jury that the whole indictment was unjustified."[36] After an appeal by prosecutors to the Russian Supreme Court, the case was referred in September 2009 back to the Procuracy, where it lingered for another year and a half with little happening.

Vera Politkovskaya voiced her exasperation with the incompetence of the investigators in an October 2009 interview:

> Today it is three years since Mama was murdered. And how the investigation has unfolded from the beginning, forgive me for such words, but it has messed up our brains: "now [they say] everything is going quickly, you are great, helping us, things are going well, fast, soon everything will be fine, we will catch everyone." . . . And they have no one. . . . If there had been the political will, then the mistakes the investigators made would not have happened. What can be said when we open one of the volumes of the criminal case and look at a page, and it turns out they have incorrectly reported the time that it took to carry out the murder—from the moment the killer arrived to the moment the killer left?[37]

What was becoming increasingly clear was that the Russian government did not want to solve the case, but rather intended to drag it out for so long that the public would lose interest.

Amazingly, Rustam Makhmudov, accused of firing the shots at Politkovskaya, suddenly materialized. (One wonders whether he had been in FSB hands all along.) He was reported to have been arrested in March 2011. Then came the arrests of two others: retired MVD officer Dmitrii Pavliuchenkov in August 2011 and Chechen Lom-Ali Gaitukaev in October. (Both were also implicated in the Klebnikov murder.) Pavliuchenkov admitted his guilt, was tried separately, and in December 2012 was sentenced to eleven years in prison. The case of the remaining five defendants went to trial in June 2013. There was a series of delays, centered around problems with the jury, several of whom recused themselves or were dismissed for various reasons. It was not until May 2014, seven and a half years after the killing of Politkovskaya, that a jury found all five defendants guilty. They were sentenced in June 2014 to between twelve years and life imprisonment.[38]

The prosecution's final story was thus: Gaitukaev, a boss in the Chechen criminal underworld, had organized the killing and enlisted his three nephews, the Makhmudov brothers, to do the job. Pavliuchenkov had provided the murder weapon and hired two other persons (who were not charged) to tail Politkovskaya. All the defendants in the final trial refused to admit guilt and said that Pavliuchenkov was lying, that he had organized the entire murder himself without their participation. The lawyer for defendant Rustam Makhmudov insisted that his client was not guilty of pulling the trigger, pointing out that there was no resemblance between him and the person who appeared in the video camera in the stairwell of Politkovskaya's apartment. Further details of the trial were not made public.[39]

Most of those who followed the case closely, including Politkovskaya's family and her former *Novaia gazeta* colleagues, agreed that the five who were charged and sentenced had indeed committed the murder. But there was no established motive, aside from money and what prosecutors claimed, unconvincingly, was indignation over Politkovskaya's writings. Then there was the fact that Politkovskaya had not only been under surveillance by the killers, but also by the MVD and FSB, for a time before she was murdered. Several employees of the police and security services had been rounded up in the initial investigation of the crime, but were released.[40]

Search for the Zakazchik

Nine years after the murder, in October 2015, *Radio Svoboda* interviewed some of those who were closely involved in the case. The story was the same. Justice would not come until the person who ordered the crime was identified. As several observers have pointed out, Pavliuchenkov, Gaitukaev, and Khadzhikurbanov, as the intermediaries between the actual killers and the mastermind probably, were keeping quiet in the hopes that they would get reduced sentences. In the words of human-rights activist Lev Ponomarev: "I think that the *zakazchik* is very close to those in power, and under this political regime it will not be possible to ascertain who he is. A person risks his life when he names the *zakazchik*."[41]

Ilya Politkovskii had said initially that he did not think the Kremlin ordered his mother's murder. But his sister, Vera, thought differently. Interviewed in October 2012, she said pointedly: "In my subjective opinion, the person who ordered the murder will not be revealed until there is a change of regime in Russia."[42] Her brother eventually came around to share this view, telling an interviewer in early 2016 that he had information from high-level sources that people in the ruling elite knew who had ordered the crime but would not reveal the information to investigators: "I would suggest that those who know the name of the person who ordered the murder of Mama are simply withholding the information until a convenient time in the future."[43] Politkovskii believes that all this is part of how members of the leadership use *kompromat* (compromising material) against each other to maintain their positions.

As for the theory that Boris Berezovsky had ordered his mother's murder, Politkovskii insisted that there was absolutely no evidence of Berezovsky's involvement and that he was being used by prosecutors as a "whipping boy." (Indeed, the notion that Berezovsky, who shared Politkovskaya's passionately critical views of Putin, would have wanted her dead is absurd.) Politkovskii said that Russian authorities had put pressure on him and his sister to endorse the claims about Berezovsky so that he could be extradited back to Russia. Asked about his reaction to the February 2015 murder of Boris Nemtsov, Politkovskii said that he and his sister were horrified by the similarities between that killing and his mother's murder—as if there were a kind of blueprint for committing such crimes.[44]

Kadyrov Lurking in the Background

One of the obvious similarities between the Politkovskaya and Nemtsov cases was the fact that Chechens were charged with the crime in both instances. In this regard, there was speculation about the involvement of Chechen leader Ramzan Kadyrov, who Politkovskaya had interviewed in June 2004. Politkovskaya's face-to-face meeting with Kadyrov did not go well. He ended up losing his temper and accusing her of being an enemy of Chechnya. She later recalled: "I couldn't bear it anymore. I stood up and walked away. My tears choked me. Of course I expected a bullet in my back." As a result of this encounter, Politkovskaya wrote about Kadyrov: "A little dragon has been raised by the Kremlin. Now they need to feed it. Otherwise it will spit fire."[45]

Before her death, as said, Politkovskaya had been reporting on the human-rights abuses committed by Kadyrov's notoriously brutal militia, the so-called *Kadyrovtsy*. She had interviewed many eyewitnesses to their crimes. Two days before she was killed, Politkovskaya spoke on Radio Liberty about her investigation of Kadyrov, whose birthday happened to be that day: "Personally, I have only one dream for Kadyrov's birthday: I dream of him someday sitting in the dock, in a trial that meets the strictest legal standards, with all of his crimes listed and investigated."[46] Kadyrov will come up again in this narrative, because he is a central figure in several of the contract killings described here. But would Kadyrov, though firmly entrenched in power in Chechnya, not take his orders from the Kremlin when it comes to retribution against high-profile critics of Putin?

Lawyers for the Politkovskaya family were unhappy that investigators never called Kadyrov for questioning, given that he had a strong motive for wanting Politkovskaya dead and that there had been speculation about his involvement in other murders. Asked by a journalist about Kadyrov, the main investigator in the Politkovskaya case had this to say:

> It is not possible to effectively interrogate a person on the basis of only rumors and speculation. The investigator must have some sort of evidence against the suspect. . . . If there is not such evidence, then the interrogation is based simply on nothing. . . . Moreover, the death of Anna Politkovskaya was not advantageous for Ramzan Kadyrov. In the summer and fall of 2006 he was preparing to occupy the position of president of Chechnya, and the resonant murder, with the victim a journalist who was critical of him, brought him more harm than good.[47]

This of course was the same skewed reasoning voiced by Putin when asked about the Politkovskaya murder three days after it occurred. He claimed that Politkovskaya had only a negligible influence in Russia and that her murder did much more damage to those in power in Russia and Chechnya than her reporting had. (Kadyrov was even blunter, saying "if she had bothered us, we would have done it long ago.") Putin of course was overlooking the fact that Politkovskaya had gained a worldwide reputation. Between 2001 and 2006, Politkovskaya received fourteen prestigious international awards for her journalism.[48] And whatever Politkovskaya's readership within Russia, she doubtless managed to strike a chord within the Kremlin. Anna's colleague Sergei Sokolov explained why she was viewed as such a threat by the ruling elite: "Anna Stepanovna in this case was not killed because she wrote a specific article, but because in total she represented a danger to the existing state structure, which is tied to violence and corruption. . . . She was killed as a public figure, as a journalist, having her own views on what was happening in Russia."[49]

Just a few weeks before her murder, Politkovskaya was in London, where she often visited, and met with the group of Russians and Chechens in exile who surrounded Boris Berezovsky, including Alexander Litvinenko. According to Alex Goldfarb, they were all concerned about Politkovskaya's safety. Goldfarb had coffee with the journalist on this final visit to London and tried to persuade her not to return to Russia. But she dismissed his warnings: "It would be so easy to kill me during my trips to Chechnya, so the fact that it has not happened means that no one needs to do it."[50] Litvinenko also urged Politkovskaya to leave Russia and suggested that she live in the United States, where she had citizenship. But Politkovskaya insisted that she had a mission to help people in Russia whose rights were being violated. And also, of course, she wanted to be there for the birth of her granddaughter, who, as it turned out, she would never see. The baby would be named Anna.

Litvinenko at a televised press conference exposing the crimes of the FSB, 1998.

(Photograph courtesy of REUTERS/Alamy Stock Photo)

7

THE LITVINENKO STORY

There are three ways of influencing a person: blackmail, vodka, or the threat of murder.

Vladimir Putin, as quoted in *Sovershenno Sekretno*, February 1, 2000

According to Alexander Litvinenko's wife, Marina, and also his friend Alex Goldfarb, Politkovskaya's murder shook up the London group of exiles badly. As with the killing of Iushenkov, there was a real sense of personal loss, for Litvinenko in particular. In Marina's words, "He was just broken down because for him it was absolutely devastating news."[1] Litvinenko and Politkovskaya shared a deep concern for the Chechen cause and an intense hatred of Putin. Also, as Goldfarb observed, the two had a special sympathy for each other because they both had similar attitudes about the risks they faced: "This was not a false sense of security, like what [Mikhail] Khodorkovsky had, but a professional skill at suppressing emotions of fear in the face of reality. They urged each other to be cautious and both joked in response."[2] After Politkovskaya's death, Litvinenko had a clear sense of immediate danger. He told Daniel Quirke, an employee of a British consulting firm he did contract work for, that he would be next: "He was worried about himself, that there might be a list, or he might be on it."[3]

Litvinenko gave an impassioned speech at the Frontline Club in London shortly after Politkovskaya's murder, insisting that no one would kill someone of Politkovskaya's stature without the sanction of Putin.[4] In a little over a month's time, he would also be brutally murdered, the victim of poisoning by a lethal and rare substance, polonium 210. As evidence would later show, Litvinenko, a former officer of the FSB exiled in London, had been a marked man in the Kremlin's eyes for several years. Why did the Kremlin want him dead so badly, badly enough to create an international scandal of unprecedented proportions?

Many of the answers have emerged from the British Inquiry into the Litvinenko case. Thanks to the persistent efforts of Marina Litvinenko and her solicitors, the British Home Office finally consented, on July 22, 2014, to open the Inquiry. It had been a long process. After Litvinenko's death on November 23, 2006, more than two hundred British police officers were assigned to the investigation of the crime. They visited over sixty premises, including hotels, bars, restaurants, homes, airplanes, and hospitals; interviewed hundreds of witnesses; and asked for reciprocal legal assistance from more than fifteen countries. An inquest into Litvinenko's death was begun on November 30, 2006, but it was adjourned pending the completion of the criminal investigation.

Although the inquest was resumed in October 2011, its scope was constrained for a number of technical reasons, including that it could not accept classified government information as evidence. Sir Robert Owen, who was appointed to lead the inquest in 2012, thus submitted a request to the British Home Office to establish a formal public Inquiry, which would allow the court to consider secret evidence separately, in closed session. The Inquiry hearings began in January 2015 and lasted, with interruptions, until July of the same year. Sir Robert's much-anticipated report on the Litvinenko Inquiry was released in January 2016. Both *The Owen Report* and the transcripts and evidence from the hearings, cited extensively here, provide an in-depth picture of Litvinenko and the circumstances of his murder, the first major hit outside of Russia.[5]

Sasha Litvinenko: A Portrait

Born in 1962, Alexander Litvinenko (known as "Sasha" to family and friends) grew up in Nalchik, a small city in the North Caucasus. He was raised by his grandparents after his parents divorced when he was a baby. Litvinenko was not accepted to a university, so he joined the Soviet army in 1980 and served for a year in the Stavropol region of the North Caucasus. He then attended the S.M. Kirov Higher Military Red Banner Command School of the MVD Internal Troops in the city of Ordzhonikidze (now Vladikavkaz). The MVD internal troops, as noted, were a paramilitary force whose job was to preserve order within the country and quell disturbances in certain hot spots, as well as to guard important government facilities, including labor camps and nuclear installations. Litvinenko graduated from the school in 1985 after a four-year course of study, as a commissioned lieutenant. He then joined the elite Dzerzhinsky Special Mechanized Rifle Division of the Internal Troops, headquartered outside Moscow.[6]

According to a Russian account, and to information from the Inquiry, Litvinenko graduated from military school with an excellent record—he was intelligent and disciplined, had a good command of small arms, and was a top athlete. Thus, in 1988, he was recruited from the Dzerzhinsky Division into the Special Departments (*Osobye otdely*, or OO) of the KGB and, after a year of training with the KGB in Siberia, returned to the Dzerzhinsky Division as an OO officer in a platoon that provided security for government shipments going abroad.[7]

The Special Departments were part of the KGB's Third Chief Directorate for counterintelligence within the military and internal troops. A key job of OO officers was to watch over members of their troop units to make sure they were obeying the rules and not doing or saying anything that was politically subversive. Not surprisingly, OO officers, who were authorized to monitor phone calls and correspondence and initiate criminal prosecutions, were not viewed kindly by their military colleagues and subordinates. Indeed, during the Soviet years, and particularly during World War II, the special departments gained notoriety for their ruthlessness in administering summary justice, including death, to soldiers suspected of disloyalty.[8]

Litvinenko later explained to Goldfarb why he had chosen that line of work:

> Look, I was a young lieutenant. The security services had a powerful attraction. Something magnetic just in the secretiveness. . . . I only [in the nineties] started to realize for the first time how much people hated us for our history. After all, I was fighting against bandits and did not think about politics. And moreover, for every one person who considered us killers, there were two who considered us valiant defenders of the motherland.[9]

This makes sense, if one understands how the Soviet/Russian system worked. Litvinenko was not from a family of privileged intellectuals or high-level government bureaucrats who had access to the Western press and may have questioned the Kremlin regime. He was raised as a patriot, like most of those in his generation, not as a dissident. As Goldfarb put it to me, "Sasha became a policeman, which in his view and that of many others was an honest profession."[10]

Litvinenko rose up in the security hierarchy, leaving the *Osobye otdely* to become an *oper* (operative) in the KGB division for economic security and organized crime in 1991. (The KGB would be disbanded later that year, and its counterintelligence agency would undergo several name changes, with its functions remaining largely the same.) In 1994, Litvinenko moved to the anti-terrorism division of FSK (a KGB successor organization that became the FSB in 1995). Anti-terrorist operations took Litvinenko back briefly to the North Caucasus, along the Chechen border with Russia, where the FSB was conducting a ruthless campaign to suppress Chechen separatists. Litvinenko was in the thick of things there, at one point even engaging in an operation to free Russian hostages. According to Marina Litvinenko, her husband returned home to Moscow from that particular venture shaken and ill. It took some time for him to recover. He was also beginning to question the role of Russian forces in Chechnya and their indiscriminate killing of innocent civilians.[11]

Marina and Sasha had met in Moscow in June 1993, while he was still married but estranged from his first wife and already had two children, Alexander and Sonia. Marina, a beautiful dance teacher who was the same age as Sasha and divorced, grew up in Moscow. They fell in love immediately. Their son, Anatoly, was born in June 1994, and they married the following October, after Sasha was divorced. In 2012 testimony for British investigators, Sasha's son Alexander recalled: "Until 2000, before he went to London, father used to visit us—my mother, Sonia, and me—about once a week. Father loved me and Sonia very much and treated my mother with great respect, despite the fact that father lived with his new wife Marina at that time." He added that he had some sort of a falling-out with Marina and that, after Sasha and Marina moved to London, he and his father stopped seeing each other. But his father continued to call him, sometimes talking for hours, and Sonia visited their father and Marina in London many times.[12] Sasha was clearly a family man.

Turmoil for Litvinenko in the FSB

Litvinenko became close to oligarch Boris Berezovsky, moonlighting as his part-time bodyguard after he allegedly saved Berezovsky from being assassinated in 1994. (Moscow was a rough-and-tumble world and Berezovsky, with his various entrepreneurial enterprises—the auto industry, broadcasting, airlines, and oil—not only was very rich, but had many enemies.) Litvinenko started meeting with Berezovsky regularly (apparently with the approval of his FSB superiors) and even accompanied him on a trip to Switzerland in March 1995, to provide security. Litvinenko came to Berezovsky's defense that same month when Berezovsky was about to be arrested by the FSB as a suspect in the murder of television host Vlad Listev. According to Marina Litvinenko, her husband rushed to Berezovsky's office and threatened the FSB officers at gunpoint, whereupon they departed.[13] Berezovsky was hugely grateful: "That Sasha was brave enough to help me without any regard for his own safety or position was a gesture that I deeply appreciated. . . . I believe Sasha saved my life."[14]

In August 1997, Litvinenko was transferred to the top secret Division of Operations Against Organized Crime (URPO) of the FSB. This division engaged in kidnappings and extrajudicial killings of mafia figures and rebel Chechens. Goldfarb recalled much later that "when he told me about URPO, Sasha was aware that his revelations cast a measure of suspicion on him. . . . He did not deny that he had been told to do illegal things before, but the URPO was a totally new world. Orders were verbal, there were no records, deniability was essential."[15] Litvinenko had entered a dark world.

Some months later, Litvinenko and several colleagues were secretly enlisted by rogue members of the FSB to murder Berezovsky, but they refused, and Litvinenko informed Berezovsky about the plot. Here is Berezovsky's rendition of what happened: "In July 1998, Vladimir Putin, who at that time was little known, replaced Nikolai Kovalyov as head of the FSB and I revealed the plot to him and arranged for Sasha [Litvinenko] to meet him, which he did."[16] The meeting between Putin and Litvinenko was bizarre, to say the least. As Litvinenko described it: "He came out from behind the desk . . .

to greet me. Apparently he wanted to show an open, likeable personality. We, operatives, have a special style of behavior. We do not bow to each other, do without pleasantries—and so everything is clear. Just look into each other's eyes and it becomes clear, do you trust the person or not. And I immediately had the impression that he is not sincere."[17] Litvinenko handed Putin a detailed report he had prepared, outlining the corruption within the government and the FSB. Putin feigned interest and said he would look into the matter, but nothing happened, except that Litvinenko was suddenly put under FSB surveillance.

Frustrated with Putin's lack of reaction, Berezovsky wrote an open letter to the newspaper *Kommersant* (which he controlled) and then arranged for Litvinenko and his colleagues to reveal the plot to kill him at a televised press conference. According to Berezovsky, "the target of the complaint was not Mr. Putin, and he was not an 'enemy': rather, we appealed to him as the new head of the FSB to address corruption. However, these events left Mr. Putin embarrassed and he criticized the whistleblowers. The fact that Sasha chose to align himself with me against the FSB sealed his fate as an 'enemy' of the FSB and a traitor."[18] For Marina Litvinenko, the press conference, which generated huge publicity, was a complete surprise: "I was shocked. Sasha had not told me beforehand."[19]

Escape

Litvinenko paid for his insubordination by being fired from his job and twice sent to prison on trumped-up charges, but managed to be released in late 1999. In the meantime, a Russian journalist and historian living in the United States, Yuri Felshtinsky, befriended him and started seeing him on visits to Moscow. Felshtinsky was part of the Berezovsky entourage and was planning to write a biography of the oligarch, although he had disapproved strongly of Berezovsky's advocacy of Putin as the next Russian president. In an effort to protect

Litvinenko from further reprisals by the FSB, Felshtinsky, who apparently had connections in Russian security circles, met with Litvinenko's former boss in URPO, General Igor Khokholkov, in May 2000. According to Felshtinsky, Khokholkov told him that "Litvinenko committed treason, that he is going to enter prison [again] anyway, and if he [Khokholkov] actually sees him by chance, you know somewhere in a dark corner, he would kill him with his own hands."[20] Felshtinsky then convinced Litvinenko that he needed to leave Russia, lest he be sent back to prison or, even worse, killed.

Litvinenko was reluctant: "What am I going to do abroad? I don't speak any languages." But at the end of September 2000, he made his escape to Georgia. The rest was a cloak-and-dagger tale, with Berezovsky micro-managing it from his extravagant villa in the south of France. Felshtinsky flew over from Boston and met Litvinenko in Tbilisi. He contacted the American Embassy there about the possibility of asylum for Litvinenko, against Berezovsky's wishes, but to no avail. Litvinenko was distraught, incautiously walking the streets of Tbilisi, where the Russians had agents everywhere. Meanwhile, Marina and their six-year-old son Anatoly were waiting things out in Malaga, Spain. Finally, a decision was made for the Litvinenkos to meet up in Anatalya, Turkey, via Berezovsky's private plane.[21]

For Marina, this turn of events was overwhelming. Although she had known that her husband worked for the security services when she married him in 1994, Marina was in the dark about most of the details, and her husband's imprisonment and sudden escape from Russia threw her for a loop. She needed a lot of persuasion to leave her beloved country, and her family, forever. She and Sasha talked over the phone many times while she was in Spain. Marina thought it was best for all of them to return to Russia, even if it meant another prison term for her husband. But Sasha convinced her that if they went back to Russia, her life and that of their son would be in jeopardy. As Marina said in her testimony for the Inquiry: a "very serious point from Sasha was my life and life of our son in dangers [sic] as well. He said, they will put me in prison, I'll not be able to protect you."[22]

Felshtinsky stayed briefly in Anatalya and then turned things over to Alex Goldfarb, who played a major role in getting the Litvinenko family to Britain, where they gained entry in November 2000 and asylum some months later. But it was not an easy process. Goldfarb, who like Felshtinsky had American citizenship, knew influential people in Washington because of his work as a top aide to the philanthropist George Soros. He too tried to get Litvinenko asylum in the United States, driving him and his family to Ankara and bringing them to the American Embassy, where Litvinenko had an interview with the CIA. The effort did not work out. Goldfarb, at this point desperate, drove to Istanbul with the Litvinenkos, who were terrified for their safety. After consultations with Berezovsky, a decision was made for them to fly to London, where Goldfarb had to use all his powers of persuasion to calm British immigration officers at Heathrow Airport—who were furious at being dumped with a major diplomatic problem—and convince them to accept the Litvinenkos.[23]

Goldfarb later recalled how Litvinenko, during the long night drive from Ankara to Istanbul, with Marina and Anatoly asleep in the back seat, had recounted his turbulent history in the security services: "Night driving loosens lips. . . . Within three hours I knew Sasha's whole story, except perhaps for the secret that had created such a furor at the CIA."[24] Eventually Goldfarb heard an explanation from a retired American spy as to why the CIA decided against taking in Litvinenko: the Russians had found out that Litvinenko was in Turkey and seeking asylum in the United States. They apparently gave the Americans the message that, if they accepted Litvinenko, the Kremlin would retaliate and cause trouble. The Americans, in turn, must have decided that it simply was not worth the possible consequences to accept the defector. But was there a deeper reason for their refusal, perhaps relating to Litvinenko's stormy past? Goldfarb, who was to become one of Litvinenko's closest friends over the coming years in London, apparently gave up on this question and made peace with Litvinenko's dubious history as a security operative in Russia. He observed after Litvinenko's murder: "As I was coming to grips with his death, I realized that in Sasha I witnessed a miracle of transformation of the kind when black turns white, right and wrong change places, death and salvation reverse punishment and reward. Within the six short years from the time he fled Russia, a scared and confused member of a corrupt and murderous clique, he became a crusader."[25]

These words ring true. Litvinenko, living in a free society for the first time in his life and associating with people who were committed to promoting democracy in Russia, saw the light. With the same energy and commitment he had devoted to his job as an officer of the Soviet/Russian security services, he threw himself into the struggle against the Putin regime.

Litvinenko in London

Litvinenko did not find his new life in London easy. Marina and Anatoly quickly learned English, but Litvinenko's progress with the language was difficult. Marina was carving out her own life as a physical fitness expert and dancer, and Anatoly was in school. Litvinenko was more at loose ends. Obsessed with what was going on in Russia, he devoted much of his time to meeting with exiled or visiting Russians, Chechens, and Georgians, and writing scathing denunciations of Putin and the Kremlin. He was also starting to consult for private British security firms that did due-diligence appraisals for companies undertaking business in Russia.

Litvinenko was living with the knowledge that he was a marked man. In late 2002, a former FSB colleague in Moscow sent him an email saying he had heard from a highly placed FSB official that the

agency had plans to exterminate Litvinenko as a traitor. "You had better start writing your will," the colleague advised. Then in September
2004, someone threw firebombs at the London homes of Litvinenko
and Akhmed Zakaev, a former Chechen government leader. (The two
were neighbors.) The police never found the culprits. And later, in
2006, according to Marina Litvinenko, she and her husband learned
that Litvinenko's photograph was being used for target practice at a
special-forces training center in Russia where he had once served.[26]

Litvinenko took care of himself by keeping physically fit. Unlike
many Russians in his line of work, he did not drink alcohol or smoke.
(This may explain why he would survive more than three weeks after
being lethally poisoned.) And he had some loyal friends, including
Zakaev. A strikingly handsome former Shakespearean actor, who I
interviewed in London in 2015, Zakaev fought against Russia in the
first Chechen war and was briefly foreign minister of Chechnya. Having fled abroad in 2000, Zakaev, accused of being a terrorist by the
Kremlin, is one of the few Chechen separatist leaders to still be alive.
After Zakaev gained asylum in Britain in 2002 and moved to London,
the Litvinenko and Zakaev families became inseparable, seeing each
other on a daily basis and often sharing meals. Part of this bond came
from the fact that, after his history as an FSB officer in Chechnya,
when Russian forces were brutally suppressing Chechen separatists in
the mid-1990s, Litvinenko did a complete turnaround and dedicated
himself to the Chechen cause. He even converted to Islam shortly before he died, insisting on being buried with traditional Muslim
funeral rites.

On a typical day, Litvinenko would take the London Underground or bus from his home in Muswell Hill to Piccadilly Circus.
After spending considerable time talking animatedly with the Russian
man who sold *matryoshkas* (Russian nesting dolls) on the corner,
he would pop in unexpectedly at the offices of the various British
consulting firms with whom he was forging relationships, and then

perhaps meet with his contact at MI6 (British Foreign Intelligence), "Martin." He would occasionally end his day at the office of his mentor, Berezovsky, who had moved from France to Britain in October 2001.

It is not clear exactly when Litvinenko started working with MI6. Marina recounted for the Inquiry that, after a few years, maybe in 2004, £2000 were deposited monthly in their bank account from British authorities. She said she was not sure whether it came from MI5 (counterintelligence) or MI6, but other sources confirm that it was MI6. Litvinenko's relationship with this agency remains vague (the information is classified), but Goldfarb recalled that Litvinenko was consulting for MI6 on Russian organized crime in Europe.[27]

Russian journalist Iuliia Latynina later scoffed at Litvinenko as an informant for MI6: "Litvinenko's sources about the secret under-pinnings of the Kremlin were from the Kompromat.ru website . . . the most scandalous part of this story is that MI6 paid for Litvinen-ko's retellings in English, which, by the way, he did not know."[28] Whether or not Latynina is correct, the fact remains that British au-thorities were not on the ball. In retrospect, they should have at least kept a closer watch on Litvinenko, both for his own protection and to prevent a notorious crime being committed on their soil.

Litvinenko began consulting work in early 2006 for a private British security firm called RISC. He also became involved with two other security companies in London, Erinys and Titon International. One report that he handed over to Erinys in September 2006 was of particular interest: it was a dossier on Putin's ally Viktor Ivanov, at the time the head of the Russian anti-drug agency. According to this re-port, Ivanov, while working for the security services in St. Peters-burg during the nineties, was engaged in laundering money from drug cartels and other illegal activities that involved organized-crime fig-ures. Putin, then a deputy mayor of St. Petersburg, provided Ivanov with protection and even took part in these criminal operations.[29]

Meanwhile, Litvinenko became involved with an Italian parliamentary group, the so-called Mitrokhin Commission, which was investigating Russian organized crime. Litvinenko provided enough information for the commission to conclude that Putin, the FSB, and the Kremlin were deeply involved in corrupt activities, and they passed this on to the Americans.[30] The Italian consultant for the commission, Mario Scaramella, who got to know Litvinenko well, was initially thought to be connected with his murder, but was exonerated. Litvinenko was also in contact with Spanish police authorities. According to an American diplomatic cable, cited by WikiLeaks, Litvinenko "tipped off Spanish security officials on locations, roles, and activities of several Russian mafia figures with ties to Spain."[31]

Litvinenko and Berezovsky

Berezovsky took the Litvinenko family under his wing once he arrived in London, providing a house for them and giving them other financial support, including paying for Anatoly's tuition at the exclusive City of London School. Together in exile, Litvinenko and Berezovsky formed a close alliance in their mutual hatred of the Putin regime and devoted themselves to campaigning against the Kremlin. Berezovsky financed both of Litvinenko's books that came out in 2002, *The FSB Blows Up Russia*, which, as mentioned, alleged that the FSB (with Putin) was behind the September 1999 bombings, and *The Lubianka Criminal Gang*, which linked Putin directly to organized crime.

Sometime in 2005 or early 2006, Berezovsky, learning about Litvinenko's collaboration with MI6, decided to cut down on the subsidies he was giving him. According to Goldfarb, the goal was to have Litvinenko become more self-sufficient financially: "He [Litvinenko] was not upset. He was a little grouchy, in the sense that, you know, Boris could have paid more . . . initially he was not happy with the reduction in the money, but it was not dramatic."[32]

What may have helped to seal Litvinenko's fate with Putin was an article he wrote for the *Chechen Press*, which appeared in July 2006. The article was prompted by a bizarre incident in which Putin stopped to chat with a group of tourists outside the Kremlin and then went over to a small boy, lifted up his T-shirt, and kissed him on the stomach. Litvinenko wrote: "The world is shocked. Nobody can understand why the Russian president did such a strange thing," and went on to explain that Putin had been known by KGB insiders to have been a pedophile and that there were secret tapes he destroyed once he became head of the FSB showing him having sex with underage boys.[33] As Goldfarb observed: "with regard to the homosexual tape . . . in order to make an enemy, it does not necessarily have to be true. . . . I would think that if you say that . . . Mr. Putin is a pedophile, it would make Mr. Putin mad regardless of the fact whether he is a pedophile or not."[34]

It is hardly a coincidence that, shortly after this article came out, the Russian State Duma passed the earlier-mentioned amendment to a law on extremism. Because the category of persons subject to reprisals was expanded to include those who slandered Russians occupying government positions, the law seemed tailor-made for justifying Russian actions against Litvinenko. As British Russia expert Robert Service observed: "The wording [of the amendment] is so expansive as to enable the authorities, if such were to be their desire, to act against every kind of unfair criticism—or indeed any criticism that they deemed unfair."[35] In later testimony to British police, Berezovsky noted that "Sasha mentioned loads of times that this legislation of course was designed to get rid of us. . . . Moreover, he said that they would most probably try to poison us."[36]

The Accused Killers: Lugovoy and Kovtun

Andrei Lugovoy was one of those shadowy, opportunistic figures whose life was intertwined with the Russian security services and the bourgeoning "big business" of the new Russia. Born in 1966, he came from a military family and attended the prestigious RSFSR Supreme Soviet Command School in Moscow. After his graduation in 1987, Lugovoy entered the KGB's elite Ninth Directorate, responsible for protecting Kremlin officials. He continued as an officer in this capacity after the collapse of the Soviet Union, when the KGB was dismantled and new security structures were created, including in 1995 the Federal Protection Service (FSO), where Lugovoy served briefly.[37]

Lugovoy guarded Yeltsin's prime minister Egor Gaidar and also Foreign Minister Andrei Kozyrev, reportedly even accompanying them to Washington, D.C. In 1996, he left the FSO and started his own private security firm, the Ninth Wave, overseeing the protection of Berezovsky's TV station, ORT. By his own testimony, given in Moscow at the request of British prosecutors in December 2006, Lugovoy accompanied Berezovsky on a trip to Chechnya in 1998 and several times flew on Berezovsky's plane with him to the oligarch's villa in France. In short, the two men were close. It was through Berezovsky that Lugovoy first met Litvinenko in 1995. After ORT was seized by Putin in 2000 and Berezovsky fled Russia, Lugovoy continued running a private security agency, but also branched out into other business ventures.[38]

One particular episode in Lugovoy's life deserves attention. Supposedly, Lugovoy was arrested in 2001 and imprisoned for fifteen months because he had tried to help an associate of Berezovsky, Nikolai Glushkov, escape from prison. This episode served to create the impression that Lugovoy was a rebel of sorts who had, like Litvinenko, been persecuted by the FSB and thus made him appear trustworthy to the London group of exiles. Berezovsky later told British investigators: "I trusted Lugovoy completely. Because he ended up in prison on the accusation of helping my friend who was also in prison at the time . . . Lugovoy was convicted. And of course this enhanced my trust, the level of my trust in him."[39]

But several people questioned this story. Glushkov, for one, said that no one had seen Lugovoy in Lefortovo Prison during the time he was allegedly detained there. And Andrei Vasil'ev, editor of the newspaper *Kommersant,* observed: "I find Lugovoy's story a little strange. He was in prison, had a criminal record, and suddenly he is okay, is allowed to do business, still having contact with Berezovsky. It raises questions."[40]

Lugovoy earned a lot of money, apparently because wealthy and often corrupt Russians were willing to pay high prices for their *krysha* (cover or protection) and because of his connections with the Kremlin and the FSB. He also became an Anglophile, even sending a daughter to language courses in Cambridge and his son to a private British school in Moscow. (He bragged to journalist Luke Harding, who interviewed him in April 2008, that he had read all the works of Arthur Conan Doyle.)[41] Starting in 2004, Lugovoy was making regular trips to London, sometimes with his wife, Svetlana, where they shopped at exclusive stores on Bond Street in Mayfair. He also was looking for London property to buy. But Lugovoy, by all accounts, did not acquire the appearance or graces of a British gentleman, even though, on the day of Litvinenko's fatal poisoning, he was flashing a $50,000 watch on his wrist.

Lugovoy made a point of cultivating relations with both Litvinenko and Berezovsky on his trips to London. He also was close to a wealthy Georgian oligarch exiled in London, Badri Patarkatsishvili, who died, allegedly of a heart attack, in 2008. Berezovsky trusted Lugovoy so much that he hired him to provide security for a daughter who was living in St. Petersburg. Lugovoy was invited to Berezovsky's lavish sixtieth birthday party, held at the elegant Blenheim Palace in January 2006, and sat at the same table with Litvinenko and Marina. Later, in the summer of 2006, Lugovoy and his wife visited Litvinenko at his home in Muswell Hill, spending three hours there. (Marina and Anatoly were away.) Meanwhile, Litvinenko and Lugovoy started collaborating on efforts to sell their insiders' knowledge of the Kremlin to British consulting firms. Litvinenko, according to Lugovoy's unsubstantiated claims, was also encouraging Lugovoy to become an informer for MI6.

In retrospect, it is hard to believe that both Litvinenko and Berezovsky trusted Lugovoy and did not suspect that he was acting on behalf of the FSB. Dean Attew, the head of Titon International, which Litvinenko and Lugovoy were attempting to engage for consulting work, disliked Lugovoy immediately upon meeting him in June 2006: "There was something I would describe as cold, scarily cold about Lugovoy. It wasn't that I felt frightened; it wasn't that I felt in harm's way in any way. I just didn't like the characteristics of the individual or the profile that was sitting in front of me."[42]

Titon International and Erinys were in the same building on Grosvenor Square and shared a boardroom. Attew advised Erinys head Tim Reilly not to allow Lugovoy in his offices, or to do business with him, but Reilly discounted the advice. He had a more favorable impression of Lugovoy, although he pointed out that Lugovoy was an obvious "new Russian": "We would call it nouveau riche, so [he] would have all the accoutrements of the Western world, and then there would be an odd, you know, shiny tie, or something like that. It was quite funny. It sounds awful, but you could spot this straightaway, and he was on the make."[43] Reilly was convinced that Litvinenko and Lugovoy were valuable resources for potential Erinys consulting contracts with Russian gas and oil companies because of their past work for the Russian security services: "If you go into any major Russian corporation the security guy is the most important person, because in Soviet times he would be the KGB guy."[44]

For all his savvy as an operator in the world of the secret services and high finance, Lugovoy made a big mistake in enlisting his boyhood friend Dmitrii Kovtun into the venture to kill Litvinenko. Kovtun, by all accounts, was a loser—sullen and furtive, addicted to alcohol, with little knowledge of English. (Lugovoy did all the talking for the two when they were in London.) At forty-one, Kovtun had not done much with his life. His father had been a colonel in the Soviet army, and he had studied at the same elite military school that Lugovoy had attended. But after serving with Soviet troops stationed in Prague and later East Berlin, Kovtun deserted in 1992 and moved with his new Russian wife to Hamburg, where he lived from 1992 to 2003, divorcing his first wife and marrying and divorcing a second. Kovtun earned money by working as a dishwasher and refuse collector, but spent most of his time drinking. His main goal, according to one of his wives, was to become a porn star. It is not clear what Kovtun did after he returned to Moscow in 2003—he lived with his mother, a veterinarian—but at some point he reconnected with Lugovoy, joining him to work on some of his business ventures, including a drinks company.[45] Apparently Lugovoy chose Kovtun as partner in his mission to poison Litvinenko because he was a loyal friend. But as it would turn out, Kovtun's ineptness helped to ensure that the two men would be exposed as the killers of Litvinenko.

Moving in on Litvinenko

Why was it so important to kill Litvinenko with such haste after he had been in Britain for six years? In addition to his Chechenpress piece, one explanation might be his work with Spanish security services in their efforts to combat Russian organized crime in Spain, which he had started at least a year before, making trips to Spain for that purpose. Litvinenko had not only provided Spanish authorities with information linking high-level Kremlin officials to the Russian mafia in Spain. He had also revealed evidence of business connections between the Tambov criminal mafia and members of the Ozero cooperative, the elite group that formed part of Putin's inner-circle. Litvinenko was planning to travel to Spain in November to give testimony to a Spanish prosecutor that would include information about

Putin's ties to organized crime. Significantly, Lugovoy knew about this because Litvinenko had suggested to Lugovoy that he accompany him. Litvinenko cancelled the trip on his deathbed.[46]

We also know from the Inquiry that shortly before his death, Litvinenko made the mistake of handing over to Lugovoy a copy of the highly damaging report on Putin's crony Viktor Ivanov that Litvinenko had submitted to Erinys, apparently so Lugovoy would have an idea of the type of product British firms were interested in. The report was actually written by Yuri Shvets, a former KGB officer living in the United States. According to *Novaia gazeta*, Lugovoy, returning to Moscow from London in September 2006, was caught red-handed with the Ivanov dossier and was detained for two hours at Sheremetevo Airport, where he was "worked over" by Russian authorities.[47] But it is more likely that Lugovoy, already collaborating with the FSB, handed the report over to this agency on his own initiative and was not interrogated at the airport.

Shvets was convinced that the Ivanov report was the final nail in Litvinenko's coffin. Here is some of what he had to say in his testimony to the British Inquiry:

> **Question from the solicitor:** If this report had got into the wrong hands—and that's to say hands connected with Mr. Ivanov, and linked to Sasha's name—do you think that that posed a risk, and a risk of physical harm to Sasha, that he might be at risk himself?

> **Shvets:** Yes, I do, I do, and unfortunately there are proverbial words in the report, the Ivanov report, which shows that Mr. Ivanov is vindictive and he comes back to the source of negative information on him with a vengeance. This is unfortunately exactly what happened to Sasha. So the report itself is an unfortunate confirmation that that is

correct. The reason is not negative information on Mr. Ivanov himself, but the report contains negative information on Mr. Putin as well. I mean the information which alleges Mr. Putin's involvement in drug-related business when he worked in the office of the mayor of St. Petersburg, and I believe that this is the last thing Mr. Ivanov or Mr. Putin wanted, to have somebody in the West . . . investigating the details of this alleged involvement. . . . It is my understanding that they have it in line already, the process for killing people which doesn't require a lot of preparation.

When I worked with the first chief directorate [of the KGB], I remember I had a personal experience, there was a lab in Moscow, at that time it was located at Academician Varga Street number 2, which was manufacturing poisons, drugs, different kind of drugs, and other deadly substances which could alter minds and which could kill people. So basically, they had the tool to kill people and at any time, at any minute.

The issue is how to organize, how to deliver the tool to the target, and it looks like there the people who were in charge, they were in a hurry, because apparently they didn't want the source of this report to continue this kind of reporting. . . . So they had this polonium ready to go to be used and then [disposed of]. The only thing was to organize the delivery, and here they have an individual, Mr. Lugovoy, who has access to Mr. Litvinenko on basically a daily basis. So it didn't appear very much complicated organizationally.[48]

However uncomplicated the plot may have seemed, it did not work out as planned. As the veteran Kremlin watcher and sociologist Olga Kryshtanovskaia observed to Luke Harding: "My FSB friends told me that this [Litvinenko's bungled poisoning] would have never happened under Andropov [former KGB head and later Communist Party chief]. They told me that the KGB was much more efficient at murdering back then."[49] Strictly from the standpoint of tradecraft, the FSB was remiss in assigning the job of killing Litvinenko to these two very questionable men. And Putin, apparently driven by a thirst for vengeance against Litvinenko, was reckless in not ensuring that the FSB carried out "Operation Litvinenko" more professionally. Putin had thus far been able to distance himself from the mounting number of political killings that were occurring on his watch. Now the world would entertain the possibility that he had actually ordered this assassination.

The accused killers: Dmitrii Kovtun and Andrei Lugovoy.

(Photograph courtesy of SERGEI ILNITSKY/EPA)

8

THE POISONING

For Putin, everything is personal.

Marina Litvinenko, author interview, April 2014

We talked about nothing . . . only just "how are things going?" . . .
All was normal. That was it.

Andrei Lugovoy, on his last meeting with Litvinenko at the Pine Bar of
London's Millennium Hotel on November 1, 2006

Prelude to a Murder

Lugovoy and Kovtun first tried to poison Alexander Litvinenko on October 16, 2006, the day that they arrived together from Moscow at London's Gatwick Airport. At Immigration Control, they had a twenty-minute interview with detective Spencer Scott, who questioned them about the purpose of their visit. Lugovoy explained, in broken English, that they were in London on business and had a meeting with a company called Continental Petroleum on Grosvenor Street. Scott found Lugovoy evasive and so called the contact at that company, who confirmed the appointment. The two men were then allowed to pass through immigration, carrying with them a small vial of the world's most deadly and rare radioactive poison—polonium 210.[1]

When Lugovoy and Kovtun showed up later at the Best Western Hotel on Shaftesbury Avenue, the manager was amused: "We found them to be quite comical, really, on account of how they were dressed and the excessive jewelry that they were wearing . . . silk and polyester suits and shirts . . . the colors didn't match, the suits were either too big or too small, they just didn't look like people who were used to wearing suits."[2] Little did he know that just weeks later, these same Russians would emerge as prime suspects in what would not only be an assassination, but also an act of nuclear terrorism.

That afternoon, Litvinenko and the two men met at the boardroom of the firm Erinys with its director, Tim Reilly. Later it was revealed that the room registered high levels of polonium contamination—the lethal radioactive material has a half-life of 138 days—suggesting that Lugovoy and Kovtun had tried to poison Litvinenko there. On the night of October 16, Litvinenko was sick and vomited. He attributed his symptoms to food poisoning, but hair samples taken from Litvinenko after he was hospitalized in November indicated a poisoning at around this time.[3]

Reilly could not remember all the specifics of the boardroom meeting, but he said the Russians had joked about the English always drinking tea and suggested that they have some. Reilly prepared tea and went off to the bathroom. While he was gone apparently either Lugovoy or Kovtun slipped polonium into Litvinenko's cup when the latter was not looking. Litvinenko possibly had a small sip of the tea or simply breathed the vapor. It was not enough to kill him, but it was enough to make him ill.[4] Both rooms that Lugovoy and Kovtun stayed in at the Best Western on the night of October 16 were later tested and revealed high levels of polonium. In Lugovoy's room, no. 107, tests made on December 22, 2006 showed extensive traces of the poison in the lower drain of the bathroom sink, suggesting, as the Inquiry report noted, that either Lugovoy or Kovtun had prepared a solution in the bathroom in preparation for poisoning Litvinenko and poured some of the solution down the sink.[5]

Lugovoy returned on his own to London from Moscow on the evening of October 25. The trip had been planned hastily, with the hotel and air bookings made only the day before. We know Lugovoy had polonium with him because the plane he traveled on later revealed contamination, as did his hotel room, 848, at the Sheraton, where he stayed for three nights. The highest readings were in the bathroom wastebasket and on towels discovered in January 2007. Experts concluded that "contamination was consistent with an accidental spillage, perhaps followed by an attempt to clean up and/or dispose of the solution."[6]

Although Lugovoy met with Litvinenko during this visit to London, it was only briefly, in the bar of the Sheraton Hotel and then perhaps the next day. This was not made clear during the Inquiry. Lugovoy did pay two other important calls, however. On October 26, a driver took him to Badri Patarkatsishvili's lavish mansion in Surrey, where he spent the entire afternoon with the Georgian oligarch. The two had known each other since 1993, when Lugovoy had headed security at ORT, the television channel owned jointly by Patarkatsishvili and Berezovsky. Subsequently, Lugovoy had provided security for Patarkatsishvili on trips to Georgia, and the two continued to have a close association. The passenger seat Lugovoy had occupied in the hired car that took him to Surrey was later tested for radiation, and secondary contamination was discovered.

Later that afternoon, or possibly the next day, Lugovoy paid a visit to Berezovsky's office in Mayfair (where the couch he sat on subsequently revealed high levels of polonium contamination). As the Inquiry report noted: "It seems clear that as late as the end of October 2006, Mr. Berezovsky regarded Mr. Lugovoy as a trusted associate—someone who was 'one of us' in his dispute with the Putin regime."[7] The same, it would seem, applied for Litvinenko. Although he had spent a career as a sleuth and knew the ways of the FSB backward and forward, it evidently did not occur to him to question Lugovoy's motives until he was on his deathbed.

Kovtun's Failed Gambit

The hapless Kovtun showed up in Hamburg on the morning of October 28, 2006. His ex-wife Marina Wall and her partner, accompanied by her children, picked him up at the airport, and he stayed the night with them. Kovtun seemed at loose ends and was broke: he borrowed the credit card of Marina's partner to book a flight to London for November 1. Marina obviously still retained some affection for Kovtun, although he had been an unsuitable husband. She later told German investigators: "Every woman finds Dmitrii charming. It is just he does not fancy working and he is not a family man. He is more a man about town. That is why we were not suited. . . ." She added that "I had to do everything. I had to set up the letters on the computer. He was not able to do this. Dmitrii was no handyman. He could not even bang a nail into the wall."[8] Moreover, we learn, Kovtun did not have a driver's license. He failed the test repeatedly because he was close to blind in one eye after a brawl with some fellow Russians.[9] This was the man, also with a serious drinking problem, who the FSB had hired to carry out a high-level political murder in the center of London, using one of the world's most lethal poisons!

Marina Wall's mother, Elenora Wall, was fond of Kovtun and picked him up outside her daughter's flat the next day so he could spend the night with her. He brought gifts, including Russian vodka, chocolate marshmallows, and pickled mushrooms from his mother, which Elenora especially liked. They spent the evening talking in the kitchen, and the next day, October 30, Kovtun went back to central Hamburg to meet with a friend from a restaurant where he had worked, Il Porto.

There was a special purpose for the meeting. Kovtun had asked his friend (only identified as D3 in the Inquiry documents) to put him in contact with a former restaurant cook living in London, telling D3 outright that he had an assignment to kill a traitor with poison and needed help. According to testimony by D3, who invited Kovtun to spend the night with him: "Dmitrii said he had a very expensive poison and needed the cook to administer it to Litvinenko. I did not take seriously what Dmitrii said. I thought it was just talk."[10] Kovtun managed to get the telephone number of the cook (C2 in the Inquiry documents) from another former restaurant employee and then returned to Marina Wall's home, where he spent the night before flying off early to London on November 1. He had, apparently unwittingly, spread polonium in all the various places he visited in Hamburg.

Once he arrived back in London on November 1, Kovtun decided to follow up with C2, who he hoped would poison Litvinenko. Using Lugovoy's cell phone, because his own was out of minutes, Kovtun put in a call to C2 at around 11:30 A.M. In later oral testimony to the Inquiry, C2 said that, while he knew Kovtun slightly because the two had worked together at the Il Porto Restaurant, he had had no contact with him for six years. C2, a native Albanian, was working at a coffee shop in East London, far from the city center. He told Kovtun that he was busy and could not meet him right away. That was the only conversation they had.[11]

Kovtun, in a much later statement to the Inquiry, claimed that he had tried to contact C2 because he wanted him to come to Moscow and work as a chef at a restaurant he and Lugovoy were preparing to open. (And in fact they apparently did open a restaurant, called Ded Pikhto, which Lugovoy later developed as a chain of eating establishments.) But why would Kovtun try to recruit an Albanian—who he hardly knew and who did not speak a word of Russian—to come to Moscow? In the words of the Owen Report: "the elaborate explanation that Mr. Kovtun has given for the call that he made to C2 . . . amounts to a tissue of lies." As for D3, Kovtun's response to his testimony was that D3 was using heroin at the time the two met in Hamburg.[12]

It might be added that Kovtun contradicted himself more than once on the reason for his London visit of November 1. In his most recent statement, made to the Inquiry in 2015, he insisted: "I have declared repeatedly that I arrived in London by chance on 1 November . . . I had not contemplated a trip to London." Yet earlier he claimed that he had come to deliver a report to one Alexander Shadrin, the CEO of Continental Petroleum Ltd.[13]

Lugovoy, meanwhile, had decided to mix business with pleasure. On the morning of November 1, he brought with him to London (along with a vial of polonium) his wife, two daughters, a daughter's boyfriend, his young son, and an associate in his security business, Viacheslav Sokolenko. The ostensible purpose of the visit was that the whole group was attending a football (soccer) match that evening between Britain's Arsenal and CSKA Moscow. Berezovsky's son-in-law, Egor Shuppe, had arranged for the tickets.

The Polonium Trail

Where had the polonium that Lugovoy and Kovtun obtained come from? As *The Owen Report* observed: "It is self evident that the isotope polonium 210 is a very rare substance . . . the isotope is difficult to produce and dangerous to handle." The Inquiry established, from scientific experts, that the production of polonium in Russia begins at a nuclear reactor at the so-called Mayak facility, near Ozersk, where bismuth 209 atoms are bombarded with neutrons. The recovery of polonium 210 from the irradiated bismuth takes place at another facility called Avangard in the city of Sarov. Small quantities of polonium 210 are then exported to the U.S. for use in devices such as anti-static guns, which remove static electricity from surfaces. The Avangard facility is the only commercial producer of polonium 210 in the world.[14]

Interviewed on November 28, 2006 (apparently without prior advice from the Kremlin), the head of the Russian Atomic Energy Agency (Rosatom), Sergei Kirienko, had this to say:

> Russia exports 8 grams [of polonium 210] every year. 8 grams is a large quantity for polonium 210. We used to supply it to Britain. I think supplies to English companies were stopped in 2001 or 2002. We still supply 8 grams a year to American companies. Each time such companies are obliged to provide an official document, the end-user's certificate and assurances that it is only used for industrial purposes. . . . The polonium produced in Russia for exports . . . is controlled very strictly. There is just one producer and it is produced under tough control in line with international agreements. . . . Therefore I do not believe that someone has stolen it at a producing facility. . . . Besides, this is a very hazardous substance. It is transported in strictly protected containers. Even if you touch it via pores, via your skin, it penetrates into the body and settles in bones and lungs. And this means death. Therefore I cannot quite understand as to who was ready to steal it.[15]

What Mr. Kirienko did not say—and what unfortunately was not brought out in the Inquiry—is that the responsibility for ensuring the security of nuclear facilities, including Avangard, is assigned to the FSB. The FSB's anti-terrorism division, as well as its counterintelligence division, are officially tasked with thwarting the theft of nuclear materials.[16] Significantly, in 2001, Nikolai Zelenkin, deputy head of the FSB office in Sarov, announced that the FSB had developed new, very restrictive measures for access to the Avangard plant.[17] It thus would have been virtually impossible for Lugovoy and Kovtun to obtain polonium in Russia without the complicity of the security services.

Polonium was apparently chosen for Litvinenko's murder because it is an alpha emitter and, unlike gamma rays, alpha rays cannot be detected during the screening process at airports. According to one expert on polonium, "the choice of polonium was genius in that polonium, carried in a vial in water, can be carried in a pocket through airport screening devices without setting off any alarms . . . once administered, the polonium creates symptoms that don't suggest poison for days, allowing time for the perpetrator to get away."[18]

Indeed, the accused killers expected that Litvinenko would die without anyone knowing the cause. But they botched the job, mishandling the polonium and failing, on November 1 at the Pine Bar of the Millennium Hotel, to administer to Litvinenko a dose that would have killed him more quickly. Had he not been so physically fit, Litvinenko doubtless would not have survived so long. His lengthy and painful deterioration enabled the doctors to finally identify the poison just as he succumbed to its effects on November 23, 2006.

But a key question remains. In deciding on polonium 210 as the poison for Litvinenko, why did the FSB not give Lugovoy and Kovtun at least some basic information and training on how to handle the substance, warning them of its lethality? Most probably because, in the eyes of the FSB, the two Russians were expendable. If they contaminated themselves and, inadvertently, others in the process of killing Litvinenko, the adverse health effects would take time to emerge. And the intention was for Litvinenko to die quickly, before the cause could be discovered. In that case, no one would have known that others had been harmed by the poison that killed Litvinenko. Above all, if the FSB had given Lugovoy and Kovtun a notion of how dangerous the poison was, they might have refused to carry out their mission.

The Pine Bar

The morning of November 1 started as a routine day for the Litvinenko family. Marina dropped Anatoly at the Underground station to get a train to his school, and then she went off to visit a friend. Litvinenko told her he was going into the city by bus to meet a business contact and later Mario Scaramella, his Italian associate in his work for the Mitrokhin Commission, and Lugovoy. At 2 P.M., Litvinenko arrived at the Grosvenor Street offices of Dean Attew, company director for Titon International Ltd. According to Attew's later testimony: "We . . . discussed work commitments. He was there for about thirty minutes. Alex was his usual self, happy, healthy, as he always was."[19]

At 3 P.M., Litvinenko met Scaramella at Itsu, a Japanese restaurant near Piccadilly Circus. Scaramella was in a panic because he had just received emails in English from a former Russian intelligence officer named Evgenii Limarev, reporting that Litvinenko and Berezovsky were about to become the next victims, after Anna Politkovskaya, of the Kremlin's vengeance. Much to Scaramella's dismay, Litvinenko did not appear to take the threat seriously: "It doesn't matter, if it's from Evgenii, it means not credible . . . it's shit if it's from Evgenii." Litvinenko was preoccupied with eating his beloved sushi and told Scaramella that he would have his son Anatoly translate the emails and get back to him in a few days.[20]

Litvinenko's next meeting, which was to prove fatal, was with Lugovoy and Kovtun in the Pine Bar of London's Millennium Hotel at around 5 P.M. The two had been sitting at a table for about half an hour before Litvinenko arrived, and had already ordered alcoholic drinks, along with a pot of green tea. Lugovoy told Litvinenko that they were in a hurry because they had tickets to attend a football match. According to Litvinenko's deathbed statement: "Lugovoy said 'If you want some tea, then there is still some left here, you can have some of this.' I could have ordered a drink myself, but he kind of presented it in such a way that it's not really need [sic] to order. I don't like when people pay for me, but in such expensive hotels, forgive me, I don't have enough money to pay that." Lugovoy ordered a clean cup, and Litvinenko had a few sips of the tea. After a few minutes of conversation, they all got up to leave, with promises to meet the next day. Lugovoy's young son, Igor, appeared and Lugovoy introduced him to Litvinenko, saying "this is Uncle Sasha," whereupon the two shook hands. (If even a minuscule amount of the poison had gotten on Igor Lugovoy's hand, it could have been absorbed through his skin and into his bloodstream.)[21]

We now know, thanks to recovered videos from surveillance cameras at the hotel, that, while they waited for Litvinenko, Lugovoy and Kovtun made separate trips to the gentlemen's "loo," presumably to measure out polonium into receptacles. Later tests revealed high levels of polonium in two of the stalls. And a teapot later proved to be heavily contaminated with polonium, even though, several weeks after the poisoning, it had been washed many times. (Polonium 210 is virtually impossible to remove from surfaces.)

Lugovoy claimed initially in an interview with *Ekho Moskvy* on November 24 (the day after Litvinenko died) that Litvinenko had had nothing whatsoever to drink at their meeting at the Pine Bar, saying unconvincingly that they were all in too much of a hurry to eat or drink anything: "This is absolutely definite, 100 per cent sure: he didn't order anything and we did not offer him anything either." But in an interview that same day with the London *Daily Telegraph*, he was more equivocal: "We had nothing to eat, but I can't remember if he had tea or not."[22]

In early December 2006, during a joint interview with *Der Spiegel*, both Lugovoy and Kovtun agreed that green tea and gin had been consumed at the Pine Bar.[23] Finally, in a much more recent statement, provided from Moscow to the Inquiry, Kovtun recalled that Litvinenko "grabbed the teapot on the table and, without waiting for an invitation, poured himself some tea . . . he gulped down two cups of hot tea one after the other . . . [and] then had a coughing fit." Of course, the accused killers should have known that the bar bill, paid by Lugovoy, would tell all. It included four Gordon's gins, three teas, and a champagne cocktail.[24] Their inconsistencies reflected their growing awareness that the investigation, centered on that fatal half-hour meeting with Litvinenko, was closing in on them.

After saying good-bye to his two Russian colleagues, Litvinenko made his way to Berezovsky's office. As noted, his relationship with the wealthy businessman had become somewhat strained because the latter had been cutting back on his financing of Litvinenko; but, nonetheless, he was always free to visit. By this time, after his meeting with Lugovoy and Kovtun, Litvinenko began to realize the significance of the emails Scaramella had handed over to him. Here is what Berezovsky, who was flying out of the country that night, later recalled:

> I did not spend any time with him because I was in a hurry. I saw him using the photocopier in the print room. He came up to me and handed me two or a maximum of three pages of paper. He told me that they were very important and that it was absolutely confidential. I do not remember if I read the photocopies, but I remember that they had several names on them. . . . I then again passed Litvinenko in the corridor, on doing so he said to me, "Boris, it's very important you should pay attention to that." I said, "Don't worry, don't worry." He said, "I know that you are leaving but don't forget, please, you should pay attention to that." I said, "Okay." He then left. I do not know where he went after this as I went back into a meeting.[25]

The next time Berezovsky would see Litvinenko would be several days later, when Litvinenko was on his deathbed.

Litvinenko's friend Zakaev picked Litvinenko up from Berezovsky's office to take him home in the early evening of November 1. Zakaev, who often gave Litvinenko lifts in his Mercedes when
the two were in the city, was driving, and a Chechen friend, Yagari
Abdul, was next to him in the front seat. Litvinenko sat in the back.
He did not yet show any signs of illness, but by this time was extremely agitated over the messages he had received from Scaramella
and urged Abdul to translate them into Russian so he would not have
to wait for his son Anatoly to do it. Abdul did his best, but Zakaev told
me that at the time they just thought Litvinenko was making a big deal
out of nothing. He tried to calm Litvinenko down as he dropped him
off at his house. The usual drama with Litvinenko, so Zakaev thought;
he was lovable and earnest, but easily excitable.[26]

An Agonizing Death

The next day, when Zakaev called Sasha, as was his routine, he
learned from a very concerned Marina that her husband was feeling
ill. In fact he had been vomiting heavily all night. A day later, on November 3, an ambulance took him to the hospital. From that point
onward, until Litvinenko's death on November 23, Zakaev—along of
course with Marina and later Alex Goldfarb and Litvinenko's father,
Valter—stood vigil at his bedside.

It did not take long for Litvinenko to conclude that Lugovoy and
Kovtun had poisoned him, but he did not want to make his suspicions public because he wanted to keep his killers off guard. (In
fact, they left Britain two days after Litvinenko drank the fatal dose.)
Zakaev was shocked when Litvinenko told him that Lugovoy and
Kovtun were the probable source of the poison. Despite his closeness
to Zakaev, Litvinenko had never before mentioned to him his association with the two men. Why? Litvinenko, with his subsidies from
Berezovsky cut back considerably, was desperate to get more contracts from British consulting firms. He evidently thought that team-

ing up with Lugovoy would help him, but he also must have known that Zakaev would disapprove because of Lugovoy's background in the security services. As Zakaev realized, Litvinenko had been playing with fire.[27]

The identification of Litvinenko's mysterious illness was a nearly impossible challenge for his doctors. At first they suspected food poisoning; but as his condition worsened, they began to look for other causes. Meanwhile, Goldfarb arrived from the United States and was alarmed to learn that Litvinenko was neutropenic, meaning that his immune system was not working. This could not have been caused by either an infection or food poisoning. Goldfarb contacted Britain's top toxicology expert, Dr. John Henry, who had helped diagnose the poisoning of Ukrainian President Viktor Yushchenko, an attack he survived but which left him disfigured by facial lesions. Henry agreed to intervene.[28]

Henry was puzzled when he examined Litvinenko. The hair loss was consistent with poisoning by thallium, a radioactive substance, but thallium also caused muscle weakness, and Litvinenko's handshake was strong. It was not until November 23, the day of Litvinenko's death, that Dr. Henry was able to conclude, after extensive research and consultations with other experts, that the poison in Litvinenko's body was polonium 210. Had Goldfarb not enlisted Henry, Litvinenko might have been buried without anyone knowing the cause of his death, except that it was poison.[29]

Marina Litvinenko's description to me of the day Sasha died, after three weeks of agony in a London hospital, is etched clearly in my memory. Once the police learned that her husband had been poisoned by polonium, and that in the days he had been sick before entering the hospital he had unwittingly contaminated their home, Marina and Anatoly were told that they could not even return to get their belongings. For Marina, of course, the shock of this news compounded her grief over losing her husband.[30]

Marina was unhappy about the letter her husband sent from his deathbed, which was published worldwide, accusing Putin of her husband's poisoning. Goldfarb and a lawyer named George Menzies had drafted the letter, with her husband's concurrence, and released it only after consulting a reluctant Marina. For her at that time, it was about the loss of her husband, not retribution, and the letter resulted in a constant barrage of inquiries from journalists for months, just as she and Anatoly were trying to recover from the shock of what had happened. Yet Marina holds no grudges (as far I could tell) and she eventually decided that the best way to honor her dead husband was by publicity. She became a fierce and very successful advocate in efforts to hold the Kremlin, and Putin himself, to account for her husband's murder.

Repercussions

As noted, the two accused killers clearly knew very little about the poison they had handled. Otherwise, they would not have been so careless, contaminating themselves, and leaving traces of the poison everywhere they went—"like the crumbs spread by Hansel and Gretel," in the words of a British authority—which is how the police were able to identify them as the culprits. Lugovoy and Kovtun were both so contaminated with polonium 210 that upon their return to Russia they had to check into Moscow's Special Clinic Number Six for several weeks. Kovtun, who lost most of his hair, was the more severely affected. The conclusion of British experts, who obtained their medical records from Moscow, was that both men had no immediate health consequences, but in the longer term had an increased risk of cancer over the normal population. Scotland Yard sent investigators to question them at the Russian clinic, and the records of the interrogations are now available. As might be expected, both suspects denied, unconvincingly, that they had anything to do with the killing. Later, they would suggest that either Berezovsky or MI6 poisoned

Litvinenko and claim that they got second-hand contamination from him.[31]

It is important to note that both Lugovoy and Kovtun also endangered their family members, along with a host of others who were at the homes, offices, hotels, and restaurants they visited in London. As Marina Litvinenko's attorney expressed it: "It was an act of nuclear terrorism on the streets of a major city which put the lives of numerous other members of the public at risk."[32] German authorities found significant polonium contamination at Marina Wall's residence, as well as that of her mother Elenora, in Hamburg. At the Millennium Hotel, where the whole Russian group had stayed, several rooms had high levels of radioactive contamination. Even on the plane returning to Moscow on November 3, several of the seats Lugovoy's family had sat in registered high polonium counts. Lugovoy later acknowledged publicly that his family had been tested for polonium and "the results were distressing."[33]

As the names of Lugovoy and Kovtun emerged in connection with Litvinenko's poisoning, both men tried doing damage control. They went to the British Embassy in Moscow to proclaim their innocence in the affair and gave a press conference in Moscow on November 24, denying their culpability. Kovtun called his ex-wife Marina in Hamburg late in November to ask her if she had heard about the murder and his possible involvement. She recounted the conversation: "I answered no and I said I didn't know what he meant. He said the newspapers were full of it. I asked what it was about and he said it involved the poisoning of Litvinenko. I said I had no idea who that was and what it was about. He said I would perhaps hear something which concerned him but this was not true."[34]

The day after Litvinenko died, Lugovoy called Marina Litvinenko, twice, to express his condolences. She did not pick up, so he left voicemail messages.[35] He began calling Badri Patarkatsishvili soon after he returned to Moscow. According to Patarkatsishvili, "I had a number of phone calls from Lugovoy. In a short period he called many times. On the first occasion, he said 'look, Badri, I inform you that I did not kill Litvinenko.' I think he understood that someone was listening to his calls and his comments were for his benefit."[36]

Lugovoy also called his contact at Erinys, Tim Reilly, shortly after Litvinenko's death. Reilly (who incidentally fell quite ill on the evening of October 26, after he, Litvinenko, and Lugovoy met in his offices) recalled: "He called me up and it was as if he was anticipating the sort of international storm; so in other words he was saying: 'I was not involved in this, Tim, as you know, and I don't know why I'm being involved in it, but I like Sasha am as shocked as you are.' "[37]

On February 7, 2007, Lugovoy telephoned Berezovsky from Moscow and asked him if he believed the story that he, Lugovoy, was involved in Litvinenko's death. Berezovsky replied that he could not say for sure, but that Lugovoy should come to London and give evidence if he was innocent. Berezovsky even offered to pay for his lawyer.[38] But by this time, Berezovsky must have begun to grasp that the man in whom he had put so much trust was likely a murderer. And what's more, he was doubtless aware that at some point, he too could become another Putin victim.

Reaction in Russia

In the meantime, President Putin did his own version of damage control during his annual press conference on February 1, 2007. Asked about the Litvinenko murder, he observed: "Alexander Litvinenko was dismissed from the security services. Before that he served in the convoy troops. There he did not deal with any secrets. . . . There was no need to run anywhere, he did not have any secrets. Everything negative he could say with respect to his service and his previous employment, he already said a long time ago, so there could be nothing new in what he did later."[39] These words, of course, were meant to convey the message that Litvinenko was not significant enough to matter to the Kremlin and that the Kremlin would supposedly have had no motive to kill him. But those who understood the Putin regime knew that Litvinenko was considered a traitor who deserved the highest punishment.

In May 2007 the British Crown Prosecution Service formally charged Lugovoy with Litvinenko's murder and issued a warrant for his arrest. Kovtun was not charged until November 2011. (Both are on international wanted lists but they have been protected by the Kremlin from extradition to Britain.) On May 31, 2007, Lugovoy and Kovtun gave another press conference in Moscow, adding more to their story, which was crumbling in terms of credibility.[40] Lugovoy did most of the talking: "The English offered me to gather incriminating information about the Russian president, V. Putin and members of his family. . . . I do not count myself an ardent admirer of President Putin, and I have my own reasons for that, which many can probably guess. But I was taught to defend my motherland and not to betray it." Lugovoy went on to describe an elaborate effort to get him to work for MI6, and claimed that Berezovsky had been a British agent since the time he had been in the Russian Security Council in the late 1990s.

In Lugovoy's somewhat confusing rendition of the Litvinenko affair, Berezovsky, in collusion with MI6, had poisoned Litvinenko because the latter was blackmailing Berezovsky. Lugovoy and Kovtun were framed by being deliberately contaminated with polonium. In Lugovoy's words: "we were marked with polonium on purpose, for subsequent use in the political scandal." Both Lugovoy and Kovtun had bitter complaints about how they had suffered because of the murder case. Lugovoy claimed that in one business deal alone "with a famous world company," he had lost $25 million. Kovtun lamented that he could never go back to Germany because he would be arrested.[41]

Interestingly, Lugovoy said in a December 2008 interview with the Spanish newspaper *El Pais* that, when he had studied at an elite military academy [in Moscow], he made friends with people who later became high-ranking officials in the FSB: "one of the people closest to me is the deputy director of the FSB, a general with huge potential and resources." Lugovoy added that "when the British agents started to approach me, one of the first things I did was to inform the FSB so that they wouldn't accuse me of being a traitor or a spy."[42] Thus Lugovoy confirmed that the FSB officials knew well about his travels to London and his dealings with Litvinenko and Berezovsky. It is hard to imagine that they would not have pressured Lugovoy to collaborate with them in furthering their objectives vis-a-vis these two putative Russian traitors, Litvinenko and Berezovsky.

Final Judgements

Far from being viewed as a criminal, Lugovoy was treated like a celebrity in Russia. In September 2007, LDRP leader Zhirinovsky announced at a press conference with much fanfare that Lugovoy would occupy the second position on his party's ticket. Zhirinovsky may have been hoping that with Lugovoy on the ticket, the LDRP would gain some steam in its political campaign for the 2007 Duma elections. Interestingly, a U.S. embassy cable observed: "Throughout the press conference Lugovoy appeared uncomfortable in his new role as straight man for Zhirinovsky. It also appeared that he had been reprimanded by his new boss about the rank order in the party. Lugovoy pointedly retracted a statement of a day earlier that he had ambitions to run for president, coyly saying that every Russian would want to be the leader of such a great country, before gamely insisting that Zhirinovsky had the mettle to replace Putin."[43]

Lugovoy has become a highly visible and wealthy member of the Duma, as well as a TV personality. (Kovtun has fared less well, and he and Lugovoy severed their relationship in 2009.) Lugovoy's wife divorced him shortly after the episode with Litvinenko, not surprisingly, given that polonium had tainted their entire family because of his venture. He remarried a go-go dancer in 2013, with a lavish wedding on the Black Sea.[44] According to Russian media reports, his new, very young and beautiful bride had no idea that her new husband was a suspect in the murder of Litvinenko when she married him.[45]

With financial help from Berezovsky, Litvinenko's father, Valter, moved to Italy with his second wife to join his son Maxim (Litvinenko's half-brother), who owned a restaurant on the Adriatic coast. Initially, Valter was convinced that Putin was behind the murder and said so publicly. But he gradually changed his mind and in early 2012 gave an interview to a Russian television station, sobbing, in which he apologized for blaming his son's death on Russian authorities.[46] Subsequently, he gave a deposition from Italy for Russian prosecutors in which he voiced the conviction that Boris Berezovsky (along with Alex Goldfarb) had killed his son: "It [his son's murder] was a result of Berezovsky's activity. It was him didn't want Alexander, after coming back to Russia, to be able to tell somebody about what he had done and about his business in London. I believe that the polonium was used just to mislead everyone and that it was skillfully placed everywhere in London where Alexander was present."[47]

Luke Harding visited the Litvinenko family in Italy in 2010. Both he and Goldfarb had the same explanation for Valter's change of mind on his son's murder. Valter and his family there (which by then included a daughter, her husband, and children) had fallen into dire financial straits because Maxim Litvinenko's restaurant business had failed. Valter's wife died in 2011 and he was grief-stricken, still not having gotten over his son's murder. Also, Berezovsky had cut the family off financially, after initially being very generous in his support. In Goldfarb's words, from his testimony for the Inquiry: "Well, he's [Valter] an old man, he had a tremendous loss . . . his second wife died and he was devastated . . . and also there were financial problems, this I know, because some time before . . . Valter complained publicly that he was cut off by Berezovsky from financial support and that Berezovsky stopped taking his calls."[48] Not surprisingly, for Marina Litvinenko, Valter's sudden turnaround "was absolutely shocking for me." (Especially painful was that Valter called his son a traitor.) Marina has not communicated with him since then.[49] She rightfully feels a strong sense of betrayal, but grief has strange ways of manifesting itself, and Valter was undoubtedly a victim of deliberate disinformation and intense pressure on him exerted by the Kremlin.

It is significant that the Kremlin would put such great effort into having Valter Litvinenko interviewed almost six years after the murder. Given that British inquest proceedings into Litvinenko's death were resumed in late 2011 after a long interval, Russian authorities were doubtless preparing a case in defense of Lugovoy and Kovtun. In December 2012, the Russian Investigative Committee applied for "interested person status" in the inquest and it was thereafter formally represented by British solicitors at both the inquest and, later, the Inquiry hearings.

However much the Russian Investigative Committee would have liked to obstruct the progress of the Litvinenko Inquiry, it only was successful insofar as it prevented transcripts of interviews by British police of Lugovoy and Kovtun in Moscow from being admitted as evidence. (The interviews themselves, conducted in Moscow in December 2006, were hampered greatly by the lack of cooperation on the part of Russian authorities.) Also, the length of the Inquiry hearings was prolonged by Kovtun's indication that he would appear as a core participant to answer questions via video link from Moscow. Later, supported by legal arguments put forth by the Russian Investigative Committee, he backed out.

When Sir Robert produced his report on the Litvinenko Inquiry in January 2016, his judgment against Lugovoy and Kovtun was unambiguous: "I am sure that Mr. Lugovoy and Mr. Kovtun placed the polonium 210 in the teapot at the Pine Bar on 1 November 2006. I am also sure that they did this with the intention of poisoning Mr. Litvinenko . . . I am sure that Mr. Lugovoy and Mr. Kovtun were acting on behalf of others when they poisoned Mr. Litvinenko." As for the possible role of Putin, Sir Robert was equivocal, concluding that "The FSB operation to kill Mr. Litvinenko was probably approved by Mr. Patrushev [head of the FSB] and also by President Putin."[50]

The reaction in Russia was predictable, given that the majority of Russians rely on state-sponsored television for their news. Over 50 percent of those polled by Russia's Levada Center rejected Owen's conclusions, opting instead for the Kremlin's version—that Berezovsky had killed Litvinenko in collusion with the British security services.[51] Even those who accepted the British judgment made their loyalties to the Kremlin clear. In fact, just after the murder, Russian parliamentary members had chimed in to say that Litvinenko got what he deserved. On November 24, 2006, Sergei Abelstev said on the floor of the Russian Duma: "The deserved punishment reached the traitor. I am sure his terrible death will be a warning to all the traitors that in Russia treason is not to be forgiven." He added that "I would recommend to citizen Berezovsky to avoid any food at the commemorative feast for Litvinenko."[52]

According to Russian journalist Alexander Baunov: "Public opinion is the complete opposite of that in Britain. The view here is that these guys [Lugovoy and Kovtun] are heroes because they punished a traitor."[53] In taking this stance, Russians were following cues from Putin, who in March 2015 conveyed a presidential medal of honor on Lugovoy "for services to the motherland" in the midst of the London Inquiry proceedings that were producing daily evidence of Lugovoy's role as a killer of Litvinenko. Putin, again, had managed to deflect blame for the assassination of an opponent, in a killing he had sponsored. As usual, suspicions of his involvement were widespread, due to overwhelming circumstantial and forensic evidence, but there was no smoking gun.

Stanislav Markelov.

(Photograph courtesy of ZUMA Press, Inc./Alamy Stock Photo)

Natalia Estemirova.

(Photograph courtesy of Matthew Ford/Camera Press/Redux)

9

CONTINUED ONSLAUGHT AGAINST KREMLIN CHALLENGERS

Markelov's murder is a declaration of war. Now the question is, whose side is the state on?

—**Natalia Estemirova, January 2009**

I am deeply shocked by the brutal murder of the well-known human rights activist and journalist Natalia Estemirova Husainovna. This crime will be investigated thoroughly and the perpetrators punished. Natalia Estemirova Husainovna defended the universality and indivisibility of all human rights.

—**Dmitri Medvedev, telegram to the Memorial Office in Grozny,**
Chechnya, July 18, 2009

The murder of Litvinenko in November 2006 did, at the time, elicit what seemed to be a strong reaction from the West. But, in the end, there were few long-term repercussions for Russia. In May 2007, Resolution 154 was introduced in the U.S. House of Representatives, and it was finally passed on April 1, 2008, while Bush was still the president. The resolution read as follows:

Expresses the sense of Congress that: (1) the fatal radiation poisoning of Alexander Litvinenko raises significant concerns about the potential involvement of elements of the Russian government in Mr. Litvinenko's death, and about the security and proliferation of radioactive materials; (2) the use of such radioactive materials demonstrates a threat to the safety and security of the people of the Russian Federation, the United Kingdom, the United States, and other countries; and (3) the President of the United States and the Secretary of State should urge Russian President Vladimir Putin and other officials of the Russian government to cooperate fully with the British government in its investigation into Mr. Litvinenko's death and to ensure the security of the production, storage, distribution, and export of polonium 210 as a material that may become dangerous to large numbers of people if utilized by terrorism.[1]

Also in May 2007, the House introduced Resolution 151, on the unexplained deaths of Russian journalists, including Ivan Safronov, a correspondent for *Kommersant*. Safronov had written an article about the failure of a Russian ballistic missile test, reportedly offending Putin and his military leaders, and was about to report on planned Russian arms sales to pariah states Syria and Iran. Safronov fell to his death from a window in his apartment in March 2007. Russian prosecutors deemed the death a suicide, but Safronov's family and colleagues suspected murder. House Resolution 151, passed in June 2007, called upon President Bush to offer Putin U.S. law enforcement assistance in investigating the many unexplained murders of Russian journalists.[2] Meanwhile, in Britain, Prime Minister Gordon Brown announced in July 2007 that the UK was expelling four Russian diplomats in response to Russia's refusal to extradite Litvinenko's accused killer, Andrei Lugovoy.

Unfortunately, these Western measures had little effect. They did not stop the killings. Putin knew full well that the West's overriding need to engage Russia in many pressing global matters would prevent a confrontation over what he was doing to his own people. There was a lull in 2008, but shortly after Barack Obama took office in January 2009 the murders began anew, aimed against Kremlin critics of Russia's repressive actions in Chechnya. As I have discussed, both Politkovskaya and Litvinenko exposed the terrible human-rights abuses that occurred in Chechnya. But Western governments continued to put the Chechen issue on the back burner, in the interest of diplomacy with Russia.

As one American Russia expert observed in: "Russia's moves to crush separatist sympathies in Chechnya were deftly transformed by the Putin government into the larger Global War on Terror. . . . While never openly stated, a deal of sorts was worked out whereby Russia would agree to assist the U.S. in its fight against global terrorism, in exchange for silencing the rhetoric over indiscriminate Russian force in Chechnya."[3] With Politkovskaya and Litvinenko dead, it was up to other Russian reporters and human-rights activists to call the Kremlin to account for its war crimes in Chechnya. But, as might have been predicted, the most forceful of these critics would also become victims of the Kremlin's vengeance.

Stanislav Markelov

Stanislav Markelov, married and the father of two small children, was a Russian human-rights attorney. Born in 1974, he graduated from the prestigious Moscow State Juridical Academy in 1996 and quickly gained prominence as a respected legal authority and political activist. In 1997, he became a member of the Inter-Republic Collegium of Advocates and the International Union of Advocates. Beginning in 2006, he was president of the prestigious Russian Rule of Law Institute. Markelov took up many controversial cases tied to military-crime, human-rights, and ecological issues. According to his friend Tanya Lokshina of Human Rights Watch: "Stas [Markelov] was one of those people prepared to give his life for the cause."[4]

Markelov had been a lawyer for the families of victims of the 2002 Dubrovka Theater hostage crisis. He also had acted on behalf of Mikhail Beketov, editor-in-chief of the paper *Khimkinskaia pravda*, who was brutally beaten in 2008. Beketov, who died in 2013 as a result of injuries he never recovered from after the beating, had campaigned against the plans of authorities to build a highway through the Khimki Forest to connect Moscow and St. Petersburg. In addition, Markelov, working with Politkovskaya, was instrumental in the conviction of Sergei Lapin, a special-forces officer in Chechnya who tortured to death a twenty-six-year-old Chechen man and was sentenced to eight years in prison for the crime.

Significantly, Markelov also represented the Kungaev family, whose daughter Elza, an eighteen-year-old Chechen, was kidnapped, raped, and murdered in March 2000 by a Russian military officer serving in Chechnya, Iurii Budanov. Budanov, the commander of the Russian 160th Tank Regiment, was, by all accounts, drunk when he and his soldiers entered the Kungaev home and abducted Elza Kungaeva, claiming that she was a sniper. Back at his encampment, Budanov interrogated Kungaeva alone and ended up strangling her to death after he raped her.

The Budanov case created a sensation in Russia, polarizing the Russian military/security establishment against human-rights activists. Budanov was immediately arrested after the murder but was not charged with rape, much to the outrage of many Chechens, who consider rape a worse crime than killing. His trial did not begin until a year later, March 2001, and lasted until July 2002. Clearly, the Russian military was reluctant to prosecute a senior officer at a time when it was waging a bitter struggle against Chechen separatists. Budanov's defenders claimed that he was "temporarily insane" at the time of his crime and had acted under the stress of combat.[5]

A temporary judgment exonerating Budanov of murder was reached by a Russian court, with the recommendation that he undergo psychiatric treatment. In December 2002, Budanov was acquitted of murder charges. As a result of pressure from lawyers for the Kungaev family, human-rights groups, and Russian democrats, the Russian Supreme Court overruled the verdict and a new trial was convened. Budanov was convicted of murder in July 2003 and given a sentence of ten years' imprisonment. He was released on parole on January 15, 2009 and two years later was shot to death on the streets of Moscow.[6]

Assassination

On January 23, 2009, just days after Budanov's release, Markelov gave a press conference, where he spoke out against Budanov's parole and vowed to bring charges against him before the European Court of Human Rights. The conference was attended by members of the Kungaev family. Markelov added that he had more facts about crimes Budanov had committed in Chechnya. After Markelov left the conference, accompanied by Anastasia Baburova, a young intern at *Novaia gazeta*, he was walking to his car when he was gunned down on the street, just a short distance from the Kremlin, and died on the spot. Baburova was also shot and died later at a Moscow hospital.

Iurii Budanov claimed that he had nothing to do with the murders of Markelov and Baburova, but many observers considered the assassinations to be directly tied to the Budanov affair. According to Amnesty International, Markelov had received a text message on his mobile phone a few days earlier. The message read: "You brainless animal . . . again sticking your nose into Budanov's case.??!! Idiot, you couldn't find a calmer method of suicide???"[7]

Amazingly, no one in the Kremlin spoke about the murders of Markelov and Baburova for over a week, although there was a huge public outcry with several street demonstrations. (In the city of Grozny, the capitol of Chechnya, more than three thousand people gathered to protest the murders and demand that the killers be brought to justice.) Finally, on January 29, the Russian president at the time, Dmitri Medvedev, met in the Kremlin with the editor-in-chief of *Novaia gazeta*, Dmitri Muratov, and expressed condolences to the families of the two victims. He explained, feebly, that the delay in the Kremlin's response was due to the fact that it did not want to influence the investigation.[8] But one wonders whether the security services and the Kremlin were simply in disarray over how to represent this terrible crime to the public.

In April 2011, at the end of a three-month trial, a jury handed down a guilty verdict against Nikita Tikhonov and his alleged accomplice Evgeniia Khasis for the double murder. Tikhonov, it was said, had intended only to kill Markelov, but also shot Baburina because he did not want her to identify him later. The evidence against them consisted of surveillance cameras, witnesses, and the murder weapon found at their home. Tikhonov had initially confessed to the shooting, saying he killed Markelov because "he defended Chechen women suicide bombers and got the Russian army officer Iurii Budanov convicted." But he later retracted his confession, claiming he had been tortured. Tikhonov also supposedly had another motive: Markelov had been investigating Tikhonov's role in the murder of an anti-fascist activist.[9]

Though the case seemed clear-cut, questions remained. It was brought up in court that others were involved in the murder, including members of ultra-nationalist groups, yet no names were mentioned. Several jury members recused themselves during the trial, and one of them claimed that there had been attempts to "brainwash" him. Also, a key witness withdrew his statement and fled to Germany.[10] More recently, in December 2013, the Investigative Committee of Russia announced that the so-called Combat Organization of Russian Nationalists, known under the acronym BORN, might have been the initiators of the Markelov–Baburova murders. The aim of the group, of which Tikhonov was a member, was "murder motivated by ideological and national hatred."[11]

But some observers expressed doubt that the murderers were neo-Nazis or right-wing radicals, so-called skinheads. The murder was too professional, in the view of former FSB officer Mikhail Trepashkin. And the weapon that fired the shot, a Makarov pistol, is banned from sale in Russia and is only available to the military or security services. The For Human Rights movement noted that the killing could have been a provocation by "those forces, who want to scare society, and justify the introduction of new, strict police powers."[12] As Pavel Felgenhauer, a columnist for *Novaia gazeta,* observed, "the Russian security services or rogue elements within these services are the prime suspects. The boldness of the attack, by a single gunman in broad daylight in the center of Moscow, required professional preliminary planning and surveillance that would necessitate the security services, which closely control that particular neighborhood, turning a blind eye."[13] Whoever organized and ordered the killings of Markelov and Baburova, these acts served the Kremlin well, sending a shock wave of fear throughout the community of Russian journalists and human-rights campaigners.

Natalia Estemirova

Natalia Estemirova, a representative of the human-rights group Memorial in Grozny, attended Markelov's funeral on January 26, 2009, along with Luke Harding, to whom she said "I think criminals are comfortable with the kind of government we have now. It's less comfortable for human-rights advocates."[14] Harding met up with Estemirova a month later, when both attended the trial of the four alleged killers of Politkovskaya. She told Harding that the trial was a farce: "We don't have a killer. And we don't have the people who are really behind it. This isn't a real trial. It's simply meant to give the impression of justice."[15] Five months later, Estemirova herself would be murdered, and her killers would never be found.

Estemirova, a widow with a teenage daughter, was born in 1959 in the Sverdlovsk Region of Russia, to Chechen and Russian parents. After earning a degree in history from Grozny University, she taught at a local high school. In the meantime, she started working as a reporter for local newspapers and television stations and produced several documentaries. She joined the Chechen branch of Memorial in 2000 and devoted herself to gathering evidence about the brutalities committed against civilians in Chechnya. She also wrote frequently for *Novaia gazeta* and *Kavkazkii uzel* (Caucasian Knot), a Caucasian news website.[16]

Estemirova received numerous awards for her journalism and human-rights work, including the Swedish Right Livelihood Award in 2004, the Robert Schuman Medal from the Group of the European People's Party in 2005, and the first Anna Politkovskaya Award by Reach All Women in War (RAW) in 2007.[17] Freelance Russian journalist Shura Burtin met Estemirova in Chechnya two months before her death. This is how he described her: "Her character immediately caught the eye. A beautiful, statuesque woman, not hiding her figure, on high heels, without a headscarf and a clear sense of self-esteem in her movements. She stood out sharply against her background. An ordinary woman in today's Chechnya is unnoticeable in a headscarf and a dark, formless dress."[18]

Abduction and Murder

Estemirova was leaving for work from her apartment in Grozny on the morning of July 15, 2009 when she was abducted by several men in a white car. Neighbors heard her shouting "I am being kidnapped" as she was carried off. Her body was later discovered fifty miles away on the side of a highway in Ingushetia, a neighboring republic. She had been shot in the head and chest.[19]

Human-rights groups worldwide condemned the Estemirova murder, along with many world leaders, including members of the U.S. Helsinski commission, the U.S. State Department, the UN secretary-general, and German Chancellor Angela Merkel. Rallies attended by several hundred people were held in both Grozny and Moscow on July 16. Human Rights Watch director Kenneth Roth observed that "it seems to be open season on anyone trying to highlight the appalling human-rights abuses in Chechnya."[20] For Estemirova's daughter, Lana, it was of course a devastating personal loss. She told Luke Harding, when he visited Grozny a few days after the murder, that Anna Polit-kovskaya and Stanislav Markelov had often stayed at her mother's flat when they came to Chechnya and that they and her mother would talk animatedly late into the night. She had lost the three most important adults in her life.[21]

In October 2009, I attended a memorial service for Estemirova in New York City, sponsored by the PEN American Center and several human-rights groups. The large auditorium was filled to the last row. Salman Rushdie spoke and read Estemirova's seminal piece that she wrote for *Novaia gazeta* in April 2007, titled "Wild Garlic Gatherers." The subject of the piece was the Chechen women, "tired with weather-beaten faces," who go into the forests to pick wild garlic to sell in the markets. The forests are strewn with landmines, and on one particular occasion there were Russian troops with submachine guns who fired on the women, killing teachers from a local elementary school.[22] Such was the nature of the everyday tragedies Estemirova recorded in her chilling, evocative prose.

Further Reactions

The presumption of most observers from the outset was that Estemirova was killed for her professional activities in Chechnya. In the weeks before her death, she was documenting several high-profile cases, including a public execution of alleged Chechen rebel Rizvan Albekov by members of Ramzan Kadyrov's police force in the Kurchaloi region, the burning of rebel homes, sometimes with inhabitants inside, and abductions of innocent civilians. She passed all this information on to the media, human-rights organizations, and the MVD. The execution of Albekov was particularly significant, because Estemirova, along with Tanya Lokshina, went to his village to investigate what had happened, and then Estemirova gave an immediate interview to the online media outlet Caucasian Knot.[23]

Not surprisingly, Estemirova's reports put Kadyrov into a fury. She had already sparked anger in him in March 2008 when she spoke on REN-TV about the compulsory wearing of women's headscarves in Chechnya, saying that it was a violation of women's rights. The mayor of Grozny called Estemirova to his office after her television appearance. According to Lokshina, "Ramzan Kadyrov entered the room and immediately began to talk with her in a raised voice. He called her an indecent woman, told her he knew where her relatives lived, grabbed her by the arms, and said obscene things. He demanded an end to all that she was doing, in the interests of her family." Fearing for her life, Estemirova went to London with her daughter and stayed for several weeks.[24]

Not long before Estemirova's death, the "human-rights ombudsman" in Chechnya, Nurdi Nukhazhiev, summoned the head of the Grozny office of Memorial and told him that Kadyrov was very angry at the group and that he was "afraid something might happen." Svetlana Gannushkina, head of the non-governmental organization (NGO) Citizen's Assistance, was told by a Chechen official close to Kadyrov that the "chief is in a rage," especially at Estemirova.[25]

The chairman of Memorial, Oleg Orlov, had no doubt that Kadyrov was behind the killing and said so publicly:

> I know, I am sure, who is responsible for the killing of Natalia Estemirova. We all know that man. His name is Ramzan Kadyrov, president of the Chechen Republic. Ramzan already threatened Natalia, insulted her, believed her to be his personal enemy. We do not know whether it was Ramzan himself who ordered to kill Natalia or his close associates, to please their ruling authority. And President Medvedev seems satisfied to have a murderer as head of one of Russia's republics.[26]

Orlov added that shortly before Estemirova was killed, Kadyrov had a private meeting with her and told her: "My hands are indeed covered in blood. And I am not ashamed of it. I killed and will kill bad people. We fight against enemies of our republic."

According to Gannushkina, Kadyrov, not surprisingly, was unnerved by the accusations and called Orlov that same day, declaring his innocence: "It seems as though Kadyrov called Oleg to find out what evidence he had."[27] Kadyrov also gave a television interview in which he defended himself. He soon was reassured by the Kremlin. President Medvedev immediately condemned the crime publicly and acknowledged that Estemirova was killed because of her professional activities. He vowed that authorities would apprehend the killers. But he also insisted that Kadyrov was not involved in the crime, thus ensuring that the Chechen president would be protected by the Kremlin and not held accountable.[28]

As for Prime Minister Putin, he showed his loyalty to Kadyrov by traveling to Grozny on August 24, 2009, just hours before a demonstration in honor of Estemirova took place in Moscow and at the exact time that mourners gathered in Grozny to mark the traditional

forty days since her death. Together with Kadyrov in a much-publicized
ceremony, Putin laid flowers at the grave of Kadyrov's father, the
ruthless former Chechen president, Akhmat Kadyrov. Tanya Lokshina
and journalist Elena Milashina were at Estemirova's gravesite. They
knew, as they recounted later, that Putin would not come to the site
because Estemirova, like Politkovskaya, was a personal enemy of both
Kadyrov and Putin.[29]

Kadyrov later filed a civil defamation suit against Orlov for
accusing him of being responsible for Estemirova's murder, and won.
He then went on to file a criminal complaint against Orlov, seeking a
three-year prison sentence. After a nine-month trial, Orlov was acquitted by a Moscow court in June 2011. During the trial, Kadyrov
was asked to testify via video link from Chechnya. He had this to say
about Estemirova: "I did not see anything saintly or useful to the
Chechen people in her work. She did not protect human rights. She
gabbed and talked, but did not protect rights."[30]

Investigation of the Estemirova Case

Aleksandr Bastrykin, chief of the Russian Investigative Committee,
should by now be a familiar character to the reader. A master at spin
and deception, he took the case of Estemirova under his personal control, appointing Igor Sobol' as the senior investigator, who led a
group that included employees of subordinate investigative commit-
tees in both the Chechen and Ingushetia republics. But, as it turned
out, the very people in Chechnya who were giving operational support to the Estemirova investigation were those who were under suspicion for her murder—Chechen police.

Deputy Russian MVD chief Arkady Edelev, a close associate of
Kadyrov, was the point man in the case until he was dismissed in February 2010. Edelev initially put out several possible versions for the
killing: rebel bandits wanting to discredit the Chechen leadership and

law-enforcement agencies; robbery (Estemirova allegedly received "foreign funds" on behalf of Memorial); and a possible "failed personal relationship." A vendetta against Estemirova by Kadyrov or his police was not even considered. This despite the fact that the car of rebel bandits who seized Estemirova would have had to pass through several checkpoints and show I.D. to get into neighboring Ingushetia—a virtual impossibility without police complicity.[31]

By January 2010, an official version of the murder had evolved and was put forward as definitive. A Chechen rebel named Alkhazur Bashaev, who allegedly led a jihad group (jamaat) in the village of Shalazhi, had murdered Estemirova. The investigators based their findings on the claim that the weapon used to kill Estemirova had been found in an empty house belonging to Bashaev, along with a forged police identity card with his photograph. The motive for the murder was said to relate to a visit Estemirova made with a colleague to Shalazhi to investigate a kidnapping and robbery by Bashaev's group of militants, and three subsequent reports about Bashaev's recruitment of young men to "go into the forest" to fight the Chechen regime that were posted on Memorial's website. According to this theory, the crime was committed in revenge for the reports. Bashaev was, by the official version, conveniently dead. He had allegedly been killed in November 2009 during a "special operation," an airstrike carried out by Kadyrov forces, which resulted in the death of several militants.

In February 2010, police authorities discovered a vehicle in an underground garage in Grozny that they traced to Bashaev. In the car, they found a gun silencer that they claimed had been used in Estemirova's murder because it matched a rubber fragment found at the crime scene. Forensic examiners also said that they discovered plant material underneath the car that matched plants where the murder had occurred. This was presented as conclusive evidence against Bashaev. The case was closed.

A Human-Rights Team Takes On the Case

A team of researchers from *Novaia gazeta*, Memorial, and the International Federation for Human Rights decided to do its own investigation, with the help of Estemirova's sister Svetlana, a lawyer. The team delved deeply into the case and was able to refute much of the official version in a report produced in September 2011.[32]

First, Estemirova never met Bashaev or interviewed him. It was unclear why he would single her out to be killed for writing about him and the Shalazhi Jamaat, given that the reports, which she did in fact write, were unsigned and he could not have known that she was their author. The team noted that Estemirova's notebook computer was missing from the murder site and that investigators had seized her work computer. Thus it would have been possible for them to identify her as the author of the reports from an analysis of the hard drives of these computers.

As it turned out, the forensic results showed that the fragment of the silencer found at the crime scene did not match the gun silencer found in the vehicle belonging to Bashaev. And the bullets collected at the murder site had not been fired through the silencer that was discovered in the car. Furthermore, there was no physical evidence found in the vehicle—fingerprints, blood, hair or pieces of clothing—to link it to the crime. The team concluded:

> If we assume that it was indeed this VAZ-2017 vehicle that was used to kidnap Natalia Estemirova, then the logic of the criminals becomes somewhat confusing. Before abandoning the car, they must have tried to thoroughly destroy all of the evidence. However, for some reason, they left the vehicle's government license plate in the trunk, allowing the car to be traced . . . to Bashaev. Meanwhile it would have been IMPOSSIBLE to completely eradicate all traces of the kidnapping from the car. The negative results from the foren-

sic analysis allow us to come to what seems like an obvious conclusion: it is unlikely that the discovered vehicle was used in the kidnapping of Natalia Estemirova.[33]

As to the fake identity card with Bashaev's photograph pasted on it, found in a cache of weapons next to the gun used to kill Estemirova, the team concluded that, while the card was indeed forged, anyone, particularly the police, could have obtained Bashaev's photograph and created a false I.D.

The most important finding of the independent group concerned the issue of DNA evidence, and it proved to be dramatic. Russian investigators had collected DNA from several different sources, including the sweat on a comb found at Bashaev's former home; sweat stains found on the blouse Estemirova had been wearing when she was murdered that were not hers; DNA from three individuals (two men and a woman) extracted from material found under Estemirova's fingernails; and DNA obtained from exhumed remains of those allegedly killed in the above-mentioned November 2009 airstrike, who were said to include Bashaev.

Members of the research team traveled to France, where Bashaev's brother Anzor was living, and were able to obtain a sample of his DNA and have it analyzed by a forensic expert in Switzerland. The presumption was that Anzor Bashaev would have many of the same genetic markers as Alkhazur. They then took the results, along with the DNA profiles of possible killers from the case file, to an independent laboratory in Russia. They received an analysis from one of Russia's most prominent geneticists, Professor Igor Kornienko.

Kornienko found a complete lack of concurrence between the DNA profile of Anzor Bashaev and any of the DNA profiles found on other materials. This meant, according to the research team, that "neither the DNA extracted from the exhumed remains [of the victims of the airstrike by Kadyrov forces], nor the DNA obtained from traces of sweat on Natalia Estemirova's blouse, nor the DNA obtained from the sweat on the comb, belong to the genotype of Alkhazur Bashaev."[34]

Interestingly, Russian authorities claimed to have found Bashaev's passport, completely clean, with no traces of blood, among the fragments of the bodies that were strewn around after their special operation against the militants. It was displayed on Chechen television after the attack. But this is the only evidence that Bashaev was indeed killed, and it could easily have been manufactured. The research team concluded that in fact the vehicle that was blown up contained bodies of murdered residents from a local town, not Shalazhi, where Bashaev was from.

As the team pointed out, the official investigation made no attempt to use comparative DNA analysis to determine the complicity in the crime of other individuals, particularly members of the security services and police. Among the potential suspects were members of the MVD from the Kurchaloi region, who had carried out the execution that Estemirova had reported on.

In sum, the report concluded that evidence produced by investigators to prove Bashaev's guilt "is more indicative of a very crude attempt to construct a version of the crime implicating the militants of Shalazhi Jamaat, and leading the criminal investigation down a false trail. Indeed, the criminal investigation is gladly following this trail, ignoring the findings of their own experts. . . . We demand that the administration of the Investigative Committee stop violating the standards of the Russian Criminal Code and the rights of the victim."[35]

While some might attribute the flawed results of the official investigation of Estemirova's murder to incompetence, it seems clear that in fact there was a concerted effort to cover up the facts and that Bashaev was just a convenient person to pin the crime on. The evidence points to Kadyrov as the one who arranged the killing. But then we must go back to the same question: Would Kadyrov have done this on his own initiative, without the okay of Putin? Not likely, given that Estemirova was so prominent that even world leaders condemned the crime. As for Medvedev, he perhaps deplored the murder, but he was in no position to do anything about it.

The U.S. "Reset" with Russia

It is ironic that just a week before Estemirova was killed, President Obama visited Russia for the first time. It seemed like a successful trip. Obama and Medvedev, who had assumed the Russian presidency a year earlier, agreed to cuts in nuclear arms, and Obama indicated that he might compromise on the planned NATO missile shield in Eastern Europe, much to the dismay of the Czech and Polish governments. In a speech at Moscow's New Economic School on the second day of his visit, Obama spoke of a fresh start in relations between the U.S. and Russia, calling for a "reset": "America wants a strong, peaceful and prosperous Russia . . . on the fundamental issues that will shape this century, Americans and Russians share common interests that form a basis for co-operation."[36]

Obama met with Russian opposition leaders on that day, and sent a U.S. delegation to a memorial service for Paul Klebnikov. Speaking on Obama's behalf at the service, the Undersecretary of State for Political Affairs, William J. Burns, said: "After five long years, we urge the Russian authorities to redouble their efforts to bring justice to those responsible."[37] Obama also attended a conference on civil society (Medvedev declined to go) and spoke about the importance of press freedom and the rule of law. But, as *The New York Times* observed, "His comments throughout the day were calculated to recognize Russian resentment of American scolding. 'I come before you with some humility,' he said. 'I think in the past there's been a tendency for the United States to lecture rather than to listen.' "[38]

Whatever motivated Obama's policy of reset with Russia, it was doomed to fail. As Russia expert Mikhail Zygar explained:

"Although the Obama administration was ready to renounce the role of global policeman and other excesses of the Bush era, it still harbored familiar old American prejudices against Russia. Medvedev, for his part, was never powerful enough to oversee a reset. And although Putin wanted a new relationship with the West, it was not the one Obama had in mind."[39]

The Obama administration placed its hopes for improved relations with Russia on Medvedev. But the White House failed to understand that Medvedev was a figurehead who was subservient to Prime Minister Putin because Putin still controlled the security services. Medvedev portrayed himself as a "liberal" and there was much talk in Russia and the West about a clique that had formed around him composed of men who genuinely favored democratic reform. As it turned out, this was a farce. From the very moment that Medvedev took office in 2008, it was predestined that Putin would return to the presidency four years later. (According to the Russian Constitution, Putin could not serve more than two terms consecutively.) In fact, Putin and Medvedev later revealed that it had been their plan all along to have Putin take back the presidency after Medvedev's term ended. Moreover, the Kremlin changed the Constitution to extend the length of a presidential term from four to six years, which means that Putin can now run again in 2018, and remain the Russian president until 2024.

In the words of one commentator, "The 'reset' was primarily built around the good personal relationship between Obama and Medvedev, and thus when Putin re-assumed the office of Russian president, the main building block of the policy was shattered. Perhaps the Obama administration was too short-sighted or idealistic and placed a clearly risky bet on Medvedev while framing policy."[40] Back in office as Russian president in 2012, Putin not only showed little interest in cooperating with the U.S. and its Russian partners on key global issues, he also initiated a new crackdown at home.

Although Obama and his foreign policy team "talked the talk" about human rights in Russia, they were not able to have significant influence on the Kremlin. Testifying in July 2011 before the House Foreign Affairs Committee, Ariel Cohen, a research fellow at the Heritage Foundation, observed: "There is good reason to believe . . . that Russian leaders do not take White House efforts to promote freedom and human rights seriously. They know that the U.S. administration is chained to the 'reset' and will do little more than verbally object to the Kremlin's abuses of human rights and the rule of law. The talk of democracy is 'for domestic [U.S.] consumption,' said one official Russian visitor to Washington last fall."[41]

Obama's failure to press the issue of human rights as he reached out to the Kremlin caused dismay among democratic activists and journalists in Russia, as well as among human-rights groups in the West. Of course, it is highly likely that, even if Obama had been more forceful in condemning the violence against Kremlin critics and the increasing crackdown on press freedoms and civil liberties, it would not have affected the Kremlin's behavior in any significant way. But at the very least he would have offered moral support to those who had the courage to oppose Putin's domestic policies and sent a message to Russia that its human-rights abuses were not going unnoticed in the West.

Nowhere were those abuses more horrifyingly evident than in Chechnya. As Tanya Lokshina pointed out, Putin and his entourage were directly responsible for Chechen President Kadyrov's brutalities, including the killing of Estemirova. In the first years of Kadyrov's rule, he and his men had kept rebel insurgencies under control, but the repressiveness of the Kadyrov regime gave little hope to young men in Chechnya who increasingly, out of desperation, "went into the forest." There had been a new rise of insurgency after 2008, and the Kadyrovites responded with escalating violence. Anyone suspected of even the slightest sympathy for the rebels was subjected to extreme reprisals. A virtual reign of terror began in Chechnya, which Estemirova bravely documented, while the Kremlin continued to give Kadyrov free rein.[42] And Washington turned a blind eye.

In July 2012, Human Rights Watch urged Russia's international partners to call Russian authorities to task: "European Union member states and the U.S. should speak with one voice, calling for justice for Estemirova and an end of the entrenched impunity for killings and attacks on human-rights defenders in Chechnya and the broader region."[43] But the official investigation of Estemirova's murder went nowhere, while the human-rights situation in Chechnya continued to deteriorate. After Estemirova's murder, Memorial closed its offices in Chechnya and *Novaia gazeta* stopped sending journalists there, deeming it too dangerous. But some months later, civic activists from several organizations created a Joint Mobile Group, which started sending rotating teams of lawyers to Chechnya to give legal assistance to victims of abuse by local law-enforcement and security agencies. Members of the Mobile Group were harassed and threatened repeatedly in attempts to get them to cease their work.

In March 2016, the Commissioner for Human Rights of the Council of Europe intervened on behalf of the relatives of Estemirova, who had filed a complaint in September 2011 in the European Court of Human Rights against the Russian government over its handling of her case. The commissioner observed that the murder of Estemirova should be seen against the backdrop of the broader pattern of violations of human rights in Chechnya and the Russian government's failure to react appropriately.[44] In July 2016, activists from Amnesty International and Memorial gathered outside the building of the Russian Investigative Committee in Moscow with placards marking the anniversary of Estemirova's death. They told reporters that they were demanding a resumption of the investigation, and they wanted Ramzan Kadyrov to be questioned. A female passerby came up to one of the demonstrators and asked: "I know nothing about her [Estemirova].

Did they kill her just like they killed Anna Politkovskaya?" Upon hearing the answer, the woman responded: "This is politics, and no one should get involved! We cannot obtain justice. But now I must look her up on the Internet."[45] This reaction is probably typical. Even if members of the general population recognize that critics of the regime are singled out far death, they often accept this as inevitable. But with every such crime, their eyes are slowly opening.

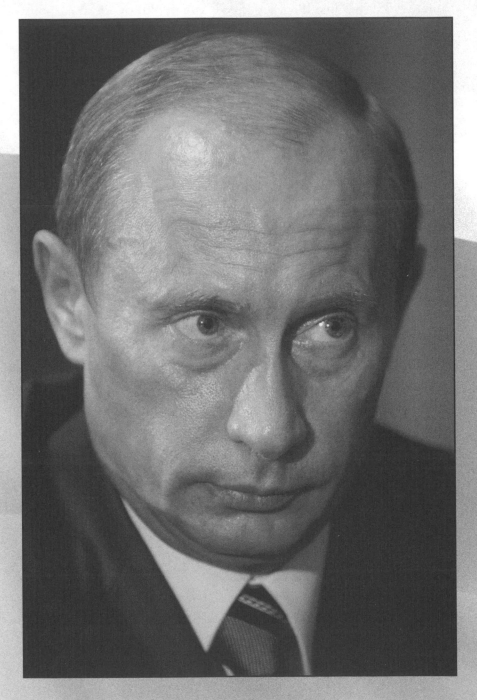

Vladimir Putin.

(Photograph courtesy of Dmitri Astakhov/AFP/Getty Images)

10

BORIS BEREZOVSKY: SUICIDE OR MURDER?

The relationship between Putin and Berezovsky is beginning to resemble that of Stalin and Trotsky. This affair risks ending up with Berezovsky getting a bullet in the head.

Russian political commentator Andrei Pointkovsky, November 2000

Vladimir Putin's third stint as Russia's president got off to a rocky start, with nationwide protests challenging the legitimacy of the March 2012 presidential vote. In fact, popular opposition to Putin had been mounting since the December 2011 parliamentary elections, which brought a victory for Putin's United Russia party. After election observers claimed that there had been widespread ballot-stuffing and other forms of fraud, tens of thousands took to the streets in Moscow and other cities. (Putin blamed the December events on Hillary Clinton, who as U.S. Secretary of State had voiced criticism of the elections.) Protests broke out anew at the time of Putin's May 2012 inauguration, and police arrested hundreds of oppositionists, including Boris Nemtsov and Aleksei Navalny. Despite a crackdown by

Boris Berezovsky.

(Photograph courtesy of BERTRAND LANGLOIS/AFP/Getty Images)

Russian authorities, close to fifty thousand Russians showed up for an anti-Putin demonstration in Moscow the next month.

These protests, understandably, unnerved the Kremlin. Putin and his allies were all too aware that when people took to the streets in the neighboring states of Georgia and Ukraine, their governments were overthrown. And similar unrest was occurring in the Middle East with the Arab Spring. In the meantime, Putin had not forgotten about his nemesis in London, Boris Berezovsky, who continued to speak out loudly about the criminal nature of the Putin regime.

Berezovsky and Putin

In July 2010, a Moscow-based associate of Boris Berezovsky named Rafael Filinov visited the oligarch in London and handed him a gift—a black T-shirt. On the front of it these words were emblazoned: "Polonium 210, London-Hamburg. To be continued." On the back of the shirt was "CSKA Moscow, radioactive death is knocking on your door," together with a red Communist star and a symbol of radiation danger. The T-shirt was from Litvinenko's accused killer Andrei Lugovoy, a known fan of the Russian soccer team CSKA, who had received tickets from Berezovsky to attend a football match between CSKA and London's Arsenal on the day of Litvinenko's fatal poisoning. According to Michael Cotlick, a former personal assistant to the oligarch, Berezovsky asked him to hand the "gift" over to the British police. Although at the time Berezovsky did not view Lugovoy's message as a huge threat, in retrospect it was a clear warning.[1]

The real danger, of course, was not from Lugovoy, but from Putin, who apparently could not get Berezovsky off his mind. In the years following Litvinenko's murder, the Kremlin persisted in blaming Berezovsky for many of the political murders that occurred under its watch. As Radio Free Europe/Radio Liberty analyst Robert Coalson observed: "Berezovsky was an easy target for demonization thanks to his questionable business dealings, his penchant for secrecy and closed-door skullduggery, his unprincipled melding of business and politics, and the tendency of his business rivals and personal enemies to meet violent ends. His long list of sins seemed somehow to cancel out in the public mind startlingly similar accusations against Putin and his inner circle."[2]

The relationship between Berezovsky, a former mathematician, and Putin went back a long way. The two first met in October 1991, when Berezovsky, then a successful entrepreneur as head of Logo-VAZ, a highly profitable car dealership, brought an Oklahoma oilman to meet the mayor of St. Petersburg, Anatolii Sobchak. Putin, who was working for Sobchak, helped Berezovsky develop LogoVAZ's business in the city and the two became friendly. Reportedly, they even skied together in Switzerland.[3]

As Berezovsky accumulated more and more wealth, including investments in Aeroflot, the aluminum industry, the television station ORT, and the oil giant Sibneft (his ownership of Sibneft shares later became a matter of dispute), he gained political influence as well. After working to promote Yeltsin's successful campaign for re-election in 1996, Berezovsky became a part of Yeltsin's inner circle, and in 1996 Yeltsin appointed Berezovsky deputy secretary of the Russian Security Council, where he served for a year, after which he became secretary of the Organization for Coordinating the Commonwealth of Independent States (CIS). In 1999 he was elected to the state Duma as a deputy from the Karachay-Cherkessia Republic. As noted earlier, Berezovsky, who viewed himself as a kingmaker, was instrumental in getting Putin appointed to head the FSB in July 1998. A year later, with presidential elections looming on the horizon and Yeltsin's approval ratings in the single digits, Berezovsky pushed to have Putin appointed prime minister. He then used ORT to promote Putin's candidacy for the Russian presidency in the March 2000 elections.

Putin won by a landslide. Boris Nemtsov later recalled in his 2007 autobiography that Berezovsky paid him a visit not long after the presidential elections and told him: "There is nothing more to be done. We did everything we could do. Putin has won. And everything is under control. What a bore. I don't know how to occupy myself." According to Nemtsov: "I almost fell off my chair: 'Borya, there is no need to be bored. Putin will change very quickly. He will never forgive you for the fact that you saw him as weak and supplicating and graciously supported him. . . .'" Nemtsov went on to observe: "After the monstrous murder in London of KGB officer Litvinenko, Berezovsky [now] expects killers from Lubyanka and is afraid of his own shadow. I think he curses a hundred times the day when he decided to support a man from the KGB."[4]

Confrontations with Putin

Soon after his election, Putin apparently decided that he did not want the oligarchs, including Berezovsky, to play the political role they had played in the past. A key to curbing their power was to gain control over the media. On May 11, 2000, just four days after Putin's inauguration, security police, wearing black masks and carrying guns, raided the Moscow offices of Media-Most, Russia's largest private media empire, which included the influential NTV; radio stations; a newspaper, *Segodnia*; and numerous other publications. The raid appeared to be in retaliation for the media group's criticism of Putin and his associates, as well as of the war in Chechnya, in the months leading up to the election. NTV had also aroused the ire of the Kremlin by conducting its own independent investigation of the 1999 apartment bombings. And Putin was thought to have resented being lampooned on NTV's popular satirical puppet show.[5]

Vladimir Gusinsky, president and founder of Media-Most (and a close friend of Berezovsky), expressed his dismay about the raid: "It is simply a pity that just a few days after the new president of Russia took office—the president on whom many people pin hope for a rebirth of the country—it looks like everything is going backwards, the same masks, the same special services, the same witch hunting."[6] Unfortunately for Gusinsky, the raid was only the beginning of a nightmare. On June 13, he was arrested on charges of theft of state funds in a privatization deal and incarcerated in the notorious Butyrka Prison. After an international outcry, Gusinsky was released and placed under house arrest. In July, he was confronted with a choice by Russian authorities: either sell all his media assets, or face further criminal charges. He agreed to sell his holdings and left Russia immediately for Spain, never again to return. (Subsequent requests by the Russian government for Gusinsky's extradition were denied by Spain.)

Meanwhile, Berezovsky was getting into his own trouble with the new Russian president. As part of a drive to tighten control over Russia's eighty-nine provinces and ethnic republics, Putin introduced legislation in May 2000, creating seven new supra-federal districts. The heads of the districts, appointed by Putin directly and drawn mainly from the police, military, and security services, were to have sweeping powers over Russia's regions. On May 31, Berezovsky, then a Duma deputy, published a lengthy open letter to Putin in *Kommersant* protesting the legislation. Berezovsky said that the project, if implemented, would represent a threat to Russia's territorial integrity and democracy. In his words:

> The directive that was issued and the package of federal laws are intended to strengthen vertical power. However, they are an attempt to solve the real problem by inadequate methods. The proposed changes are anti-democratic, in that if adopted, they violate the system of the balance of internal power necessary for the functioning of any democratic state and market economy, greatly expand the power of the executive over the legislature, and restrict the participation of citizens in a representative government.[7]

He ended by saying: "Vladimir Vladimirovich, your personal experience in St. Petersburg and Moscow, I am sure, has shown that democracy itself is imperfect, and each step toward the democratic development of society requires huge effort, because in contrast to dictates, you are obliged to convince (and not order) millions of citizens that you are right. Please do not hurry in deciding questions of historical proportions for our vast, seriously flawed country."[8]

This was a direct challenge to Putin and his plan to establish strong centralized political power, bypassing democratic procedures. More was to come. On August 12, 2000, the Russian nuclear submarine *Kursk* sank during naval exercises in the Barents Sea. It took the Russian navy more than sixteen hours to locate the vessel, and divers spent the next four days trying to open the escape hatch. It was not until the fifth day that Putin authorized the navy to accept help from the Norwegians and British, long after the 118 crew members had perished. Initially, Russian naval commanders tried to blame the disaster on a collision with a NATO submarine. But in fact two explosions on board had caused the submarine to sink.

As the rescue efforts were going on, Putin was shown on television enjoying himself at a holiday villa on the Black Sea. He did not respond publicly until ten days after the sinking, when he met with families of the deceased sailors near a naval base on the Barents Sea. He was not well received. By all accounts, the meeting was hostile and contentious, with Putin very much on the defensive. In short, the *Kursk* affair was a public relations disaster for the Russian president, and his approval ratings plummeted.[9]

Putin was quick to blame independent Russian media for the crisis. During his meeting with the families on August 22, he came close to losing his composure when talking about the reporting on the *Kursk*: "They are liars. The television has people who have been destroying the state for ten years. They have been thieving money and buying up absolutely everything. . . . Now they are trying to discredit the country so that the army gets even worse." In an interview on government television the next night, Putin lashed out again, with obvious reference to Gusinsky and Berezovsky: "They'd better sell their villas on the Mediterranean coast of France or Spain. Then they might have to explain why all this property is registered in false names under front law firms. Perhaps we would ask them where they got the money."[10]

Open Conflict Between Putin and Berezovsky

Berezovsky did not hold back. On September 2, ORT (where Berezovsky was a major shareholder) broadcast an hour-long special on the *Kursk*, hosted by Sergei Dorenko, a prominent journalist known for his in-depth reporting. (He was dubbed by Alex Goldfarb "the Peter Jennings of Russian television.") The program was an unflinching indictment of Putin and the Russian military establishment, and included footage of Putin's disastrous meeting with families of the victims. Dorenko ended by saying "The story of the *Kursk* is not over. The main conclusion is that the government does not respect any of us, and so it lies. And the important thing is that the government treats us like this because we all allow it to."[11] (Dorenko was later fired from ORT and arrested on bogus charges of hooliganism.)

In October 2000, Putin gave an interview to the French newspaper *Le Figaro*, in which he suggested that media oligarchs were blackmailing him. He addressed a warning specifically to Berezovsky and Gusinsky: "The state has a cudgel in its hands that you use to hit just once, but on the head. We haven't used this cudgel yet. We've just brandished it. . . . [But] the day we get really angry, we won't hesitate to use it."[12] Then on November 1, Russian prosecutors ordered Berezovsky, who was residing at his villa in Cap d'Antibes, France, to return to Moscow for questioning in a fraud case involving Aeroflot. Berezovsky refused to comply. Instead, he responded by publishing a long statement in *Kommersant*:

Today I took a difficult decision—not to return to Russia for questioning. I decided on this step due to the ever-increasing pressure put on me by the regime and President Putin personally. In essence, I was forced to choose—become a political prisoner or a political emigrant. The so-called Aeroflot case was thought up by [former prime minister Evgenii] Primakov and now revived by Putin, who is unhappy with my criticism of his politics. Putin, as a presidential candidate, was absolutely not bothered when the profits of Swiss companies working with Aeroflot were used to finance the "Unity" bloc and [his] presidential campaign. But Putin, as president, shamelessly has arranged to transfer me from a witness to a defendant in the Aeroflot case, and then threatens me with a blow on the head just because ORT told the truth about the tragedy of the submarine *Kursk*. . . . The president is trying to establish control over the major media outlets in order to establish a regime of personal power. And finally he has put the country at the mercy of the secret services and officials who stifle the freedom and initiative needed for Russia to progress. . . . I am certain that, if Putin continues his politics that are destructive for the country, his regime will not last until the end of his first constitutional term.[13]

According to Alex Goldfarb, who visited Berezovsky at his French villa several days after the oligarch received the Russian prosecutor's summons, Berezovsky had fully intended to fly back to Russia to appear in court and would have done so if it had not been for Goldfarb's stepping in: "Boris, in a bout of apparent madness, wanted to go. His plane was waiting at the airport. I literally pulled him out of his car."[14] As Goldfarb learned, the main reason Berezovsky had intended to go to the court hearings was because his loyal manager of

Aeroflot, Nikolai Glushkov, was a hostage of Russian authorities. Berezovsky thought that if he did not answer the summons, it would make things worse for Glushkov.

In fact, Glushkov was arrested three weeks later. The price of his release, it turned out, was Berezovsky relinquishing his 49 percent ownership of ORT. Russian oligarch Roman Abramovich, who owned a villa not far from Berezovsky, conveyed a message from Putin: if Berezovsky sold his ORT shares to Abramovich for $175 million (a ridiculously low price), Glushkov would be a free man. Berezovsky had no choice but to agree to the deal. But, as it turned out, Glushkov remained in prison anyway.[15]

Berezovsky Pursues His Agenda

Berezovsky moved to London and applied for asylum in October 2001. In the meantime, he had already launched an important initiative. His new Berezovsky Foundation (later called the International Foundation for Civil Liberties, or IFCL) was formed with the intention of creating a grassroots network of opposition to the Kremlin. The first grant, three million dollars, was given to Elena Bonner, the widow of the famous Soviet dissident and physicist Andrei Sakharov, as an endowment for the Sakharov Museum and Civic Center in Moscow. As Goldfarb, who was put in charge of the foundation, put it: "The grant to the Sakharov Center was meant to underscore the continuity of Soviet oppression under Putin and the permanence of dissidents' resistance."[16]

According to Goldfarb: "By May 2001, the IFCL had awarded 160 more grants to NGOs across Russia, which collectively represented, Boris hoped, 'crystallization centers,' for protest movements: antiwar groups like Soldiers' Mothers, supporters of prisoners' rights, the Greens, defenders of ethnic minorities, and local human-rights watchdogs."[17] And then of course there was the formation of a new political party, Liberal Russia, by Berezovsky and Sergei Iushen-

kov, announced in May 2001. As mentioned earlier, the party's plat-
form was anti-Putin and included as its central purpose revealing
the truth about the 1999 apartment bombings.

Needless to say, Berezovsky's initiatives did not sit well with
the Kremlin. In September 2001, the Procurator-General of Russia
indicted Berezovsky *in absentia* on three counts: complicity in
fraud, failure to return currency proceeds from abroad, and money
laundering. He was put on the Russian federal wanted list. In August 2002, Russian authorities opened a criminal investigation of
Berezovsky, along with his two former partners, Badri Patarkatsishvili and Iulii Dubov, for the theft of 2,323 cars when the three
owned the car dealership LogoVAZ in 1994 and 1995. The funds
they received from the sale of these cars were allegedly used for the
purchase of homes in the Moscow region, totaling more than seven
million rubles in value, as well as shares in media outlets.[18]

And so it went. In October 2002, Berezovsky was charged by
Russian authorities with large-scale embezzlement and put on the international wanted list, along with Dubov, who was also in London,
and Patarkatsishvili, who was residing in Georgia. The next month,
Russian prosecutors sent British authorities a formal request for the
extradition of Berezovsky and Dubov. After subsequent hearings
on the matter, Berezovsky and Dubov were granted political asylum
in Great Britain in September 2003, and Russian requests for their
extradition were officially refused.[19]

As noted, Berezovsky was an enthusiastic supporter and financier of Litvinenko's ventures, including his book *Blowing Up
Russia,* which blamed Putin and the FSB for the 1999 bombings in
Russia. "I'd give a lot to see Volodya's [Putin's] face when he reads it,"
the oligarch told Goldfarb.[20] One wonders, however, if Berezovsky
did not feel some culpability for these attacks, given his key role in
catapulting Putin to the Russian presidency. As a member of the "family"
that surrounded Yeltsin and therefore privy to many of the Kremlin's

darkest secrets, did he not suspect right away that Putin and the FSB were behind the attacks, while independent Russian journalists were voicing these suspicions left and right?

Whatever his past, after he left Russia, Berezovsky did everything in his power to make up for his sins. In January 2006, he told a correspondent for AFP that he was planning a coup against Putin: "President Putin violates the constitution and today any violent action against him would be justified. This concerns a forcible seizure of power, and that is what I am working on. The last year and a half we have been preparing to take power in Russia by force."[21] Berezovsky said that the operation would be financed by him personally, with funds that in the past five years had grown into billions of dollars. He voiced similar views on *Ekho Moskvy* Radio the same day, prompting a warning from British Foreign Minister Jack Straw that he could lose his refugee status if he continued to make such incendiary statements.[22]

Berezovsky's support for the Orange Revolution in Ukraine was doubtless another issue that rankled the Kremlin. Reportedly he transferred fifteen million dollars to the campaign of Viktor Yushchenko, who won a victory over Kremlin-backed Ukrainian President Leonid Kravchuk in December 2004. Berezovsky apparently hoped that a victory for the Orange Revolution would trigger a similar revolution in Russia and bring the Putin regime down. Of course, in the end the Orange Revolution failed to meet expectations. Berezovsky did not live to witness the second people's revolution in Ukraine, in December 2013 and January 2014, which led to the ouster of Viktor Yanukovich, a successor to Yushchenko.

In June 2007, Berezovsky was told by Scotland Yard that they had arrested a Russian man on charges of conspiracy to commit murder and that he was the intended victim. British authorities sent the man back to Russia. At a press conference, Berezovsky stated: "I think the same people behind this plot were behind the plot against Alexander Litvinenko. Not only people in general but Putin personally."[23] The Kremlin did not let up on Berezovsky. By the end of January 2010, Russian authorities had initiated a total of twelve criminal cases against Berezovsky—for fraud, embezzlement, money-laundering, and a host of other charges.[24]

The Death of Patarkatsishvili

Everyone knew him as Badri, and he was by all accounts a flamboyant character. Born and raised in Georgia, Badri started accumulating his substantial wealth when he hooked up with Berezovsky and LogoVAZ in the mid-nineties, and later became a senior executive at ORT. Like Berezovsky, Badri was under constant fire from Russian prosecutors for various alleged financial crimes, and he finally left Russia to settle back in Georgia in 2001. He balanced his time between Georgia, where his major business interests were, and Britain, where he maintained a lavish home in the London suburbs. As mentioned earlier, he relied on the services of Litvinenko's accused killer, Lugovoy, for security when in Georgia. Badri and Berezovsky were the closest of friends, in addition to their business partnerships, so when Badri died suddenly on February 12, 2008 at his home outside London, it must have been a terrible blow for Berezovsky.

Badri was only fifty-three years old and had not complained of health problems. His death was from a reported heart attack, but of course there was the usual speculation. He was, after all, on Putin's black list, and only a week earlier a conversation Badri had had with a Georgian official about Putin had been leaked to the Russian press.[25] In this conversation, Badri recalled how down and out Putin had been when his mentor Sobchak lost the mayoral election in St. Petersburg in 1996. He said that Putin wore the "same dirty green suit every day." Putin had provided Badri with a *krysha* for his business activities in St. Petersburg and urgently needed Badri's help in return to get him a sinecure in Moscow. According to Badri, "Putin called me twice a day and pleaded, saying I don't want to stay here."

Badri said that he managed to get Putin a job as the assistant to Pavel Borodin, the Kremlin's property manager, and later, according to Badri, Putin became prime minister, and Yeltsin's designated successor, partly because of his efforts, along with those of Berezovsky. Badri then talked in the conversation about how badly Putin had handled the *Kursk* submarine affair, which was doubtless something Putin did not want to be reminded of. This leaked transcript, shortly before the March 2008 presidential elections, with Putin's designated candidate, Dmitri Medvedev, set to replace him, must have infuriated Putin. Although there was no evidence of foul play in Badri's death, Putin was probably gratified to have him out of the picture.

Berezovsky versus Abramovich

In October 2011, Roman Abramovich, forty-six years old and the third-wealthiest man in the United Kingdom, with a fortune estimated at over twelve billion dollars and the world's largest yacht, entered a London courtroom. He was the defendant in a civil suit filed by Berezovsky. As the owner of the Chelsea football club since 2003, Abramovich was spending most of his time in Britain, although his cordial relations with Putin meant that, unlike Berezovsky, he was always welcome in Moscow.

Berezovsky, twenty years Abramovich's senior, had not fared as well financially. The vast sums he had spent in support of Russian opposition groups, and the millions of dollars he had been ordered to pay his ex-wife Galina Besharova in a divorce settlement, had taken a heavy toll on his finances. As Masha Gessen, who attended the court proceedings, observed: "This year Berezovsky fell off the *Sunday Times* list of the thousand richest people in Britain. Unless he receives an infusion of capital, he will not be able to afford his lifestyle much longer and will be a very poor excuse for an oligarch."[26]

Berezovsky and Abramovich had met for the first time in late

1994, on a sailboat in the Caribbean. Abramovich had a plan for making large amounts of money by buying two Siberian oil businesses that were part of the state-owned oil conglomerate Rosneft and creating a new private oil company. He wanted Berezovsky to be his partner in the venture, and Berezovsky agreed. The two men set about getting a line of credit that would enable them to bid at an auction for shares of government oil companies—as part of Yeltsin's controversial "loans-for-shares" scheme, which many would later say robbed ordinary Russians of what was rightfully theirs (the auctions were rigged) and created a new class of super-rich oligarchs.[27]

As part of the plan to create what would be called Sibneft, Berezovsky went to Yeltsin and persuaded him to support the Sibneft venture in exchange for Berezovsky using funds from the venture to take over the main state television channel and promote Yeltsin's reelection in 1996. Berezovsky used his close personal relationship with Yeltsin's daughter Tatiana and her future husband Valentin Yumashev in order to help persuade Yeltsin to agree to his plan. He also enlisted Yeltsin's chief bodyguard, Aleksandr Korzhakov, to lobby on his behalf.

In fact, it was never clear who ended up owning Sibneft. At the 2011 London trial, Berezovsky claimed that he and Badri Patarkatsishvili each gained 25 percent of Sibneft shares and Abramovich 50 percent. But it was a gentleman's agreement with Abramovich, because Berezovsky was heavily involved in politics and did not want it to be known that he was a shareholder. Abramovich disagreed with Berezovsky's version, saying that he had sole ownership of Sibneft and that the substantial payments he subsequently made to Berezovsky and Patarkatsishvili were payback for their using their influence to help him acquire Sibneft. He said that he made the final payment of $1.3 billion to them in 2001.

It was Berezovsky's word against that of Abramovich, because there was no documentation of the financial deal they had made in

1995. And the judge, on August 31, 2012, dismissed Berezovsky's case. She had this to say about Berezovsky: "On my analysis of the entirety of the evidence, I found Mr. Berezovsky an unimpressive and inherently unreliable witness who regarded truth as a transitory, flexible concept, which could be molded to suit his current purpose."[28]

Meanwhile, Berezovsky had been doing some soul-searching. In February 2012, well before his legal case against Abramovich collapsed, Berezovsky wrote a "letter of repentance" to be posted on his blog at *Ekho Moskvy*. But the editors, accused of "extremism" by deputies of the pro-Kremlin United Russia Party for posting Berezovsky's previous inflammatory statements, refused his submission. Berezovsky then put his letter on his Facebook page. Here is part of what he had to say:

> I have led a long and wonderful life, and on the way I have inevitably made a lot of mistakes. Some of my wrongful actions I did intentionally, but even more of them when I did not know what I was doing. . . . I repent and ask forgiveness for greed. I longed for riches, with no hesitation. . . . I was not alone in doing this, but that does not excuse me. I repent and ask forgiveness for bringing Vladimir Putin to power. For the fact that I was obliged, but unable, to see in him a future greedy tyrant and usurper, a man who trampled on freedom and stopped the development of Russia. Many of us did not recognize it then, but that does not excuse me. I understand that repentance is not only a word, but also a deed. And that will follow.[29]

The last two sentences were puzzling. What deed was to follow? A single-handed effort to bring down Putin? The act of suicide? This letter was written months before the judge handed down the verdict in his suit against Abramovich, which Berezovsky expected to win. So he still had something to live for. Nonetheless, his reference to his "long and wonderful life" had a note of finality to it. At the very least, he was becoming contemplative, although he was still obsessed with Putin.

Death of an Oligarch

At approximately 3:20 P.M. on Saturday, March 23, 2013, Berezovsky was found dead by his bodyguard of six years, Avi Navama, hanging from a shower rail in the bathroom of his mansion outside London. (The home actually belonged to his ex-wife.) His black cashmere scarf was tied around his neck. Navama had last seen Berezovsky the night before, at 9:05 P.M. The initial determination of investigators was that the death was a suicide. There were no signs of trauma suggesting force had been used. No intruders were seen on the CTV cameras that surrounded the home.

Although Berezovsky did not leave a note, there was good reason to assume that he had taken his own life. He had, by several accounts, been depressed. In fact, according to his son Artem, Berezovsky had been taking anti-depressants but had stopped shortly before he died because they were affecting his liver. Both Artem and Navama said that Berezovsky had talked frequently of suicide ever since he lost his suit against Abramovich. He asked Navama: "Should I jump, or should I cut my vein?"[30]

The day before he died, Berezovsky had an interview with the editor of *Forbes* Russia, Il'ia Zheguliev, at the Four Seasons Hotel in London. As Berezovsky had stipulated, the interview was just to be a conversation with nothing recorded. The oligarch had not given any interviews since the ruling on his court case against Abramovich had been announced the previous August. When Zheguliev asked him if he missed Russia, Berezovsky responded: "There is nothing that I want more than to return to Russia. . . . The main thing that I underestimated was how dear to me Russia is, that I cannot be an emigrant. . . . This does not mean that I have lost myself. I have been through a lot more times when I have had to re-evaluate things and [lived through] disappointments. . . . I have lost the meaning of life." Berezovsky ended by saying that he did not want to engage in politics any more, adding that "I am sixty-seven years old and I do not know what to do next."[31]

Berezovsky's death seemed a straightforward suicide until new evidence was introduced at an inquest a year later. Professor Bern Brinkmann, a German forensic scientist retained by the Berezovsky family, concluded in no uncertain terms that the marks on Berezovsky's neck were not consistent with strangling through suspension: "The strangulation mark is completely different from the strangulation mark in hanging."[32] Also, the paramedic who arrived on the scene revealed that his radiation alarm went off as he entered the property, and he was puzzled by the fact that Berezovsky's face was purple, when usually faces of people who hang themselves are "quite pale." There was also a mystery fingerprint found in the bathroom that police were unable to identify.[33] In light of these developments, the coroner left open the question of whether the death was a suicide or murder. "I can either return a verdict that Boris Berezovsky has committed suicide, or that he was killed. Any of these versions should definitely be supported with evidence."[34]

On March 25, 2013, two days after Berezovsky's death, the Moscow weekly the *New Times* (*Novoe vremia*) published an interview with Berezovsky's longtime girlfriend, Katerina Sabirova, in which she discussed the couple's imminent plans to meet in Israel. Sabirova, who was living in Moscow, could not get a visa to come to the UK. "He was definitely planning to come to Israel, I know that for sure," she said. They had last spoken late on the previous Friday evening, to discuss the logistics of their meeting at Tel Aviv airport, after which they had planned a vacation on the Dead Sea. According to Sabirova: "There was nothing extraordinary in the conversation, except that his voice sounded better than usual. His mental state was always reflected in his voice. And I had the impression that he was better." Sabirova said that Berezovsky was planning on seeing his daughter Nastia on the Saturday, when he was found dead, and Avi, his bodyguard, was supposed to pick her up in London. She insisted that it was not possible that Berezovsky had taken his own life.[35]

Sabirova confirmed what President Putin's press officer, Dmitrii Peskov, later claimed—that Berezovsky had written a letter to Putin not long before his death, asking to be allowed to return to Russia: "I saw the written text. He read it to me. He apologized [to Putin] and asked to be allowed to return. . . . He asked me what I thought of the letter. I said that if they published the letter, he would look bad. And it would not help him. He said he didn't care, that they had already hung all these sins on him and it was his only chance."[36]

Marina and Anatoly Litvinenko stayed close to Berezovsky after Sasha's death. He treated them like family and continued to pay for Anatoly's schooling. They told me that they have no doubt that Berezovsky was murdered. While acknowledging that Berezovsky was depressed before he died, after losing the lawsuit against Abramovich, Anatoly, who spent a lot of time with him, observed: "It just was not his style [to kill himself]. He was not the type of man who could do such a thing to himself. . . . Besides, hanging himself would have been difficult because he did not really have a neck." Marina added that Berezovsky had a lot to live for, especially his six children and his elderly mother, to whom he was devoted, along with his lady friend, Sabirova.[37]

Akmed Zakaev concurred in an interview with the *Sunday Telegraph* soon after the murder: "I can assure you that Boris was not the kind of person who would harm himself. His friends and family can confirm that as well. He loved life and was not planning on leaving it any time soon."[38] It is true that Berezovsky was deeply in debt at the time of his death. He reportedly had assets of around £34 million and owed creditors £309 million.[39] But his close friend Iulii Dubov did not think that would have caused Berezovsky to take his own life: "He had financial problems his entire life. . . . He never had enough to do what he wanted. But he was not one of these people who let material concerns unsettle him."[40]

Berezovsky's death remains a mystery. But Alex Goldfarb, Berezovsky's close associate for years, put the issue into perspective when I spoke with him recently. Goldfarb himself thinks that Berezovsky probably did kill himself, because he was very depressed. Yet in the end, as he put it to me: "It does not matter whether Boris killed himself or not. In the final court, one way or another, Putin was responsible for Boris's death. It was Putin who drove him to this condition of hopelessness."[41]

Postscript: Alexander Perepilichnyi

Not long before Berezovsky's death, another London-based Russian tycoon died. In November 2012, Alexander Perepilichnyi, married and the father of two young children, dropped dead at age forty-four while jogging at his lavish estate in Surrey. He had earlier in the day flown into London after a three-day trip to Paris. The cause of his death was reported to be a heart attack, and police insisted that there was no foul play involved. But further events suggested otherwise.

It was learned, during prolonged on-and-off inquest proceedings, that Perepilichnyi took out a $5 million life-insurance policy not long before he died. (A requirement for the policy was a medical exam, and Perepilichnyi received a clean bill of health.) The insurance company ordered forensic tests that revealed the presence in his stomach of a rare and deadly fern called *Gelsemium elegans,* known to have been used in previous assassinations. It also emerged that the oligarch had received more than one anonymous death threat.

Perepilichnyi was a whistleblower, or what Russians call a "super-informer," on Russian money laundering. Before he fled to

Britain in 2010, Perepilichnyi had managed money for certain officials from the Russian MVD and the tax police, who had ties to a mafia gang run by one Dmitrii Kliuev. Once in exile, Perepilichnyi claimed that members of the Russian government, including a senior tax official named Olga Stepanova, had siphoned off $230 million in tax money paid to the Russian government by the American William Browder's investment company, Hermitage Capital. The money ended up in a Credit Suisse account in Switzerland. (Sergei Magnitsky, the earlier-mentioned Russian lawyer for Hermitage who died in prison in 2009, first drew attention to this tax fraud.) As a result of Perepilichnyi's revelations, Stepanova was put on the so-called Magnitsky list and forbidden entry into the United States.[42]

A prime suspect in what now appears to have been the poisoning of Perepilichnyi is Russian lawyer named Andrei Pavlov, who was reportedly acting as a go-between between the victim and Olga Stepanova and her business allies. Pavlov was in Britain on the day Perepilichnyi died, and he flew out of Heathrow the next day. Speaking at a pre-inquest hearing in May 2016, a lawyer for the company that took out life insurance for the oligarch said: "Pavlov was in the country at the time of Mr. Perepilichnyi's death. He was a prominent member of the Kliuev organized crime group. He is certainly in any view a candidate for the killing of Mr. Perepilichnyi."[43] (Pavlov later denied that he had been in Britain when Perepilichnyi died. He claimed that he flew in and out of Heathrow the day afterwards.)[44]

As *The Guardian* observed about the case: "Whether he was a whistleblower who had gone to the police after his conscience got the better of him, or a corrupt financier who had ratted on his associates after he fell into financial ruin, there is no doubt that Perepilichnyi had powerful enemies."[45] In September 2016, British authorities postponed the ongoing inquest into Perepilichnyi's death on the grounds that sensitive documents in the case would pose a threat to Britain's national security if they were revealed publicly. In response,

William Browder had this to say: "The coroner is not able to do his job. This is where it gets confusing. The police are saying there is nothing suspicious about the death. The government is saying it is a matter of national security. Those two things are mutually inconsistent. I would like to see a full ventilation of the facts. I believe that will lead to the conclusion that Alexander Perepilichnyi was murdered. That means people are getting away with murder in the UK."[46]

The issue of national security and the so-called Public Interest Immunity of certain documents was finally resolved in May 2017. Unlike the Litvinenko case, where a public inquiry allowed the judge to consider secret intelligence material in closed sessions, the Perepilichnyi case will proceed as an inquest, set to begin on June 5, without the coroner using secret documents to reach his findings. The coroner has stated that the absence of these documents will not hinder him in ascertaining how Perepilichnyi died. Whatever the outcome of the inquest, it could have serious implications for Britain's relations with Russia.[47]

Tamerlan Tsarnaev. *(Photograph courtesy of Unknown)*

11

THE BOSTON MARATHON BOMBINGS: RUSSIA'S FOOTPRINT

"The Russians have been very cooperative with us since the Boston bombing. . . . I've spoken to President Putin directly. He's committed to working with me to make sure that those who report to us are cooperating fully in not only this investigation, but how do we work on counterterrorism issues generally."
—**President Obama at a White House press conference, April 30, 2013**

"I will die young."
—**Dzhokhar Tsarnaev on Twitter, April 20, 2012**

Tamerlan Tsarnaev

In the four years that followed the attempted reset by the Obama administration in 2009, relations between Washington and Moscow did not improve. As noted, Putin's sudden announcement in September 2011 that he would run again for the Russian presidency made it clear to the West that Medvedev, the supposed liberal in the government, had just been holding a place for Putin and was never a leader in his own right. Russia was losing its status as a powerful player on the global scene and also was beset with terrorist attacks by insurgents from the North Caucasus. In November 2009, an explosion on the train between St. Petersburg and Moscow, the Nevsky Express, killed twenty-eight people and injured many others. In January 2011, a suicide bomber at Moscow's Domodedovo Airport left thirty-eight dead and many others injured. There were many other incidents of terrorism in the North Caucasus.

Putin had secured the Winter Olympic games for Russia, to be held in Sochi in February 2014, but the terrorism issue was making Olympic officials nervous about the safety of the games. The Kremlin needed to distract Western attention from Russia's insurgency and show that other nations faced the same problem. Enter the Tsarnaev brothers, who carried out bombings at the Boston Marathon, resulting in three dead and 260 wounded on April 13, 2013.

On November 6, 2011, Tamerlan Tsarnaev, the older of the two brothers who would carry out the bombings in Boston, purchased a one-way ticket on Aeroflot from New York's Kennedy Airport to Moscow. Although the FBI had been warned earlier in the year by the Russian FSB that Tamerlan was a security risk because of his politically extreme views, U.S. agents concluded, after interviews with him and his family, that the FSB message did not warrant anything more than putting Tamerlan's name on a watch list of the Customs and Border Protection Service (CBP) in the event of his international travel. But the FSB had apparently given two incorrect birth dates for Tsarnaev, and the transliteration from Cyrillic of his last name that appeared on the watch list was Tsarnayev, with an extra *y*. On the day of his travel, January 12, 2012, the CBP was apparently overtaxed with possibly suspicious travelers, so Tamerlan went through customs and immigration unimpeded. He arrived at Moscow's Sheremetevo Airport the next day and was back six months later, on July 17, 2012.[1]

According to a report by the U.S. House Homeland Security Committee issued in April 2015: "Customs and Border Protection [CBP] failed to place Tamerlan Tsarnaev into secondary screening upon exiting and re-entering the United States. Additionally, it is unclear as to whether a CBP JTTF [Joint Terrorism Task Force] officer notified the FBI Agent who had conducted the Tamerlan Tsarnaev assessment regarding his travel."[2] In other words, U.S. security authorities missed the boat.

Now, more than four years after the bombings, Tamerlan Tsarnaev's sojourn in Russia has remained a mystery. But a close look at the facts surrounding his 2012 trip, as well as his contacts in Boston, point strongly to Russian involvement in the terrible tragedy that occurred in Boston. I have already demonstrated, with the 1999 bombings and other attacks in Russia, how the Kremlin, through its extensive infiltration into the underground insurgent movements in the North Caucasus, has used terrorism to further its own political goals. I believe the Boston Marathon case is another example of this strategy, this time exported to the United States.

The Tsarnaev Family

By all accounts, the Tsarnaevs, originally from Russia's North Caucasus region, were a highly dysfunctional family whose efforts to forge a successful life in the Boston area failed miserably. As author Masha Gessen has pointed out, history was not in their favor. The volatile and politically uncertain nature of the Soviet Union, and then Russia, resulted in constant moves for the parents, Anzor and Zubeidat—back and forth from Central Asia to the North Caucasus, then finally to the United States. Neither Anzor nor Zubeidat was able to adjust to the transitions. Unfortunately, their four children, Tamerlan, Dzhokhar, and two sisters, were the victims of what eventually became almost pathological behavior, particularly on the part of Zubeidat. She and her husband quarreled constantly, while

Tamerlan, the adored first child, showed growing signs of extreme narcissism, violence, and impulsivity.[3]

I focus here on Tamerlan because he, of the two brothers who committed this terrible crime, was without doubt the one in charge. As we know, Tamerlan was killed when his brother ran over him with a car during a confrontation with police four days after the bombings, while Dzhokhar was found guilty of multiple murders at a trial in Boston which began in March 2015. He was sentenced to death, a sentence that is being appealed. In Chechen culture, the older brother always has the dominant role, and Dzhokhar was seven years younger. Dzhokhar worshipped his brother and did everything he said, despite the fact that he, Dzhokhar, seemed to have adjusted much better to life in Boston than Tamerlan had. More importantly, it was Tamerlan, not Dzhokhar, who became the "object of interest" on the part of the Russian security services, well before the FBI allegedly knew who was.

Zubeidat Tsarnaeva was a Muslim, a member of the Avar ethnic group, from Makhachkala, the capital of Dagestan, which borders Chechnya in the North Caucasus. Her husband Anzor was a Chechen who was born and grew up in Kyrgyzstan in Central Asia, where hundreds of thousands of Chechens were deported by Stalin in 1944. After marriage in Siberia, the couple moved to Kyrgyzstan and then in the early 1990s to Chechnya, but the war there forced them to move back to Kyrgyzstan. In the late 1990s, they relocated to Makhachkala with Tamerlan, born in 1986, Dzhokhar, born in 1993, and two daughters. But the region was then so rife with violence that had spilled over from Chechnya that the Tsarnaevs decided to seek a new life in the United States. The Tsarnaevs gained asylum as Chechen refugees, arriving in the United States just a few months after the September 11, 2001 terrorist attacks. This was, as Gessen notes, a new era, "when the United States stopped viewing Chechen rebels as freedom fighters and started seeing them through Russian optics, as likely Islamic terrorists."[4]

Tamerlan stayed with relatives in Kyrgyzstan after his family moved to Boston and did not join them there until 2003, when he was sixteen. Their home was a small third-floor apartment—crowded, noisy, and chaotic. Tamerlan entered the local school, Cambridge Rindge and Latin, as a sophomore and began training as a boxer. In 2009, Tamerlan reached the national boxing competition in Salt Lake City, but then he was denied the possibility to compete at that level because he was not yet an American citizen, and his boxing career came to an abrupt halt.

Tamerlan, who Gessen says started dressing like an "Italian gigolo," dropped out of community college, married a young American woman named Katherine Russell, and quickly fathered a baby with her. As Gessen puts it: "By 2011 Tamerlan was neither a boxing champion nor a music star nor even a college student, but a twenty-four-year-old father living with his parents, his siblings, and his own family in a three-bedroom apartment."[5] He made a bit of money delivering pizzas and selling pot. In the words of Scott Helman and Jenna Russell, the authors of *Long Mile Home*, "Tamerlan had been unsuccessful at virtually every one of his endeavors in America."[6] In other words, he was a perfect target for recruiters of would-be terrorists.

Tamerlan's Journey Into Radicalism

Meanwhile, tensions were rising within the Tsarnaev household, partly because the family was constantly broke and on public assistance, and also because Anzor (who made a small living repairing cars) had developed serious health problems. In 2011, the parents started divorce proceedings and Anzor began to make plans to move back to Dagestan. Tamerlan, with no steady job and his wife working as a home healthcare worker, found himself alone caring for their baby and started cruising the Internet. According to *Long Mile Home*, Tamerlan pasted a link on his Facebook page to an article from an online Chechen news agency which claimed that the U.S. government was engaged in an all-out war against Muslims and urged them to take up arms against America.[7]

In addition to the internet, it is possible that Tamerlan became attracted to militant Islam because of contacts he made in the Boston area. The Chechen, or North Caucasian, diaspora in the area was small and hardly a hotbed of radicalism. Although highly religious Chechens, devoted to Islam, might well have felt sympathy with the rebels back home who were fighting the Russians, this did not ordinarily translate into the desire for a global jihad against the West. But there may have been exceptions.

Tamerlan had a Chechen acquaintance, Viskhan Vakhabov, who emigrated to the United States in 2004 and could have influenced him in some way. Tamerlan called Vakhabov on his cell phone just after he had shot and killed an MIT patrol officer in the hours following the bombings. Vakhabov was interviewed by the FBI and reportedly gave inconsistent statements. He was called as a witness at the trial of Dzhokhar but refused to appear, citing his fifth-amendment right against self-incrimination.[8] We know nothing more about him.

Another émigré friend of Tamerlan was Magomed Dolakov, a Russian who first entered the United States in June 2012 and moved to Cambridge, Massachusetts the next month. He met Tamerlan at a local mosque in August 2012 and continued his acquaintance with him. Dolakov was known to the Russian FSB: he had been detained by its officers on more than one occasion in Russia. When interviewed by the FBI after the bombings, Dolakov said that Tamerlan had expressed radical views and told him that he was planning on joining the mujahidin. Although Dolakov saw Tamerlan just three days before the bombings, at which time he had gone to his house and then to the gym with him, he did not appear at Dzhokar's trial because authorities could not locate him.[9] Dolakov's interview with the FBI shortly after the bombings was cited at the trial but was not made publicly available, despite the fact that he would clearly have been a key witness at the proceedings.

It is important to note that the Russian Foreign Intelligence Service, the SVR, has "illegals" posing as Americans, green-card holders, or tourists throughout the United States. Their job is not only to collect intelligence but to infiltrate and indoctrinate vulnerable people.[10] Thus the SVR might have used either Vakhabov or Dolakov to rein force in Tamerlan any tendencies he had toward radicalism. This could also have been the role of the mysterious "Misha," an Armenian man whose name came up often as a friend of Tamerlan, and who allegedly had considerable influence on him. According to one expert on Russian Islamists: "Misha may very well have recruited Tamerlan as the circumstances were favorable. Tamerlan came from a nation that is entirely Muslim. The only thing that was required from the recruiter was to convince Tamerlan of the injustice that some people inflict on Islam worldwide."[11]

Significantly, Tamerlan's uncle, Ruslan Tsarni, the brother of Anzor, who lives outside Washington, D.C., also mentioned "Misha," an Armenian who Ruslan claimed had radicalized Tamerlan beginning in 2009. Tsarni told CNN on April 25, 2013 that he was so concerned about Tamerlan being brainwashed that he even asked a friend from Cambridge to look into the problem.[12] And Tamerlan's parents also acknowledged after the bombings that Misha, a Russian speaker, was a frequent visitor to their house and had a strong religious influence on Tamerlan and their family. According to Tamerlan's mother, Zubeidat: "I wasn't praying until he prayed in our house, so I just got really ashamed that I am not praying, being a Muslim. . . . Misha, who converted [to Islam], was praying."[13]

Zubeidat's sister Shakhruzat Suleimanova testified at Dzhokar's trial about how drastically changed Zubeidat's appearance seemed the last time she visited Dagestan not long before the bombings. Suddenly Zubeidat went from colorful clothes that flattered her figure to a black burqa and hijab: "She came and she was all covered up. We were all shocked. We were all in pain. We were very scared. We never had people like that in our family."[14] This apparently was a result of Misha's influence, too.

Elmirza Khozhugov, the former husband of Tamerlan's sister Ailina Tsarnaeva, testified for the defense at the trial of Dzhokhar on live video from Almaty, the capital of Kazakhstan. He claimed that Tamerlan had been heavily swayed toward radical Islam by a conservative Muslim named Misha, who often visited the Tsarnaev apartment in Cambridge and discussed Islam with Tamerlan: "I wouldn't call it formally a lesson, but he was teaching him and suggesting books to read . . . expressing his own views about that faith to Tamerlan."[15] Khozhugov added that Tamerlan stopped boxing, taking acting classes, and even listening to music after Misha convinced him that those activities were not in keeping with Islam.

Misha, it turns out, was Mikhail Allakhverdov, who was tracked down a few weeks after the bombings by the American journalist Christian Caryl.[16] Misha was living in Rhode Island with his elderly parents after moving from Boston a couple of years earlier. Misha did not want to discuss Tamerlan with Caryl, except to say that "I wasn't his teacher. If I had been his teacher, I would have made sure he never did anything like this." He also asserted that the FBI had interviewed him and they were about to close his case. But questions remain. Why had Misha converted to Islam and started to attend mosque daily at the time he met Tamerlan, though he came from a Christian family that had no connection to Islam? Significantly, Caryl noted that when he came to interview Misha, he was greeted not only by Misha's family, but also by his girlfriend, who was wearing shorts and shook his hand, something unheard of among devout Muslims, as Misha professed to be to the Tsarnaevs. And why did Misha spend so much time with Tamerlan, who was twelve years his junior, and his family? Inexplicably, Misha did not appear as a witness at Dzhokar's 2015 trial.

The FSB on Tamerlan's Trail

Tamerlan was on the radar of the Russian security services as far back as 2010. (Unconfirmed reports say that Tamerlan was mentioned to the FSB by a radical Islamist, William Plotnikov, a Russian-born Canadian, who had moved to Dagestan and was interviewed by the FSB in 2010. Supposedly Plotnikov, a boxer, had earlier been in contact with Tamerlan over the Internet.)[17] On March 4, 2011, the FSB sent the FBI a message, mentioned above, requesting information on Tamerlan. Here is what the FBI press office stated on April 19, 2013, six days after the bombings: "In early 2011, a foreign government [i.e., Russia] asked the FBI for information about Tamerlan Tsarnaev. The request stated that it was based on information that he was a follower of radical Islam and a strong believer, and that he had changed drastically since 2010 as he prepared to leave the United States for travel to the country's region to join unspecified underground groups."[18]

In fact, the message from the FSB, still classified as secret, said much more than that. In May 2013, members of the House Committee on Homeland Security, including its chairman Mike McCaul and Boston congressman William Keating, went to Moscow to seek more information about Tamerlan and his six-month trip to Russia in 2012. Congressman Keating, who I later interviewed by telephone, told me that the delegation met with FSB officials and asked to see the March 2011 memorandum.[19] These officials refused to give the lawmakers a copy but did agree to read it out loud. Here is what the House Committee later reported:

> In the letter, the Russian government expressed concern that he [Tamerlan] had become radicalized and that he might return to Russia and join extremist groups there. While lacking compelling derogatory information on exactly why he posed a threat, the letter contained detailed biographical

information on Tamerlan Tsarnaev and his mother, including physical addresses, marital status, [and] online social
media profiles, and discussed his history as a boxer. The letter also noted that he had previously hoped to travel to the
Palestinian territories to wage jihad, but decided not to go
because he did not speak Arabic. The letter requested that
the FBI notify the Russian government if Tamerlan Tsarnaev attempted to travel to Russia.[20]

One question that immediately arises is why and how the FSB had
gathered so much information on Tamerlan and his family, given that
they had lived outside Russia for several years. Clearly, the FSB had
earmarked Tamerlan for surveillance, but for what purpose? Did the
Russian security services send this memorandum as a sort of "fishing
expedition" to find out what the FBI knew about him? They gave the
wrong birth date for Tamerlan: Why? Was it just a careless error?[21]

After receiving the March 2011 warning about Tamerlan from
the FSB, the FBI initiated an investigation. Here is what the FBI press
office later reported:

In response to this 2011 request, the FBI checked U.S. government databases and other information to look for such
things as derogatory telephone communications, possible
use of online sites associated with the promotion of radical
activity, associations with other persons of interest, travel
history and plans, and education history. The FBI also interviewed Tamerlan Tsarnaev and family members. The FBI
did not find any terrorism activity, domestic or foreign, and
those results were provided to the foreign government [Rus-
sia] in the summer of 2011. The FBI requested but did not
receive more specific or additional information from the foreign government.[22]

In April 2017, the FBI released a report on an interview its agents had with Tamerlan on April 22, 2011. Tamerlan told them that, although he attended a mosque regularly, he had no interest in radical Islam and did not engage in violence.[23] But after following up on the interview by sending the FSB three requests for more information, the FBI did not hear another word from the FSB about Tamerlan or his visit to Russia. (According to Congressman Keating, the FSB insisted to his delegation that they had never received requests from the FBI for further information on Tamerlan, but that appears to be not the case. The FSB apparently just ignored the requests.) The FSB did, however, send a message to the CIA in September 2011, reiterating the earlier message to the FBI about Tamerlan. As a result, the CIA had the National Counterterrorism Center (NCTC) add Tamerlan's name to its watch list, but since, as mentioned earlier, his date of birth and the transliteration of his name were incorrect, he slipped through the cracks.[24]

One thing is clear: had the FBI known of Tamerlan's trip to Russia, things would have played out very differently. According to an Intelligence Community report issued in April 2014, the special agent in charge of the Boston Joint Terrorism Task Force said that if she had learned about Tamerlan's Russia trip, it would have "changed everything." And the LEGAT (FBI legal attaché in Moscow, who was the first to receive the FSB's March 2011 memorandum) characterized Tamerlan's travel as "huge" and said that, if he had known about it, he would have requested the FBI and CIA to do a reassessment of Tamerlan and to pressure the FSB for more information on him.[25]

It was not until several days after the bombings that the FSB communicated again with the Americans, suddenly sending the FBI and CIA transcripts of two telephone conversations Tamerlan had in 2010—one with his mother and one with an unidentified person from the North Caucasus. These transcripts have not been made available outside the U.S. intelligence community, but the North Caucasian mentioned by the FSB reportedly turned out to be Ibragim Todashev, a Chechen who had been close to Tamerlan in Boston before moving to Orlando, Florida.[26]

This last FSB message was apparently what prompted the FBI to re-open an unsolved 2011 triple murder, outside Boston, of three young men who were friends of both Todashev and Tamerlan. The FBI burst in on Todashev in Orlando in May 2013 and started interrogating him. After allegedly confessing to the murders, and Tamerlan's involvement in them, Todashev suddenly became violent and was shot dead by an FBI agent. Whether Todashev's confession was truthful, and Tamerlan was actually a participant in the murders, is unclear. Authorities have apparently concluded that the killings were drug-related and not directly connected to the bombings. But with Todashev dead, it is unlikely we will ever know why the FSB put him on the FBI's radar screen after the bombings.[27]

Tamerlan in Russia

There has been no credible explanation of Tamerlan's decision to go to Russia in January 2012, leaving his wife and baby daughter behind, apparently with little money. How did Tamerlan get funds to pay for the costly air ticket to Moscow and back, or for his travel from Moscow to Makhachkala, Dagestan? (Congressman Keating, when I asked him, suggested that maybe Tamerlan had money from selling marijuana, but whatever he earned from that enterprise he presumably used to help support his wife and daughter.)[28] Why did Tamerlan tell people he was returning to Russia to get a Russian passport and yet did not follow through in doing so? Tamerlan's father told reporters after the bombings that his son also had gone to Dagestan to attend a cousin's wedding, "but it did not work out." In fact, the wedding had taken place before Tamerlan arrived.[29]

More important, of course, is why Russian authorities would let Tamerlan, in their eyes a possible terrorist, enter their country unimpeded. While we know from the Homeland Security Report on the bombings that U.S. authorities inadvertently let Tamerlan slip through the cracks when he made his trip to Russia and back, it is simply inconceivable that the Russian security services would have allowed him into Russia without conducting extensive interviews with him. Anyone who goes to Russia knows that even with ordinary businesspeople, those visiting families, or tourists, the protocol involves questioning—about the purpose of the visit, financial means, and the length of the planned stay there.

FSB agents knew—because they doubtless were still monitoring Tamerlan's communications, as well as his postings on social media, and had informants in Boston—that he was a vulnerable, disenchanted school dropout who smoked a lot of pot, with little hope for a successful future in the United States—or anywhere else, for that matter. He was the ideal young man to recruit as a jihadist who would return to his country of residence and commit a terrorist act. In short, a Chechen who would show the world what the Kremlin had been saying all along—that its long and brutal war against Chechen and Dagestani rebels was justified because they are global jihadists.

One crucial fact overlooked by those who have investigated the Boston bombings is that Tamerlan arrived in Moscow in January 2012, but, according to his aunt, Patimat Suleimanova, he did not show up in Makhachkala, where she and the rest of Tamerlan's extended family lived, until March, and his father, Anzor, only arrived there in May.[30] Yet Anzor insisted that he had been together with Tamerlan the entire time the latter stayed in Russia. He told reporters "When he came here [to Makhachkala] he was with me, worked in the apartment, broke concrete walls. We bought an old apartment and did repairs there. He was with me. He did not go anywhere. He did not communicate with anybody."[31]

So how do we account for the period between January and March 2012? Akhmed Zakaev insisted to me that the only explanation was that Tamerlan was in Moscow during these two months, doubtless being sustained financially and interviewed continually by the FSB. As Zakaev told me, it is not difficult to see the Russians' motive, given that they had the upcoming Olympics in Sochi in early 2014 and people were beginning to question the Russians' ability to keep Sochi secure. With an attack on American soil, the focus would change—to the global problem of terrorism, on which Russia and the U.S. could cooperate.[32]

Tamerlan and Global Jihad

Once in Dagestan, Tamerlan reportedly often traveled the ninety miles from Makhachkala to the small town of Kizlyar, near the border with Chechnya and—according to Masha Gessen—"a presumed hotspot of insurgent activity in the eyes of Russian authorities."[33] There, Tamerlan met on ten to fifteen occasions with a third cousin, Magomed Kartashov, who was a former policeman and the leader of a non-violent Islamic group called The Union of Just. Kartashov was a well-known activist who spoke frequently at rallies in support of Muslim rights. Thus, the Dagestani branch of the FSB would have been well aware of his contacts with Tamerlan, who stood out as a foreigner, though one of North Caucasian heritage.[34]

Kartashov, who spoke via Skype more than once with Tamerlan after his return to the United States, was arrested by the FSB at the end of April 2013 for allegedly attacking a policeman. The timing of his arrest, coming so soon after the Boston bombings, was strangely convenient for the FSB. He was subsequently, in early June, interviewed by the FBI, at the FSB's headquarters in Makhachkala. Kartashov claimed that Tamerlan had already been intent on waging jihad when he arrived in Russia: "He came to Russia with the intention of fighting in the forest. I knew what he was thinking was a dead end." Kartashov said that he had tried to dissuade Tamerlan, but the latter was "convinced of his way." When asked how Tamerlan came to develop his extremist views, Kartashov said "I know for a fact that it was the Internet site Kavkaz Center and the lectures of Anwar al-Awlaki [the American jihadist who inspired many to join Al-Qaeda and was killed by a U.S. drone attack in Yemen in 2011]."[35]

These statements were exactly the message that the FSB wanted to convey. To be sure, Tamerlan is known to have been influenced by al-Awlaki, because his Internet browsing history showed that he had watched many of the latter's videos. Tamerlan also logged on frequently to the Kavkaz Center, the website of the Caucasian Emirate, a radical North Caucasian group that has taken credit for numerous terrorist attacks in Russia. But the Center (which has been accused by Russian authorities of being financed by the CIA and the U.S. State Department, with the intention of de-stabilizing Russia) immediately denied any connection with the Boston bombings and stressed that it was at war with Russia, not the United States.

As Brian Glyn Williams, a specialist in Islamic history, observed, the Caucasian Emirate viewed the United States as an enemy of Islam, but this was never translated into advocating terrorist attacks on U.S. territory, and the group had at this time declared a moratorium on terrorism against civilians. Williams concluded that "we can thus rule out the idea that Tamerlan was actively recruited and trained to attack the United States by the Dagestani branch of the Caucasian Emirate."[36]

There were reports (apparently deliberate leaks from the FSB to the Russian media) that while he was in Dagestan, Tamerlan connected up with the above-mentioned William Plotnikov and one Mahmud Mansur Nidal, both of whom had been drawn into the wider jihadist movement. Nidal was a nineteen-year-old native of Dagestan who was shot to death by Dagestani police in Makhachkala in mid-May 2012. Plotnikov was killed in the forest outside the city by Russian anti-terrorist forces shortly before Tamerlan returned to the United States.[37] But these young men were clearly peripheral characters in Tamerlan's journey to jihad against America. And he may well have never met them.[38]

Political commentator Maribek Vatchagaev raised important questions about Tamerlan's sojourn in the North Caucasus:

> Why did Tamerlan Tsarnaev . . . not demand an end to the bloodshed in Dagestan [where his large extended family lived], but was instead interested in what happened in Afghanistan and Iraq? The casualties in Dagestan are quite comparable to the casualties in those countries. . . . Dagestan was Tamerlan's homeland on his mother's side and the place where he lived for one and a half years, in 1999–2001. So why did Dagestan not become important to him? . . . After the Boston bombings, all Chechens are asking the same question—why did Tamerlan pick the U.S. as the target of the attack? If he wanted to take revenge for Chechnya or Dagestan, he had the ideal opportunity to do so when he was in Dagestan.[39]

It seems clear that Tamerlan was dissuaded by Kartashov from going "into the forest" in Dagestan, the base of rebels who are fighting what they believe is a life-and-death struggle against Russian aggressors. But Kartashov's Union of Just, although not espousing violence per se, was an offshoot of Hizb ub-Tahrir, which calls for the creation of an Islamic caliphate as its primary goal. According to one expert: "While HT may not directly engage in violence, it certainly preaches engagement with violence. What HT peddles, in fact, is an escapist romantic fascism of a sort that appeals to members who simply want to be told what to do."[40]

While discouraging him from fighting on behalf of local insurgents, Tamerlan's cousin Kartashov and the Union of Just seem to have instilled in Tamerlan the idea of a wider cause. Significantly, in the spring of 2012, while in Dagestan, Tamerlan sent several email messages to Dzhokhar and to his wife, Katherine, often with links to radical Islamist websites. In an April message to Dzhokhar, he said: "I am educating myself more and more about Islam. We are working on spreading Islam. In order for an Islamic society to emerge, Islamic spirit and thinking must reign amongst the population. And here in the Caucasus there are still very many people who live in jahili [in ignorance]. But it gets better and better."[41]

As Brian Glyn Williams noted, the Union of Just proudly burned American flags, and its members "were also known for their globalist rhetoric attacking the United States for its occupation of the Muslim lands of Iraq and Afghanistan. By the end of his time in Dagestan, Tsarnaev's interests seemed to have shifted from local insurgency to a more global notion of Islamic struggle—closer to the one espoused by Kartashov's organization."[42]

In the meantime, the FSB must have been closely following Tamerlan's movements in Dagestan and Chechnya, which he also visited. (His mother, Zubeidat, claimed he was questioned by police in Makhachkala on at least one occasion.)[43] The FSB's Anti-Terrorist Agency has a ubiquitous presence throughout this area. As Vatchagaev observed:

> According to experts who visited Dagestan and truly experienced surveillance by the Federal Security Service (FSB), Moscow should have been aware of every step of a young man who came from the U.S. The FSB was certainly aware of all of Tamerlan's contacts and the details of his stay in the capital of Dagestan. . . . Knowing of Tamerlan's suspicious contacts in Dagestan in 2012 and having suspected him as early as 2011, it is unclear what prevented the FSB from seizing him when he was leaving Russia via Moscow's Sheremetevo Airport. What prevented the FSB from giving this information to the U.S.?[44]

Back Home

There is no doubt that Tamerlan returned to the U.S. in July a changed person. Secretary of State John Kerry observed shortly after the Boston bombings: "We just had a young person who went to Russia, Chechnya, who blew people up in Boston. So he didn't stay where he went, but he learned something where he went and he came back with a willingness to kill people."[45] As Janet Reitman noted in a piece for *Rolling Stone,* "By early summer [2012] Tamerlan was talking about holy war 'in a global context.' . . . Dissuaded from his quest to wage jihad in Dagestan, he apparently turned his gaze upon America, the country that, in his estimation, had caused so much suffering, most of all his own."[46]

However extreme Tamerlan's views might have become in Boston before his Russia trip as a result of people like Misha and others, his acquaintances observed a marked difference after the visit to Russia. This was the impression of Tamerlan from a witness, Robert Barnes, an old school friend of Dzhokar's, at the latter's trial. Barnes was sitting in a Boston pizza parlor when he saw Tamerlan walk in, and he invited him to his table. He asked him about his life, his brother Dzhokhar, old friends. Tamerlan said that he could no longer drink or smoke; he was dressed in long clothes and had a beard. His appearance was very different from the last time Barnes had seen him. According to Barnes: "He definitely got into stuff about, you know, foreign policy stuff, American foreign policy stuff, and he had some criticisms of the things, you know, what the United States government does abroad. . . . He definitely was very passionate about what he was talking about and—yeah, he spoke very emphatically. . . . I don't remember him talking about Chechnya."[47] As for Tamerlan's source of income, his friend Magomed Dolakov told the FBI that when he saw Tamerlan in early 2013 and asked if he was working, Tamerlan "said Allah sent him money."[48]

Just a few weeks after he returned from Russia, Tamerlan opened an account on YouTube, where he compiled playlists of jihadi videos. One video was titled "The Emergence of Prophecy: The Black Flags of Khorasan," about a holy army rising out of Central Asia and sweeping across the Middle East to Jerusalem. Tamerlan also posted songs from a Chechen bard, Timur Mutsurayev, who proclaimed "we will devote our life to the jihad."[49] And in the months immediately preceding the bombings, the Tsarnaev brothers spent several hundred dollars on explosive powder, ammunition, and electronic components for making bombs. They reportedly used instructions from an article called "Make a Bomb in The Kitchen of Your Mom," from a 2010 issue of an English-language Al-Qaeda publication called *Inspire*. It is not clear where the brothers got the money for the bomb ingredients, other than from "Allah," or whether anyone helped them make the devices. According to the prosecutors of Dzhokhar: "These relatively sophisticated devices would have been difficult for the Tsarnaevs to fabricate successfully without training or assistance from others."[50] But no accomplices were ever identified.

Aftermath of the Bombings

The authors of the above-mentioned House Homeland Security report complained that the FBI had not been cooperative in their efforts to learn more about Tamerlan's history:

> For several months the FBI largely denied or ignored the Committee's requests for assistance. Uncertainty continues to surround the question of which Federal agencies and investigators knew of Tamerlan Tsarnaev's travel to Russia. . . . If these agencies had proactively communicated with one another and worked to de-conflict their records, we would have had a more thorough picture of the threat Tamerlan Tsarnaev posed, and it could have presented the opportunity to review his case after his return from Dagestan, Russia.[51]

But, for all the missteps of the U.S. intelligence community, it was Russian authorities who had hidden the facts surrounding Tamerlan. And these Russian authorities emerged triumphant from the carnage in Boston. On April 25, 2013, at a news conference in Moscow, President Putin asserted that the bombings proved Russia's long-standing claims—that the rebels in the North Caucasus had a global jihadist agenda: "Common folk in the U.S. are not to be blamed, they don't understand what is happening. Here I am addressing them and our citizens to say that Russia is a victim of international terrorism too. . . . I was always appalled when our Western partners and the Western media called the terrorists, who did bloody crimes in our country, 'insurgents' and almost never 'terrorists.' "[52]

Shortly after the bombings, Putin and Obama had a "very productive" telephone conversation. Both agreed that their two countries should unite in the struggle against global terrorism. And in June 2013 former FSB chief Nikolai Patrushev, head of Putin's Security Council, was received personally at the White House by President Obama to discuss the importance of cooperation between Russia and the U.S. in fighting terrorism.[53] The Boston bombings had proved to the world that North Caucasians were a common enemy, not, as previously assumed, victims of Russian aggression and brutality. Tamerlan and Dzhokhar Tsarnaev were the poster boys for this new image. Unfortunately, with the trial of Dzhokhar, this view has been reinforced. No one, it seems, would like to think the unthinkable—the very real possibility that the two brothers, though of course murderers, were pawns in the hands of the Russian security services.

Interestingly, the Russian propaganda machine put out a message that conflicted with that of President Putin. On April 28, 2013, Zubeidat Tsarnaeva, back in Dagestan, was interviewed at length on one of Russia's main television channels, NTV, which is controlled by the Russian government. She insisted that her sons had been "framed," with the implication that this had been done by U.S. authorities. Normally in Russia, relatives of suspected terrorists would be treated with derision and not featured sympathetically on television. Yet the FSB went out of its way to protect the Tsarnaevs from unwanted journalists and to arrange their meetings with the press. In the words of one analyst, "the Russian security services appear to be courting the parents instead of persecuting them."[54]

Meanwhile, Russia continues to play its double game with terrorism emanating from the North Caucasus. Drawing on its extensive penetration of insurgency groups in that area, the FSB has been encouraging radical Islamists to take their struggle to the Middle East, in particular Syria, where they have joined ISIS in significant numbers. According to one authoritative source, 2,400 Russians, the majority from Chechnya and Dagestan, had joined the Islamic state by September 2015.[55] As of 2017, according to Russian officials, 4,000 or more Russian citizens are fighing for ISIS in Syria.[56] Michael Weiss explained this phenomenon in the *Daily Beast,* "The logic is actually straightforward: Better the terrorists go abroad and fight in Syria than blow things up in Russia."[57]

An investigation by a *Novaia gazeta* journalist, cited by Weiss, revealed that the FSB set up a "green corridor," through which rebels could go first to Turkey and then on to Syria. The exodus to Syria, where radicals from North Caucasus fight against the U.S.-led coalition there, has resulted in an estimated 50 percent decline of violence in the North Caucasus. Weiss rightly notes that "penetrating and co-opting terrorism also has a long, well-attested history in the annals of Chekist [a reference to the first security police established in 1917] tradecraft."[58] The case of the Tsarnaev brothers deserves a place in this history.

Boris Nemtsov and Vladimir Kara-Murza, with opposition leaders, March 2012.

(By Lalekseev—Own work, CC BY-SA 3.0,

https://commons.wikimedia.org/w/index.php?curid=21961428)

12

ANOTHER DEMOCRAT FALLS VICTIM: THE NEMTSOV MURDER

AND ITS AFTERMATH

"If I were afraid of Putin, I wouldn't be in this line of work."

Boris Nemtsov, interview with *Sobesednik* newspaper, February 2015

As far as the crime committed against Boris Efemovich Nemtsov is concerned, I knew him personally and our relationship was not always sour. It was he who chose the path of political struggle, personal attacks and so on. I was used to it and besides, he was not the only one. However, that does not mean you have to kill him.

Vladimir Putin, press conference, December 2015

In early 2015, the Ukrainian conflict, fueled by Russian military backing for separatists in Eastern Ukraine, was showing no sign of abating, despite a new ceasefire agreement. Russia was bolstering the dictatorial regime of Syrian president Bashir al-Assad with military aid and within months would begin air strikes against anti-Assad rebels. Russia's strategy, of course, was running directly counter to Western government efforts to defeat ISIS and bring about a peaceful settlement to the Syrian crisis. All of this created tensions for the West's relations with the Kremlin. By the end of the year, in December 2015, the U.S. Treasury would expand its list of sanctions against Russia to include thirty-four more individuals and legal entities, because of Russia's military aggression in Crimea and Eastern Ukraine. Nonetheless, neither Security Council Chief Nikolai Patrushev nor FSB chief Aleksandr Bortnikov would be among those Russian officials put on the new list, although they were both sanctioned by the Eu and Canada in 2014. As mentioned earlier, Bortnikov was a guest at President Obama's three-day conference in Washington on "countering violent extremism" in February 2015. Ironically, this was just when the Litvinenko Inquiry was taking place in London—with evidence mounting that the FSB had organized Litvinenko's murder—and a month before the Dzhokhar Tsarnaev trial began in Boston. Within just days of Bortnikov's visit to the United States, late on the night of February 27, 2015, liberal Russian politician Boris Nemtsov would be brutally gunned down just outside the Kremlin.

Nemtsov was a larger-than-life figure—handsome, charismatic, and relentlessly energetic. What immediately comes to mind when contemplating Nemtsov is that he was the complete opposite of his nemesis, Putin. Physically they were like night and day—Nemtsov dark-haired, muscular, swarthy, and much taller than the diminutive, balding, beady-eyed Putin. Putin, as we know, has gone to great lengths to portray himself as macho, riding a horse bare-chested, shooting tigers, and doing other stunts designed to showcase his virility. The telegenic Nemtsov had no need to choreograph such an image. He was by nature the very man who Putin was not. It cannot have set well with the Russian president when Nemtsov even joked in an interview about Putin's small stature, remarking that "all Russia's fierce tyrants have been small—Ivan the Terrible, Lenin, Stalin."[1]

Unlike the secretive and inscrutable Putin, the gregarious Nemtsov, fifty-five when he was killed, was completely transparent, letting everything about himself be known, including his business dealings and love affairs. (He readily admitted: "I have a problem, though I don't consider it a problem. I love women and I can't do anything about it."[2]) But of course what really set Putin and Nemtsov apart was Nemtsov's firm belief in democratic elections and a free market, and his conviction that Russia needed to adopt Western political and economic values. In the years after he became Russia's leader, Putin became convinced, particularly after the departure of George W. Bush as the U.S. president in 2009, that the West was Russia's enemy. His Kremlin supporters followed suit and embarked on an unprecedented anti-Western campaign through the television media, a campaign that continues to this day.

Nemtsov went against the grain of this approach and actively courted the West, which greatly rankled the Kremlin. His shooting, allegedly by a group of hired thugs from Chechnya, eliminated one of Putin's main political opponents. Putin's press secretary, Dmitrii Peskov, insisted on the day after the murder that Nemtsov was not important to the Kremlin: "With all due respect to the memory of Boris Nemtsov, in political terms he did not pose any threat to the current Russian leadership or Vladimir Putin. If we compare popularity levels, Putin's and the government's ratings and so on, in general Boris Nemtsov was just a bit more than an average citizen."[3] But if one considers Nemtsov's unrelenting efforts to expose the corruption, authoritarianism, and unwarranted military aggression of Putin's Russia, it is clear that Peskov's statement was far from the truth.

Nemtsov the Politician

A talented physicist, Nemtsov embarked on politics even before the 1991 collapse of the Soviet Union, running for the Russian parliament successfully as a delegate in the Gorky region (later called Nizhny Novgorod). Like many other scientists whose careers had been stifled during the Soviet period, Nemtsov, then in his early thirties, saw the new Yeltsin government as an opportunity to make positive political change in his country. As an active member of the Russian parliament, he drew the attention of Yeltsin, who appointed him governor of Nizhny Novgorod in November 1991, a post Nemtsov held until 1997 after winning the popular vote for the governorship in 1995.[4]

Nemtsov looked to the West as a model for economic development and introduced wide-ranging market reforms in his region. The author of a 1997 profile of the politician observed: "During Nemtsov's five years as governor, Nizhny Novgorod oblast [region] became a model province, according to all the indicators. It can justly claim to be the only region in Russia in which economic reforms have been pursued consistently."[5] Nemtsov did not hesitate to speak his mind, even when it meant opposing the policies of Yeltsin. After Yeltsin brought troops into Chechnya in December 1994 to subdue an increasingly violent movement for independence there, Nemtsov delivered a petition against that war to Yeltsin with over a million signatures. (So much for the Kremlin's theory that Nemtsov was murdered because he was hated by the Chechen people.) This contrarian move did not stop Yeltsin from appointing Nemtsov first deputy prime minister in 1997, a post that some, including Yeltsin, considered a stepping stone to the presidency.[6]

The 1998 financial crisis in Russia led to the resignation of Nemtsov, who had concerned himself with Russian economic affairs. But he did not give up politics. In late 1999, he ran successfully for a seat in the Duma as a leader of a new liberal-democratic coalition, the Union of Right Forces (SPS), and in early 2000 he became deputy speaker of that body. Early on, as Nemtsov recounts in *Confessions of a Rebel*, he and fellow party leader Anatoly Chubais had grave doubts about Putin as a candidate for the Russian presidency, mainly because Putin was a product of the KGB: "Both Chubais and I experienced a huge shock over the decision by the president [Yeltsin] to choose Putin as his successor."[7] But when it came to the SPS deciding whether or not to support Putin in the 2000 presidential elections, Nemtsov and Chubais disagreed. Nemtsov was against the idea, but he was out-voted by others in the SPS leadership, including Chubais. As a result of backing Putin, Nemtsov's party lost its support among the people it needed most, liberal democrats, and became marginalized. In the par-liamentary elections of December 2003, the SPS failed dismally and did not earn enough votes to be represented in the new Duma. This defeat began Nemtsov's career as an outsider who would devote all his energy to opposing the Putin regime.[8]

Nemtsov the Kremlin Critic

After his failure to be re-elected to the Duma, Nemtsov decided that the only way to unseat Putin was to publicize his transgressions, in particular human-rights abuses and the rampant corruption among Kremlin elites. This he did, through meticulous research, publishing a series of reports (*doklady*) from 2008 onward. The first such report, co-written with his colleague Vladimir Milov, was "Putin. The Re-sults" (2008), a scathing denunciation of Putin's first eight years in power. Just one citation from the report is enough to give the gist: "Assets are being removed from state ownership and handed over to the control of private people, property is being purchased with state money back from the oligarchs at stunning prices, a friends-of-Putin oil export monopoly is being created, and a Kremlin 'black safe' [slush fund] is being funded. This is a brief outline of the criminal system of government that has taken shape under Putin."[9]

As mentioned earlier, just after the report came out, I was able to meet Milov in Moscow, where he told me it had caused a huge stir in the Kremlin. This was confirmed by Lilia Shevtsova, a political analyst at Moscow's Carnegie Center, who informed me that the report was like a "bomb, which anywhere but in Russia would cause the country to collapse."[10] The report's appraisal of Putin and his administration was so damning that the Kremlin attempted, with considerable success, to block its distribution. The publisher, *Novaia gazeta*, originally planned on a first printing of 100,000. But the distributor backed out at the last minute because of strong pressure from the Kremlin. This left *Novaia gazeta* with only one place in the entire country to sell the book—its own kiosk on Moscow's Pushkin Square. As a result, only five thousand copies were printed, and by mid-March 2008 only two thousand had been sold.[10]

This publication was followed over the next years with further reports by Nemtsov, all focused on corruption in the Kremlin and on Putin's increasing authoritarianism. Of particular note was "Winter Olympics in the Subtropics," which appeared in May 2013 and described the folly of the choice of Sochi for the Olympics, the unprecedented amount of government money spent to prepare for the games, and the vast corruption that was part of the process.[11]

The report, which Nemtsov co-authored with his colleague Leonid Martynyuk, pointed out the huge costs involved in the construction for the games and the lucrative contracts that were awarded to Putin cronies. The authors predicted that the total expenditure on the Olympics by the Russian government would be $50 billion—more than four times the original estimate of $12 billion. Acknowledging that most governments spend double their initial estimates on the Olympics, they observed: "The cost of the Sochi Olympics, based on the global average, should have been $24 billion (i.e., Putin's $12 billion, multiplied by two). The remainder—$26 billion—consisted of embezzlement and kickbacks." For Putin, the fact that Russia was hosting the 2014 games was a dream come true—an opportunity to bring prestige and glory back to his country. Nemtsov and Martynyuk cast the shadow of corruption upon this event.

These writings would have been all the more devastating for Putin had they reached a wide audience in Russia. But they did not, despite the efforts of a team of Nemtsov supporters to distribute them throughout the country—at metro stations, polling places, and other venues. Nemtsov and his colleagues simply did not have the resources to get their message out to the general population and to counter the Kremlin's efforts to suppress their reports. But from the Kremlin's point of view, these publications were nonetheless a grave threat. The so-called Orange Revolution in Ukraine, prompted by mass protests against government corruption and voting fraud in 2004–2005 and Russia's own public unrest in 2011–2012, were doubtless foremost in the Kremlin's mind.

Equally offensive to the Kremlin were Nemtsov's direct approaches to Western governments with his damning information about the Putin regime. In November 2010, Nemtsov spoke at a commemoration in Washington, D.C. of the 2009 death of Sergei Magnitsky, the lawyer who had exposed high-level government corruption in Russia. Nemtsov urged U.S. lawmakers to impose targeted sanctions against specific Kremlin officials who were involved in money laundering and human-rights violations. In June 2013, Nemtsov testified before the U.S. Senate Foreign Relations Committee, calling on committee members to broaden the so-called Magnitsky Act, the bipartisan bill passed in 2012 to punish those Russian officials responsible for the death of the lawyer:

> With Vladimir Putin's return to the presidency in May 2012, Russia's authoritarian regime has transitioned to a new stage of development—from the "sovereign democracy" characterized by election fraud, media censorship, and the harassment of the opposition, to overt political repression. . . . Unfortunately, the initial public list of violators that was published by the U.S. administration in April includes only eighteen names—none of them high-ranking. Too many of those responsible for repression and human rights abuses have been let off the hook. This is a grave strategic error. I hope that it will be corrected in the nearest future.[12]

In the eyes of Putin and his allies, these actions were nothing short of treasonous. It was one thing for Nemtsov to be an active opposition-ist at home, but to engage U.S. politicians in his struggle against the Kremlin was overstepping all bounds. It would only be a matter of time before Nemtsov would be eliminated.

Finally, the Nemtsov family lawyer, Vadim Prokhorov, has mentioned another possible reason for the murder—a statement Nemtsov made about Putin at a forum in Kiev in the spring of 2014. In response to a question from a woman in the audience, Nemtsov asserted that "Putin is really fucked up." After the woman posted the statement on the internet, according to Prokhorov, "the people in power in one re-public, and in fact all over the country, and their close associates with criminal mindsets, decided that this remark required an equally strong response." The Russian Investigative Committee began a crim-inal case against Nemtsov for slandering the president, but the case was subsequently dropped.[13]

Nemtsov was very aware that he was in danger. According to his close friend Yevgenia Albats, editor of the *New Times* magazine, "He was afraid of being killed. And he was trying to convince himself, and me, they wouldn't touch him because he [had been] a member of the Russian government, a vice premier, and they wouldn't want to cre-ate a precedent. Because, as he said, [some] time the power will change hands in Russia again, and those who served Putin wouldn't want to create this precedent."[14]

February 27, 2015

It is no coincidence that Nemtsov was about to publish yet another scathing indictment of Putin, called "Putin.War," which would doc-ument Russia's covert military involvement in Ukraine. In an inter-view on radio *Ekho Moskvy* on February 27, just three hours before he was killed, Nemtsov said: "The main reason for the crisis [in Rus-sia] is that Putin started this insane policy of war with Ukraine, which is aggressive and murderous for our country. The presence of Russian troops in Ukraine is well-documented. . . . Why are Russian soldiers being killed, while you, Mr. Putin, commander-chief, disown these soldiers by lying that they don't take part in the fighting?"[15]

After his radio interview, Nemtsov had a late dinner with his Ukrainian girlfriend, Anna Duritskaya, at the Café Bosco on Red Square. According to his colleague Milov, writing on LiveJournal (*Zhivoi zhurnal*) shortly after the murder, Nemtsov usually had his driver wait for him and then take him back to his apartment when he went out in the evening. Despite the harsh weather, he and Duritskaya apparently decided they would go home without the car. But they took an unusual route. Instead of walking north to Manezh Square, where they could have taken the subway home, they decided to walk south, across the Bol'shoi Moskvoretskii Bridge, about two hundred yards from the Kremlin. It was there that a man emerged and fired shots at Nemtsov from behind, fatally wounding him. (Duritskaya, who could not give a description of the assailant, was not hurt.) The killer then escaped from the scene in a car driven by an accomplice.[16]

Several questions arise immediately. First, how did the killers know that the couple would be walking home, instead of going by car? And taking this unusual route? The only way they could have known would have been either through hacking Nemtsov's cell phone and hearing his communication with his driver, or by some sophisticated technology that would have enabled them, while Nemtsov was dining, to listen to his conversation with Duritskaya. It is clear that, given the hugely congested traffic around the Kremlin, even at that late hour, the getaway car could not have been in place—and the killer there—without advance knowledge that Nemtsov and his companion would be walking across the bridge.

It is highly unlikely that the killers would have had the means to conduct sophisticated surveillance, including possibly tracking Nemtsov's movements through his cell phone, unless they had help from the Russian security services. Indeed, it is a known fact that the FSB, as a routine, followed Nemtsov's every step. According to a report by Russia expert Catherine Fitzpatrick, "Proof that Nemtsov was under surveillance came with the publication of *leaked cellphone calls in the past,* intended to discredit him, and footage of his meetings on state TV. Michael McFaul, the former U.S. ambassador to Russia, *claimed on Twitter* that he had personally seen cars speed after Nemtsov following visits with him."[17] Nemtsov himself complained about the surveillance, which, given that he was organizing a large protest march against Russian involvement in Ukraine for March 1, would have been especially concentrated on him at this time. Russian authorities later claimed that the Chechen killers had been following Nemtsov for months. Why then would they not have been noticed by the FSB?[18]

The crime took place in an area that is normally under intense scrutiny—both with cameras and physical patrols—by the Federal Protection Service (FSO), which is under the direct control of the Russian president. This seemed an unlikely spot for the killers to choose, since Nemtsov was known to have walked the back alleys of Moscow alone at night and could easily have been shot where there were no police or surveillance cameras. Someone had told the killers that they could carry out their crime with impunity on that bridge near the Kremlin. As Milov pointed out, the police made no attempt to find the car with the killers until a half hour had elapsed after Nemtsov was shot. By this time, it was too late. The car was found hours later, abandoned in a Moscow suburb.

Nemtsov's Friends Speak Out

Milov, for one, did not spare words in laying responsibility for the crime on Russian authorities: "I have practically no doubts that the murder of Boris Nemtsov was organized by the Russian security services." He went on to say: "In some sense this might be revenge, analogous to the Litvinenko case. Nemtsov was not only considered a politician, playing this or that role in Russia, but also, in the opinion of the Kremlin, 'guilty' for the difficult situation the Putin establishment was in because of [Western] sanctions."[19]

Yevgenia Albats observed in an interview with National Public Radio:

> Let's face it: Boris Nemtsov was shot on one of the main bridges of Moscow just 100 meters [sic] from the Kremlin, which is heavily surveilled by the security cameras, which is under control of the Russian power institutions. If you try to do a photo op at the Moscow bridge where Boris was shot you would immediately face a policeman. . . . Either the so-called Russian law enforcement can't do their job—except for following the opposition, tapping their phones, and putting peaceful opposition leaders into jail—or they *don't want* to do their job, and that suggests that they were part of this plot to kill Boris.[20]

It should be mentioned that Putin's longtime St. Petersburg KGB comrade Evgenii Murov was FSO chief at this time. Recall that as far back as 2000 he was compiling hit lists of Putin's opponents. (See chapter 2.)

Anti-corruption crusader Aleksei Navalny was unable to attend the public funeral of his close friend Nemtsov on March 1, 2015 because he was under house arrest. In mid-February, he and Nemtsov had passed out leaflets together in the Moscow metro, inviting people to the scheduled opposition march against Russian aggression in Ukraine. Navalny, who had already been charged several times for demonstrating in public illegally, was arrested, while Nemtsov got off with a warning. One wonders whether the authorities' decision not to detain Nemtsov, which they easily could have done, was part of a larger plan. Arresting such a prominent political figure as Nemtsov (he had earlier been detained for dissident activities) would have made him a cause célèbre and encouraged more people on the streets in protest against the Kremlin. Killing Nemtsov a little later was a better solution.

Although Navalny was not always in agreement with Nemtsov on policy issues and strategy, the two worked together for the common cause of bringing about democracy in Russia, in the process forcing Putin out of office. As a goal, this may have seemed close to impossible, but it did not keep them from trying, despite the obvious dangers to both. Navalny, clearly shaken by the murder, shared the following thoughts for his Russian blog readers on March 1: "I believe that Nemtsov was killed by members of the government (intelligence) or a pro-government organization on orders from the political leadership of the country, including Vladimir Putin. It is only a question of how this order was formulated: 'You must kill Nemtsov' or 'you must do a hugely sensational action.' . . . This was not freelancing, but directly [the work of] Putin, Nikolai Patrushev, Sergei Ivanov [Putin's chief of staff] [and] Aleksandr Bortnikov. . . ."[21]

Navalny went on to discount the idea, spread by the Kremlin, that Putin could not have been connected with the murder because it painted him in a bad light. This theory, Navalny said, "goes into the same corner with 'murderers who were not advantageous to Duvalier' or 'the Red Terror was not advantageous to Stalin.' . . . It is advantageous to Putin. Open a history book, it is all written there." Navalny also dismissed the idea, circulated immediately by the Kremlin, that there was no point in the government murdering Nemtsov because he was not important or influential: "Boris was one of the most problematic politicians for the Kremlin. He was one of a few who exposed the corruption of Putin and his close circle, citing concrete names."[22]

Navalny added that the only thing that could refute his claim of Kremlin involvement in Nemtsov's murder would be the rapid solving of the case, with both the perpetrators and the contractors identified, and an open trial. However, it comes now as no surprise that, as in previous cases, the FSB, the MVD, and the Investigative Committee accomplished little more rounding up five suspects and coercing them by torture into confessing.

The Kremlin Responds

The day after the killing, Putin issued a formal order (published on his Russian website) to the three chiefs of his investigative agencies. The order said that they were to create a special body to solve the crime and personally oversee the case. But how were these men, all close allies of the president, to investigate a murder that may well have been ordered by him? They knew that Putin takes everything personally when it comes to his critics, and Boris Nemtsov was the most vociferous of them all. More important, would anyone dare kill such a prominent national figure as Nemtsov without the Russian president's permission?

In all probability, these security chiefs knew the secrets behind this shocking crime, but they nonetheless had to go through the motions of an investigation. Things did not go smoothly, however. The different agencies began to contradict each other—and themselves— as they spoke out about the investigation and provided leaks to various media outlets. (Indeed, the scenario that played out after the murder was almost laughable, if not for the tragic circumstances.)

The first problem arose with the issue of camera surveillance. The FSO initially claimed, falsely, that it did not have jurisdiction over the eighteen cameras located on lampposts along the Moskvoretskii Bridge, because the bridge was under the authority of the City of Moscow. After city officials denied that this was the case, FSO officials allowed that in fact the cameras were theirs, but they had been under repair at the time of the murder. (In fact, the Moscow municipality did have television cameras on the bridge for monitoring the weather, but its images were not clear enough to show the killer or the car he escaped in.)[23]

The day after the crime, LifeNews television (a Kremlin mouthpiece) produced a witness, one "Viktor M," who was allegedly on the bridge and saw Nemtsov's murder. The witness, whose face was disguised, gave the following information: the killer was a man with short, dark hair, five feet, seven inches tall, who escaped after the murder in a silver-colored VAZ-21102 with North Ossetia number plates. That was the last that was heard from Viktor M.[24] Then, a month later, the Russian newspaper *Kommersant*, citing sources from the security agencies, claimed that a twenty-seven-year-old company manager by the name of Evgenii was also a witness. His last name was not given. According to the paper, Evgenii was walking behind Duritskaya and Nemtsov, wearing headphones and listening to loud "hard rock" music, and did not hear the gunshot. He was looking at his phone screen at the time of the shooting—Viktor M, coincidentally, had the same story—but did see the shooter afterward. He described the killer as a person of medium height, with long dark hair and the getaway car as a white Lada, not a VAZ.[25]

Meanwhile, within just six days (a record for any high-profile murder), authorities had arrested five Chechens as suspects, including the alleged triggerman, Zaur Dadaev, who did not fit either of the physical descriptions given by the two supposed witnesses. A former member of Chechen President Ramzan Kadyrov's crack "Sever" (North) fighting Battalion, Dadaev confessed to the killing but later recanted, claiming he had been tortured. Russian authorities said they were still looking for two other suspects: Ruslan Makhutdinov, another Sever member, who they alleged was the organizer of the murder, and Ruslan Geremeev, deputy commander of the Sever Battalion. Both were closely connected to Kadyrov.[26]

All of these details, it seems, were designed to give the impression to the public that investigators were zealously following leads in trying to zero in on the criminals. In fact, it seemed more like a clumsy, half-hearted effort to cover up the fact that investigators knew from the beginning—indeed probably beforehand—who had committed the murder. As it later turned out, the five arrested Chechens were, in all probability, the perpetrators. But they were a sorry bunch. In November 2015, security officials leaked a curious report on the investigation to *Kommersant*.[27] Investigators had located a Moscow apartment that the criminals had allegedly been using as a base since September 2014 for conducting extensive surveillance of Nemtsov. (No matter that the Chechens had supposedly been driven to kill Nemtsov because of his sympathetic comments about the victims of the Charlie Hebdo massacre, which did not occur until December 2014.)

Interestingly, Russian security authorities claimed to have found evidence of heroin and other drugs in the apartment used by the killers. (In fact, investigators had earlier reported that the accused killer, Dadaev, was first apprehended by the Russian Anti-Drug Agency, FSKN, on narcotic charges.) This claim was presumably an effort to show that the killers were not sophisticated professionals, hired by a highly placed contractor to carry out a politically motivated murder. But how would these drug-addicted Chechens, an ethnic group that is watched closely by authorities when they travel outside Chechnya, have gone unnoticed by the FSB or MVD for all these months? As noted, the FSB was, as a routine matter, conducting its own surveillance of Nemtsov. It is simply not possible that the FSB would have been unaware that these Chechens were also following him and that they were plotting his murder.

Putin's Disappearance

Many commentators have said that Dadaev would not have undertaken such a bold assassination without Kadyrov's explicit orders. But
the chain of command still would have had to go higher than the
Chechen president. Although Kadyrov runs Chechnya like a fiefdom,
and has for years cracked down on his enemies with impunity, his
powers have clear limits in the Russian capital. Akhmed Zakaev
stressed to me that Kadyrov would never embark on a mission to kill
such a prominent figure as Boris Nemtsov without Putin's approval.
Kadyrov, he said, "can do what he wants in Chechnya, but not in
Moscow. It is most likely that Nemtsov was assassinated because it
was Putin's wish."[28] Nemtsov's colleague Vladimir Milov concurred:
"Although Kadyrov might not know some things and did not attend
university, he is perfectly aware that the decision regarding the life of
Boris Nemtsov lies in 'Daddy's' [Putin's] domain. By doing anything
to Nemtsov [on his own], Kadyrov would be crossing a red line and
entering the territory under Daddy's jurisdiction."[29]

On March 9, just two days after the arrests of Dadaev and the
other four Chechens were made public, the Kremlin, astonishingly,
announced that Putin had awarded Kadyrov a medal of honor for his
service to the Russian state. And, as previously noted, a medal was
awarded at the same time to Lugovoy, the main suspect in the Litvinenko murder. The strange timing of the awards was dismissed by
presidential spokesman Dmitrii Peskov as "just a coincidence." But in
the meantime, Putin had vanished from public view with no explanation, so it is possible that someone highly placed in the Kremlin
used this announcement to try to discredit Putin by associating him
with the murders of Litvinenko and Nemtsov. Or that Putin did sanction the awards, as a defiant signal that he would let neither Lugovoy or Kadyrov face reprisals. Putin's unprecedented ten-day
disappearance, from March 6 to March 16, gave rise to intense me-

dia speculation: Was he gravely ill? Had he been ousted from the Kremlin by his colleagues?[30]

When he finally re-emerged, Putin made light of his absence, saying "life would be boring without gossip." But there is good reason to believe that his disappearance was connected to the Nemtsov murder. Close observers of the Kremlin surmised that some of his security officials, most probably from the FSB, thought Putin had gone too far in having Nemtsov shot so close to the Kremlin and in using Kadyrov to carry out the job. Bortnikov's FSB had reportedly long objected to Kadyrov's reckless use of extrajudicial killings to go after his Chechen enemies in his own republic and abroad. The siloviki elite includes such powerful figures as Patrushev, Igor Sechin, and Aleksandr Bastrykin. Some members of this group may also have voiced dissent, causing Putin, in keeping with a long-lived Kremlin tradition during power struggles, to disappear from the scene.

As Russian political analyst Stanislav Belkovsky noted: "For the first time in his fifteen-year-long rule, Putin has run into a really serious problem: a virtually open conflict between the two pillars of his power, the federal security establishment and Ramzan Kadyrov." Belkovsky observed that Putin's power depends on his good relations with the security services, since they are responsible for carrying out his most important policies as well as ensuring his personal security. On the other hand, he is also dependent on the support of Kadyrov, who has kept a lid on the restive North Caucasus. Belkovsky concluded that Putin opted to lay low until the situation resolved itself.[31]

In the end, Putin weathered the storm, apparently unscathed. This can be explained by the fact that Putin's men in the Kremlin, whether from the security elite or not, have a huge stake in keeping him in power. By "laying low" for ten days, Putin demonstrated to them how essential he is for their survival. Putin's allies, who have benefited financially from government corruption and have carried out his repressive measures at home and abroad, would surely fall with him if he lost his hold on power and disappeared from public life.

Challenges to the Kremlin's Version

In response to their requests to investigative authorities for answers to their many questions about the Nemtsov murder case, Milov and members of Nemtsov's family have been met with obstruction. Nemtsov's daughter Zhanna, who has left Russia and now lives in Germany (she is a journalist for *Deutsche Welle*) because she fears for her own safety, said that she doubts the facts of her father's murder will ever come to light: "Russia—it's a country of secrets. Everything is secret in Russia."[32]

In October 2015, Dmitrii Gudkov, the lone liberal deputy to the Russian Duma (who lost his seat after the September 2016 parliamentary elections), sent a complaint on behalf of the lawyer for the Nemtsov family, Vadim Prokhorov, to the President's Administration. Gudkov wanted an explanation as to why the FSO had not provided surveillance videos from the cameras on the Bol'shoi Moskvoretskii Bridge the night of Nemtsov's murder to the Investigative Committee. In his complaint, Gudov noted that the bridge "is a key transportation hub in the immediate vicinity of the Kremlin, to which the FSO, in carrying out its duties, must give special attention, including 24-hour camera surveillance. The absence of video surveillance on the bridge [that night] means there are serious inadequacies in the protection of the president and other key [government] structures."[33]

Gudkov was told to address his complaint directly to the FSO, which responded to him a couple of weeks later. According to a FSO press officer, it was indeed the case that the FSO did not have CCTV cameras monitoring the bridge. Their cameras were directed toward the inside of the Kremlin wall. Gudkov was incredulous, noting on his Facebook page that this meant "any terrorist can come right under the Kremlin wall."[34]

In the meantime, Zhanna Nemtsova filed a complaint with a Moscow City Court requesting that investigators question Ramzan Kadyrov and three of his close supporters from Chechnya, all of whom were widely thought to have been involved in the murder. Nemtsova was strongly discouraged from making this request by none other than Anatoly Chubais, Nemtsov's former Kremlin colleague, currently the chairman of the technology corporation Rosnano. He also suggested that she fire her lawyer, presumably for giving her bad advice. Chubais, who posted an email exchange with Nemtsova on Facebook on September 1, 2015, is still a Kremlin insider, so he presumably had heard that Kadyrov would be kept out of the case.[35] In October, after a hearing, Nemtsova's request was denied.

Events in the Case Unfold

By July 2016, Russian prosecutors had completed their case against five Chechens, and a Moscow District military court began preliminary hearings and jury selection. (The case was assigned to a military court because one defendant was a member of the Sever Battalion, which belongs to the Internal Troops.) The accused were as follows: Zaur Dadaev, the brothers Anzor and Shadid Gubashev, Tamerlan Eskerkhanov, and Khamzat Bakhaev. According to the indictment by Russian prosecutors, in September 2014 this group of Chechens reached an agreement with one Ruslan Mukhudinov (and other unnamed persons) to kill Nemtsov for a reward of fifteen million rubles (roughly $275,000). Mukhudinov, the alleged mastermind, is still at large and is on the wanted list of Interpol. He is reportedly in the United Arab Emirates.[36]

The indictment charges that the group conducted intensive surveillance of Nemtsov in the following months, while obtaining weapons and devising a plan of attack. On the evening of the murder, Dadaev, Anzor Gubashev, and one Beslan Shavanov (who allegedly blew himself up while being captured by police) followed Nemtsov.

Dadaev alone climbed the steps to the bridge and on a signal from the other two fired six shots at Nemtsov from behind. Mukhudinov drove the getaway car. The group fled to Ingushetia in the following days and were then, with the exception of Mukhudinov and Shavanov, apprehended by the police. Mukhudinov's motives for organizing the murder remain unclear, and the source of his fifteen million rubles has not been established.

Nemtsov's family members and their attorneys filed a complaint with the Investigative Committee demanding that Putin's former chief bodyguard Viktor Zolotov, head of the Internal Troops at the time of the murder, be questioned in the case. Two of the alleged killers, Dadaev and Shavanov, as members of the Sever Battalion, were subordinate to him. The complaint noted that in August 2015, Zolotov paid a personal visit to Kadyrov, who considered the Sever battalion to be his private army. The family's lawyers were able to obtain an important document, a January 2016 memorandum sent by a senior investigator in the case, Maj. Gen. N. B. Tutevich, to Zolotov, noting that Dadaev had been on active duty in Moscow at the time of the killing. (In contradiction to this, prosecutors had claimed that Dadaev had resigned from the Internal Troops at that point.) The memorandum also stated that, after the murder, Dadaev hid in the Moscow apartment rented by the commander of the Sever battalion, Ruslan Geremeev, who had been assigned to Moscow with a personal weapon. In the memorandum, Tutevich made reference to a possible "intent to distort reality with the purpose of covering up the involvement of Dadaev in the murder of Nemtsov" and requested that Zolotov conduct an internal probe and discipline those who were guilty.[37]

It might be added that Geremeev, who was initially a suspect, was relegated to the status of witness in the case after questioning by investigators, despite the fact that Mukhudinov was his personal driver and that Geremeev rented the Moscow apartment where some of the defendants hung out. By all accounts, Geremeev is a member of Kadyrov's inner circle and therefore was protected from prosecution in the Nemtsov murder. He is a close relative of some of the most senior people in Chechnya, including Russian Duma deputy Adam Delimkhanov, his cousin, and Suleiman Geremeev, a senator and member of the upper house of the Russian parliament, who is his uncle. According to Nemtsov family lawyer Prokhorov, senior investigator Tutevich prepared an indictment against Ruslan Geremeev, but it was struck down by Bastrykin. As for Geremeev's whereabouts, Prokhorov said: "I think he is in Chechnya, someone else claims he is in the Emirates."[38]

Quite clearly the Kremlin would like the Nemtsov case to recede into the background. When the jury trial finally began in Moscow on October 3, 2016, a lawyer for the prosecution, Olga Mikhailova, noted that the investigation had been hampered by the fact that Kadyrov had not been available for questioning and that the footage of surveillance cameras at the time of the murder was missing. Also, two of the defendants, Dadaev and Gubashev, claimed that they had been coerced into giving a false confession. All of the five defendants have proclaimed their innocence.

After sixty-seven sessions, the prosecution and defense finished presenting evidence in the Nemtsov trial at the end of May 2017, with a verdict by the jury soon to follow. The lengthy trial yielded few revelations. The motives of the killers remained unclear, and two of the defendants, Eskerkhanov and Bakhaev, appear to have played only a peripheral role in the crime. It is worth noting that a Russian lawyer named Igor Murzin, who has written extensively about the case for the Russian-language website of Garry Kasparov, has argued that Nemtsov's girlfriend, Anna Duritskaia, was actually an accomplice in the murder. Murzin claims that Duritskaia was a high-priced prostitute who was recruited by the FSB to entrap Nemtsov. After giving evidence to prosecutors immediately after the murder, she was allowed to return home to her native Ukraine and has not appeared

as a trial witness.[39] Vadim Prokhorov, who has discounted Murzin's
claims about Duritskaia, says that the Nemtsov family is not interested
so much in those in the dock for the murder, as in those who ordered
and organized it. He has no doubt about the complicity of Putin's
police agencies: "The question isn't whether the security services
were involved, but what role they played—and which security services they were."[40]

Vladimir Kara-Murza

Nemtsov could have been killed in a number of other, less blatant
ways than a shooting so close to the Kremlin. The murder had the
clear purpose of intimidating democratic oppositionist. As Garry
Kasparov, now in exile in the United States, observed, the crime sent
"a chilling signal to everybody; it spread fear and terror." But
Nemtsov's allies were not to be deterred. The FSB raided Nemtsov's
apartment immediately after the murder and took away his computer,
along with his research notes for his planned report on Russian military aggression in Ukraine. Olga Shorina, who had been Nemtsov's
closest aide for many years, assured me, when I spoke with her on the
telephone in Moscow a few days after the murder, that she and her
colleagues had copies of all of Nemtsov's research, and despite his
death they published "Putin.War."[41] Without the imposing presence of
Nemtsov, their efforts lost a great deal of momentum, but they've per-
severed nonetheless.

One of Nemtsov's close collaborators and a leading member of
PARNAS, the People's Freedom Party, was Vladimir Kara-Murza,
who has played a key part in the effort to continue what Nemtsov had
been striving for—exposing the facts about the Putin regime. Educated at Cambridge University, Kara-Murza became a journalist and
author, while at the same time engaging in politics. In 2001, at only
twenty, he joined the Union of Right Forces and in 2003 ran unsuc-

cessfully for the State Duma. He is the coordinator of Open Russia, a democratic initiative established and funded by the exiled Russian tycoon Mikhail Khodorkovsky (released from prison by Putin in late 2013 and residing now in Switzerland), and a regular contributor to the journal *World Affairs*.

Like his mentor Nemtsov, Kara-Murza was a forceful advocate for the U.S. Magnitsky Law. In July 2012, he testified about the proposed law before the Human Rights Commission of the U.S. Congress, describing it as "a pro-Russian bill which provides a much-needed measure of accountability for those who continue to violate the rights and freedoms of Russian citizens. . . . The Kremlin's reaction to this [proposed] legislation shows that it hits them precisely where it hurts."[42] In late April 2015, Kara-Murza appeared before the U.S. Congress with another member of his opposition party, Mikhail Kasyanov. They presented a list of eight names of Russian television journalists who had created an atmosphere of "hate, intolerance, and violence" against Nemtsov in the months that led up to his murder and urged congressmen to add these names to the Russian persons denied visas to enter the United States under the Magnitsky Law.[43]

A few weeks later, on May 26, 2015, Kara-Murza collapsed at his office in Moscow with an undiagnosed illness. He was taken to the hospital and lapsed into a coma, which lasted over a week. His wife wanted him evacuated for treatment abroad, but he was too ill to be transferred. All his body systems shut down, and doctors gave him only a 5 percent chance of living. Miraculously, Kara-Murza survived, but not without residual complications. It was months before he could return to work. He was understandably cautious in explaining the cause of his mysterious illness, determined by doctors to be poisoning by an unknown substance. He said only that "it was not an accident" and that it was connected to his opposition activities in Russia. Later, in December 2016, Kara-Murza requested the Russian Investigative Committee to initiate a criminal case on his attempted murder, but nothing came of it.[44]

Not to be deterred, Kara-Murza continued his political campaigning as a leader of PARNAS and his work for Open Russia. In late 2016, he traveled throughout Russia promoting a film he had made in honor of Nemtsov, which was sponsored by the Khodorkovsky Foundation. The film, *Nemtsov,* was screened in several major cities. In early January 2017, Kara-Murza submitted a letter to the U.S. Senate Foreign Relations Committee, which was conducting hearings on the confirmation of Rex Tillerson as secretary of state. The letter reported that violence against opposition figures and journalists in Russia was an increasing phenomenon and seemed to be a warning about Tillerson's cozy relationship, as past CEO of ExonMobil, with members of the Kremlin elite, in particular Rosneft chairman Igor Sechin. The Kremlin, which favored the candidacy of Tillerson (he had said that he thought sanctions against Russia were ineffective) cannot have been happy about Kara-Murza's letter.[45]

Less than a month later, on February 2, 2017, Kara-Murza was hospitalized again because of poisoning, while in Moscow. His symptoms were identical to those of the prior incident, and he had to be put into a medically induced coma for almost a week. The White House had no comment on the poisoning. Indeed, on February 5, while Kara-Murza was at death's door, Trump insisted to Fox News host Bill O'Reilly that he respected Putin and when reminded by O'Reilly that Putin was a killer, responded: "We've got a lot of killers. What, you think our country's so innocent? You think our country's so innocent?"[46]

By contrast, the poisoning triggered a strong response from U.S. lawmakers, including from Senate Republican John McCain, who said on the Senate floor on February 7 that Vladimir Kara-Murza had been poisoned because "he kept faith with his ideals in confrontation with a cruel and dangerous autocracy." In a pointed rebuff to Trump, McCain had this to say: "Vladimir knew that Putin is a killer, and that he might very well be the next target. Vladimir knew there was no moral equivalence between the United States and Putin's Russia. And anyone who would make such a suggestion maligns the character of our great nation and does a disservice to all those whose blood is on Putin's hands."[47]

Kara-Murza's wife, Evgeniia, also made her views known. In an exclusive interview with ABC News the day after Trump made his comments to O'Reilly, she had this advice for the U.S. president: "[Trump] must know that such people as Vladimir Putin are not friends. And they cannot be dealt with on friendly terms."[48] Kara-Murza, thankfully, has survived this second attempt on his life, but his horrifying experience apparently did not convince Trump that he should give up his hope of a close alliance with the Russian leader.

Chechen president Ramzan Kadyrov with Putin.

(Photograph courtesy of ALEXEI NIKOLSKY/AFP/Getty Images)

13

KADYROV, PUTIN, AND POWER IN THE KREMLIN

The impunity and omnipotence of Ramzan Kadyrov depends on the support of . . . Putin. As long as Putin supports him, nobody will touch a hair on Kadyrov's head, even if he kills us all.

—**Lyudmila Alexeyeva, human-rights activist and head of the Moscow Helsinki Group**

Cops are afraid of the prosecutors, prosecutors are afraid of the Investigative Committee, the Investigative Committee is afraid of the FSB, the FSB is afraid of Kadyrov, Kadyrov is afraid of Putin, and Putin is afraid of everybody.

—**Opposition democrat Roman Dobrokhotov on Twitter, August 2016**

Ramzan Kadyrov, the president of Chechnya since 2007, has figured consistently in this narrative because of the pivotal role he has played in ensuring Putin's hold on power. As one Russia expert expressed it, "It's important to remember that the 'Chechen Scenario' has been a common theme throughout Putin's rule—in fact, he *owes* his rule to it."[1] Kadyrov has run Chechnya as his own little country, although it is a part of Russia, terrorizing its citizens with violence, kidnappings, and extrajudicial killings, carried out on his behalf by the notorious "Kadyrovtsy." All this is supported by the Kremlin, which needs to keep rebellious Chechens in check. At the same time, Kadyrov has acted as Putin's "hatchet man" in getting rid of the Russian president's troublesome critics.

Kadyrov had direct encounters with some of the victims of the political murders I have discussed. It was Anna Politkovskaya, after her terrifying face-to-face meeting with him at his residence outside Grozny in the summer of 2004, who first labeled Kadyrov "the Kremlin's Chechen dragon."[2] Natalia Estemirova, as noted, had a similar frightening experience with Kadyrov not long before she was gunned down in Chechnya in 2009. And Boris Nemtsov had also been directly threatened by Kadyrov. Nemtsov was in Chechnya in December 2002 to attend a congress of Chechen people, presided over by Ramzan's father, Akhmat Kadyrov, at the time acting head of the administration of Chechnya. The discussion centered around the future political structure of Chechnya, with a strong presidency being advocated by most of those present. Nemtsov spoke out against the idea and suggested instead a more representative form of government. As he was leaving the congress hall, he was confronted by the younger Kadyrov, his eyes blazing, who told Nemtsov that he deserved to be killed for what he had said. Nemtsov recalled: "I can't say that I was frightened, because the Chechens who were around him started to say that Ramzan was joking. But in his eyes I saw that it was no joke. In his eyes I saw hatred."[3]

Given that the killers in the cases described in this book were often Chechens who were either subordinate to Kadyrov or closely connected with him, it is highly likely that Kadyrov had a role in the murders. But what about Putin? As mentioned earlier, former Chechen government leader Akhmed Zakaev insists that Kadyrov would not have embarked on his criminal ventures without the approval of Putin. But Kadyrov, as demonstrated again and again, is a loose cannon. Is Putin not playing a dangerous game in outsourcing murders to a man who, by most accounts, is an unpredictable psychopath?

Kadyrov's Rise to Power in Chechnya

Both Akhmat Kadyrov and his son Ramzan fought on the side of Chechen rebels against Russia during the first Chechen war in 1994–96. But they switched their allegiance to the Kremlin after Russian troops invaded Chechnya in the autumn of 1999. As a reward, newly elected Russian president Putin appointed the senior Kadyrov to be the leader of Chechnya in 2000. Ramzan, then in his mid-twenties, became head of his father's security forces, which numbered around a thousand men. This force would become the stronghold for the younger Kadyrov's rise to power, although he was not able to prevent enemies of his father from assassinating him in May 2004. The only thing that kept Ramzan from succeeding his father at that time was his age. He was not eligible to run for the presidency of Chechnya until he reached thirty, so the Chechen Minister of the Interior, Alu Alkhanov, supported, of course, by Russian federal authorities, was "elected" president in August 2004.

Presumably pressured by Moscow, Alkhanov allowed Kadyrov's personal guard corps to be officially integrated into his government structure, becoming a legal armed unit, and in May 2006 he appointed Ramzan his prime minister. This power-sharing did not work well and ended up in armed confrontations between security forces loyal to Alkhanov and those loyal to Kadyrov. Kadyrov emerged the winner. In early 2007, Putin accepted Alkhanov's resignation and appointed Kadyrov acting Chechen president. A month later, Kadyrov was officially elected to that office. Thus began the complex alliance between Vladimir Putin and Ramzan Kadyrov that would carry them through a decade of mutual dictatorships over their people.

Of course, Kadyrov's fiefdom, with a population of only 1.4 million, is small, and he is dependent on the Kremlin's constant flow of money to finance his government. But he rules Chechnya with an iron hand. According to a report by Ilya Yashin, a former ally of Nemtsov and a leader of the opposition party Parnas, "Ramzan Kadyrov enjoys practically unlimited authority in the Republic of Chechnya. The parliament, the media, and the judicial system are all controlled by the Chechen leader. Kadyrov has said that Vladimir Putin is the only factor limiting his personal authority in the republic: 'I am Putin's man. His word is law for me. How can one not worship him? Putin is a gift from God.'"[4] As political commentator Dmitry Oreshkin points out: "This is an 'inside out empire,' a case in which it is not the large country that dictates its own interests but, on the contrary, it is a small colony that holds its parent country by the throat and wheedles as much money out of it as it needs."[5]

Kadyrov's Death Squads

Even before he became Chechnya's president, Kadyrov employed killers to take out his enemies, with complete impunity. The first such attack was on November 18, 2006, when Movladi Baisarov was gunned down on Leninskii Prospect, in the heart of Moscow. Baisarov had headed the senior Kadyrov's security service but then formed his own military unit in Chechnya, subordinate to the Russian FSB, after Akhmat's assassination. Under pressure from Ramzan Kadyrov's forces, Baisarov fled to Moscow, where he voiced public criticism of Kadyrov as a "khan" with "Asiatic habits" and became Kadyrov's avowed enemy.

In response to the killing, State Duma deputy Sergei Mitrokhin, a member of the liberal Yabloko party, told *Kommersant*: I don't understand how the Chechen [special forces] could act on the territory of Moscow—couldn't the

Moscow GUVD [Internal police] [or] FSB deal with it themselves? The suspicion arises that Kadyrov put out a contract
on Baisarov and that the federal authorities gave permission
for it to be carried out. The country's leadership must be
responsible for who in the country carries out operational
activities, who is allowed to carry out the death penalty in
Russia, and who Ramzan will dispose of next.[6]

This assassination was followed in September 2008 by the
murder, also on the streets of Moscow, of Ruslan Iamadaev, a State
Duma deputy from Chechnya. Iamadaev was one of three brothers
who were part of a powerful and rich Chechen clan that opposed
Kadyrov. The Iamadaevs had fought on the side of Chechen rebels
during the first Chechen war, but then, like Kadyrov and his father,
had switched to the side of the Kremlin. Ruslan, forty-seven, was shot
to death by an unknown assailant as he sat in his car during rush-
hour traffic after a visit to the Kremlin. In April 2009, a Moscow court
convicted two Chechen natives of committing the murder.

A few months later, in January 2009, Imar Israilov, a former member of Kadyrov's security guard living in exile in Vienna, was gunned
down there. Austrian police, after conducting an intensive investigation, concluded that Kadyrov and his top aide, Shaa Turlaev, were
behind the murder. A representative of Human Rights Watch said:
"The conclusions reached by the Austrian Prosecutor's Office about
Ramzan Kadyrov . . . should prompt the Russian government to finally
take the necessary steps to restore the rule of law in Chechnya."[7]

The Kadyrov forces went after another of the Iamadaev brothers,
Sulim, in March 2009, this time in Dubai. Sulim had been the commander of the pro-Moscow Vostok Division in Chechnya before flee-
ing to Dubai because of threats from the Kadyrov clan. He was shot
to death in his car in an underground garage. The Dubai government
accused Kadyrov's cousin, Adam Delimkhanov, a member of Russia's

parliament, of organizing the murder. They requested his extradition, to no avail.

In July 2009, Isa Iamadaev was the victim of an attempt on his life in Moscow, believed to have been organized by Kadyrov. He subsequently returned to Chechnya and made peace with Kadyrov. Months later, in November 2009, Viskan Abdurakhmanov, an avowed enemy of Kadyrov, was found dead on the street in Baku, Azerbaijan. Abdurakhmanov had been raising support from the Chechen diaspora in Turkey and the Near East for rebels opposed to Kadyrov's rule.

Kadyrov as Supreme Ruler

In a February 2016 profile of Kadyrov for *The New Yorker*, Joshua Yaffa observed that the Chechen leader "is a skillful and popular politician, one of the few in modern Russia, where nearly all officials tend to be charmless functionaries." He went on to say that while Kadyrov "can be brutal and severe . . . he can also appear genuine, even sensitive—another rarity in Putin-era politics." Yaffa favorably quoted Kadyrov's adviser, the journalist Timur Aliyev, as saying: "I once believed in this image of him [Kadyrov] as a brutal guy. But then I got a chance to meet him. . . . He thinks of himself not just as the head of the Chechen republic but as a person who looks after the well-being of each individual."[8]

These observations hardly square with those of human-rights activists in Chechnya or the Chechens who have suffered as a result of family members abducted and killed, or their houses burned down in retaliation for suspected opposition to Kadyrov. By Russian accounts, including a documentary produced by Mikhail Khodorkovsky's Open Russia Foundation and the report by Yashin, Kadyrov has created a huge personal army, which may number up to eighty thousand men and which he has exclusive control over, despite the fact that his republic is part of the Russian Federation. The members of his army, which includes the Sever Battalion that was implicated in

Nemtsov's murder, behave with complete impunity, terrorizing the civilian population.[9]

The human-rights group Memorial, in a 2016 report, presented a similar picture, noting that "'a state within a state' has essentially been created in the Chechen Republic, first during the long years of struggle against separatists, and then during the fight against the terrorist underground using methods of state terror. The cure turned out to be worse than the disease." Memorial went on to point out that "Chechnya's relative stability is only maintained by the constant, brutal, blatant use of force. The existence on the territory of our country of an enclave where a totalitarian regime has been established represents a serious danger for the future of the rule of law and the protection of the rights of all citizens in Russia."[10]

Kadyrov is not only the political leader of Chechnya, but also the religious leader, the "amir," of the republic, who deems it his duty to interfere in all spiritual matters of its citizens. In his television appearances, for example, he often issues instructions on how his subjects are to dress: "I tell you that a woman who goes out in black clothes, with a covered chin . . . her husband should know that we will take this woman away and look her over . . . we will force her to take off her clothes and trousers." (Such dress, in Kadyrov's view, is a sign of extremism and does not conform with Sharia law.) His security forces and clerics carry out raids on buses and cars, detaining young men whose appearances do not conform to Kadyrov's take on the dictates of Islam. Their relatives are not informed of their whereabouts, even as they are held captive for several days for "guided discussions."[11]

Among the most chilling accounts of the situation in Chechnya is a report issued by Human Rights Watch in August 2016.[12] This in-depth study, written by Tanya Lokshina, describes a new, comprehensive crackdown on residents of Chechnya who have manifested dissatisfaction with the Chechen leadership, as well as on human-rights defenders, journalists, and lawyers. Based on forty-three interviews, the report documents case upon case of abduction, torture, public humiliation, and murder by Kadyrov forces. On three occasions since 2014, the offices of the Joint Mobile Group of Human Rights Defenders in Chechnya (JMG), the sole such organization to remain in the republic, were ransacked or burned. The group was forced to withdraw from Chechnya in 2016. In March 2016, a group of Russian and foreign journalists traveling in a mini-van from Ingushetia to Chechnya was attacked by masked men, dragged out of the van, and beaten severely. The attackers then set the van on fire. Putin's press office condemned the attack and promised to investigate, but nothing came of it.

More recently, in March 2017, Kadyrov's forces began a targeted campaign against gay men in Chechnya, where homosexuality is condemned. According to *Novaia gazeta*, "the command was given for a 'prophylactic sweep' and it went as far as real murders." Tanya Lokshina noted that gay men who had been abducted "returned to their families barely alive from beatings."[13] The official line in Chechnya is that gays don't exist there, so there is no persecution. During a televised appearance with Putin in mid-April 2017, Kadyrov called the reports about a campaign against gays "libelous." The Kremlin has backed him up. Kremlin spokesman Dmitrii Peskov told journalists that there was no evidence of arrests of gays in Chechnya. This should come as no surprise, given the Kremlin's own openly anti-gay policies and Putin's apparent personal hostility toward gays.[14]

Meanwhile, Kadyrov has long assured Putin that his forces are prepared to carry out Putin's orders anywhere, at any time. In late December 2014, he called thousands of Chechen Interior Ministry troops to a sports stadium in Grozny, making a pledge that they would be at the command of the Russian president: "We are ready to pick any point in the world and to move to where our president will tell us. . . . We will fulfill his orders 100 percent."[15]

As one analyst pointed out, Boris Nemtsov, in a "chillingly prescient" post on Facebook, speculated on the meaning of this massive rally: "I can't understand what Putin is expecting when 20,000 of Kadyrov's fighters gather in a stadium in Grozny. Kadyrov said his fighters are ready to defend the regime and execute any order from the Kremlin. I believe this. So where will Kadyrov's 20,000 fighters go? What will be required of them? How should we behave? When will they arrive in Moscow?" Nemtsov would be gunned down in just two months.[16]

The Money Factor

The Kremlin regularly funnels vast sums of money into Chechnya, where unemployment is close to 20 percent, but most of it goes into Kadyrov's coffers. According to one estimate, Moscow allocates around fifty-nine billion rubles (around one billion dollars) annually to Chechnya in grants and subsidies.[17] The much-vaunted "Grozny City," established by the Kadyrov government, features five skyscrapers, but four of them remain empty. The rest of Grozny is in a sorry state. According to the Open Russia film about Kadyrov:

> The myth of the restoration of Chechnya is exactly that—a myth. The public face of a restored Grozny, endlessly shown by federal channels, is in fact only one street in Grozny, Putin Avenue. The rest of Chechnya still lies in ruins—there are traces of shells and bullets on the walls of buildings. After a few days in Chechnya, we can confidently say that billions of federal aid money has been spent on a Potemkin village, and on Ramzan Kadyrov's Arab sheikh lifestyle. Ordinary residents have seen nothing of this aid.[18]

In addition to federal funds, Kadyrov has another source of income—the Akhmat Kadyrov Foundation, named after Ramzan's father. Chechens are required to pay monthly fees to the foundation, based on their earnings. According to Open Russia experts, the fees yield about three to four billion rubles a month, a truly staggering amount to take from ordinary Chechens.[19] The alleged purpose of the foundation is to carry out social projects and provide assistance to citizens who cannot make ends meet. But in fact most of it goes to Kadyrov himself, who lives a lavish lifestyle befitting a king. He has a fleet of sports cars, including a Lamborghini and a Ferrari, estimated to be worth over three million dollars. He lives in a 260,000-square-meter palace in his native village, Tsentaroi. According to one journalist: "In 2004, he [Kadyrov] had a house in Tsentaroi. Then it became a palace. And in 2014 this had become a building of incredible size with private quarters for Putin."[20]

Kadyrov's residence even has its own private zoo, with pumas, tigers, and panthers. And Kadyrov owns more than a hundred race horses. In the words of Ilya Yashin: "It is worth mentioning that the discrepancy between official income and actual living standards is a typical phenomenon for Russian officials. Kadyrov's example, however, cannot be compared to that of any [other] governor or minister. No other representative of the Russian authorities allows himself to make such an ostentatious display of his luxurious lifestyle and to throw money around in public."[21]

Kadyrov has a penchant for adulation. He paid a reported two million dollars to Mike Tyson for his attendance at a boxing tournament in Gudermes (eighteen miles east of Grozny) in September 2005. And for his thirty-fifth birthday in October 2011, Kadyrov paid American actress Hilary Swank an undisclosed sum to be among those celebrating at an elaborate ceremony in his honor. This prompted Akhmed Zakaev to send Swank a letter, pointing out that "Russia unleashed two terrible wars on the Chechen soil that resulted in the deaths of 250,000 people, including 40,000 children. The Russian regime of terror continues to reign in Chechnya under Kadyrov's leadership."[22]

Kadyrov's Personality Cult

In April 2016, during the nationwide television program "Direct Line to Vladimir Putin," a video message appeared from a Chechen villager in which he complained that local officials were pocketing money from federal funds designated to restore housing destroyed during the war and to pay teachers. In short order, the villager, Ramzan Dzhalaidinov, received threats against his life and was forced to flee to Dagestan. A few weeks later, armed security officers broke into his home in Chechnya, abducted his wife and children, and set the premises on fire. Shortly thereafter, Dzhalaidinov appeared on Grozny television and said: "I am very ashamed of myself, and I apologize to Ramzan Kadyrov for the unfounded accusations." He also thanked Kadyrov for the reconstruction of houses in his district, which he claimed had been completely rebuilt.[23]

As Tanya Lokshina has pointed out:

Public humiliation forms part of Kadyrov's latest strategy to eradicate dissent in the republic. For close to a decade, the young leader has been exercising tyrannical rule over Chechnya. *A free press no longer exists,* and the few journalists from independent Russian and foreign outlets reporting on ongoing abuses inside the republic find themselves at great risk of harassment, arbitrary detentions, and even violent attacks by security officials and their proxies. But the worst punishment is reserved for Chechens themselves. Those who dare to post critical comments online are increasingly being tracked down and penalized.[24]

It is difficult to judge Kadyrov's popular support, because he has forbidden any political opposition. In his words: "We have no opposition, which serves only to undermine [state] authority. I will not allow [political opponents] to play with the people."[25] Because there are no alternatives, close to 100 percent of the votes go to the pro-Kremlin United Russia Party in elections at all levels. Kadyrov has built up an extensive personality cult, which he fosters through the state-controlled Grozny television and radio, the main sources of news for Chechens. He also uses social media as a tool for political control, firing off a constant stream of messages on Instagram, either bragging about himself or threatening his perceived enemies. In addition, Kadyrov maintains accounts on Facebook, Twitter, and VKontakte. His total number of followers on these different accounts was estimated by the Chechen Ministry for Press and Information in 2015 to be over two million.[26]

In the autumn of 2016, Kadyrov began starring in a reality TV show called *The Team,* which is similar to Donald Trump's *Apprentice.* As *The New York Times* observed: "Mr. Kadyrov . . . is clearly getting a hug from the Kremlin, with state-run television running what amounts to a weekly infomercial. . . . The show appears aimed at persuading more investors and Russian tourists to open their wallets in Chechnya so that Moscow will not have to. . . . The show may also be an attempt to groom Mr. Kadyrov for a national [i.e., Russian] role."[27]

Threats to Russia's Opposition

In January 2016, the leader of Chechen's parliament, Magomed Daudov, posted on Instagram a photograph of Kadyrov straining to hold a leash on his fierce-looking German shepherd, named Tarzan. The accompanying message said that the dog was "itching to sink its teeth" into certain prominent Russian opposition figures, and gave them nicknames that matched breeds of dogs.[28] Just days later, Kadyrov himself posted a video on Instagram. It showed two leaders of the opposition party Parnas, Mikhail Kasyanov and Vladimir Kara-Murza, in a sniper's crosshairs, stating "whoever doesn't get it will get it." (The video had over 16,000 "likes.") Aleksei Navalny had this reaction: "There is no longer any doubt that all such statements in recent weeks and specifically this one were approved by Putin and the Kremlin, and quite probably were inspired by them too."[29]

Responding to the uproar over the Kadyrov video, Putin's press secretary, Dmitrii Peskov, said that the Kremlin did not follow Instagram but that "we will watch this video and see what it is all about."[30] But in the meantime, on January 18, 2016, Kadyrov had come forth with a piece in the Russian government-sponsored newspaper *Izvestiia*, just days before the first anniversary of Nemtsov's murder.[31] His writing was reminiscent of the jargon of the Stalin era. The headline was "Jackals Will Be Punished According to the Law of the Russian Federation." It was a scathing denunciation of those who spoke out against Putin.

Kadyrov threatened oppositionists who had "sold their souls to the Western devil." He went on: "The non-systemic opposition and its supporters can be considered a mass psychosis. I can help them with their clinical problem. I promise that I will not spare injections [in a psychiatric hospital]. We will give them double the prescribed dose." (This presumably was a reference to the way the Kremlin had dealt with dissidents in the Soviet era.) But what was most significant about the ravings of Kadyrov was what he said in the end: "If these dogs have defenders in their own country, well, the Russian people have their own defender, the president of our country, Vladimir Putin, and I am ready to fulfill his orders, no matter how complex." A thinly veiled statement that Kadyrov would continue to use Chechen thugs to murder dissidents on Putin's behalf.

American journalist Anna Nemtsova (no relation to Boris Nemtsov), who has interviewed Kadyrov several times, wrote that "the Chechen leader, once a Putin favorite, is embarrassing the Kremlin by threatening everyone."[32] But it is more likely that Kadyrov is serving the Kremlin's purposes by intimidating Russian oppositionists and journalists on its behalf. As one observer noted, "In many ways, Kadyrov is the Putin regime's collective id. He manifests its basic instinct. Its intrinsic aggression. Its deepest, darkest desires."[33]

Kadyrov has been outspoken about other matters, saying what the Kremlin would like to say but cannot. He initially distanced himself from the Tsarnaev brothers, insisting that they never lived in Chechnya and that nobody in the republic knew them. He noted that "Tamerlan and Dzhokhar are the worst 'shaitans' [devils]. That is why I do not defend them and have no intention of saying a word of support for them."[34] But after the guilty verdict against Dzhokhar was announced on May 15, 2015, Kadyrov denounced his death sentence. He wrote on Instagram:

> No one was surprised by this news. The American security services, which were suspected of involvement in the Boston tragedy, needed a victim. They offered up Tsarnaev as a victim. . . . Tamerlan Tsarnaev was killed under strange circumstances. Ibragim Todashev [the friend of Tamerlan] was shot dead at the time he was being questioned. Dzhokhar Tsarnaev alone ended up behind bars. I do not believe that the Tsarnaevs carried out this terrorist attack—if they did carry it out—without the U.S. security services' knowledge.[35]

Kadyrov had also praised the prime suspect in the Nemtsov murder, Zaur Dadaev, as "a real soldier and patriot" on Instagram shortly after Nemtsov was killed.[36]

Kadyrov's Future

In a lengthy October 2016 report for *Novaia gazeta*, Elena Milashina, who has spent a lot of time in Chechnya despite the tremendous danger there for journalists, speculated that the ten-year "contract" between Kadyrov and Putin has expired. Milashina observed that, with terrorism now at an all-time low in the republic, the Kremlin is rethinking its unconditional support for Kadyrov, whose dictatorial methods threaten to destabilize the situation and inflame discontent elsewhere in the North Caucasus. In the words of Milashina:

> The need for revising the old contract, which has exhausted itself (the terrorist underground has been practically destroyed, and the towns and villages of Chechnya, still terribly poor, have been rebuilt), has begun to be recognized in Moscow. But the signals that the Kremlin was sending, after many years of 'hurrah, Kadyrov,' are mixed. On the one hand, Putin repeatedly pulls Ramzan down. On the other, his criticism is always followed by a 'consolation prize,' in the form of high state honors designed to soften the blow to the ego of the 'faithful foot soldier.'[37]

As Milashina noted, this dynamic was illustrated when there was a "crisis of confidence" between Kadyrov and Putin after the Nemtsov murder. This crisis played out for a year after the killing, with Kadyrov announcing in February 2016 that he would not seek re-election for a third term as Chechen president: "My time has passed." But the announcement was followed by an outpouring of support from thousands of Chechen citizens (doubtless orchestrated by Kadyrov and his circle). In rally after rally, the people said "do not leave us, our dear father." Responding to the pressure, Putin received Kadyrov in the Kremlin and announced in late March 2016 that he was appointing him acting president (his term had been due to expire on April 5) until the September presidential elections in Chechnya. But Putin added a caveat: "You and all future leaders of the republic must do everything to comply with Russian laws in all spheres of life, and I want to stress, in all spheres of our lives."[38]

Kadyrov was recalcitrant. In May, he suddenly demanded that the president of the Chechen Supreme Court, who was appointed by

Moscow, resign. Three other Supreme Court judges were detained by Chechen law-enforcement authorities and forced to sign letters of resignation. Moscow was totally unprepared for Kadyrov's latest move. But in response, Putin's press secretary, Dmitrii Peskov, gave a signal of capitulation. The resignations, he claimed, were completely voluntary and not coerced.[39]

During the summer of 2016, Kadyrov had visits from several high-ranking Russian officials, including vice-premier Igor Shuvalov, who is responsible for the economic affairs of the Russian government. On August 25, Kadyrov had a late-night meeting in the Kremlin with Putin, who renewed his blessing for Kadyrov's leadership of Chechnya. Kadyrov, for his part, thanked Putin for his "constant attention to the republic and [his] help and support in resolving the most difficult, severe, and relevant issues." Significantly, during his visit to Moscow, Kadyrov also met with Aleksandr Bastrykin, who has led the investigation of the Nemtsov murder. Kadyrov's refusal to allow investigators to interrogate Ruslan Geremeev, the presumed organizer of the crime, did not prevent him from earning Bastrykin's praise for his accomplishments in Chechnya. Indeed, Bastrykin gave Kadyrov two presents—a medal for "vigilance and bravery" and a general's dagger.[40]

Kadyrov was re-elected Chechen president with a resounding 98 percent of the vote on September 18, 2016. And some Russia experts see Kadyrov as presiding over Chechnya for the long haul. In the words of Catherine Fitzpatrick, who follows Kadyrov closely: "Moscow political and military leaders cannot hope to compete with ethnic ties and a leader who remembers the birthdays of all the police chiefs he has put in power. They would have to remove not just Kadyrov, but his extended family and all of his loyal men. And he personally, as well as all his lieutenants, are buff and ready for combat."[41] *The New York Times* even went so far as to suggest that Kadyrov is being groomed for the Russian presidency: "Mr. Putin has no

anointed heir . . . and some imagine that if a succession proves chaotic, Mr. Kadyrov could swoop in with his 20,000-strong Praetorian
Guard and claim to impose order for the good of all Russia."[42]

But the inherent instability of Kadyrov's rule should not be underestimated. There was an assassination attempt on Kadyrov by
disgruntled members of his extended clan in the early summer of
2016. Kadyrov even acknowledged the attempt during a televised news
conference that September. And, according to Ekaterina Sokrianskaia
of the International Crisis Group, attacks against Kadyrov forces by
Islamic insurgents are again on the rise, with combined casualties on
both sides rising a dramatic 43 percent in 2016. Also, Kadyrov's
brutal methods against his people—including, recently, his anti-gay
campaign—are arousing an outcry in the West that the Kremlin is
finding difficult to ignore. As Sokrainskaia describes the situation:
"If Mr. Putin continues to give the Kremlin's tacit approval to
Mr. Kadyrov's repressions, he is only storing up trouble for the
Russian Federation. The Chechen conflict has not been resolved but
merely contained by brute force and a personal bond between the
two leaders. In the long run, such an unstable situation makes a
deadly new conflict in Chechnya almost inevitable."[43]

Power Politics

Against this backdrop, the changes that Putin instituted in the Russian law-enforcement agencies in April 2016 take on added significance. Viktor Zolotov, who was in charge of the MVD Internal
Troops at the time of the Nemtsov murder and who has deep connections with both Putin and Kadyrov, is now Putin's top security
chief as head of the new National Guard. The apparent efforts of the
FSB to bring Kadyrov to heel have been successfully thwarted by Putin, for the time-being at least. Both Zolotov and Kadyrov will be
essential allies to Putin in the event that there is dissatisfaction with
the Russian president among the political elite, or unrest among the

general population, as there was in 2011 and 2012 and again in the spring of 2017, when Russians by the thousands took to the streets in some eighty cities in response to a call by Aleksei Navalny to protest against widespread government corruption.

That Putin dismissed his longtime ally Sergei Ivanov from his post as head of the Presidential Administration in August 2016 suggests that the Russian president is forming new alliances. Ivanov, who shares a background in the KGB with Putin, was viewed as the most powerful member of Putin's inner circle, aside from Igor Sechin. From 2001 to 2007, he had been Russian Minister of Defense, and after that a first deputy prime minister, until he became Putin's chief of staff in 2011. Ivanov, who is sixty-three, will retain his seat on the National Security Council but will play only a minor role in Putin's government as a special envoy for transportation and the environment.

Ivanov's replacement is Anton Vaino, forty-four, a former diplomat who later served as head of protocol for Putin. (Said to be an "absolute favorite" of Putin, Vaino is seen in one photograph carrying an umbrella over him.) Political scientist Tatyana Stanovaya observed that "Putin is gravitating toward those who serve him, and distancing himself from those who, by virtue of their resources, attempt to rule alongside Putin. He does not need advice, he needs people who will carry out his orders with as little fuss as possible."[44]

While Putin appears to be taking an assertive stance in making these changes within his ruling circle, the problem of corruption could undermine public confidence in his leadership as the 2018 presidential elections loom on the horizon. In November 2016, the former first deputy chairman of the Russian Central Bank (the post Andrei Kozlov held when he was murdered), Aleksei Uliukaev, was arrested by the FSB on charges of soliciting a $2 million bribe in exchange for approving, apparently with great reluctance, the purchase of 50 percent of the shares of the state energy company Bashneft by the Russian oil giant Rosneft. The case against Uliukaev, Putin's minister of eco-

nomic development and a reputed reformer who encouraged privatization of state assets, was initiated by Bastrykin's Investigative
Committee. The arrest created shock waves in Russia, because it was
the first to be directed at a current member of Putin's administration.[45] It was widely reported that Igor Sechin was behind the arrest
and had set up Uliukaev in a sting operation. According to a source
that follows the Russian energy sector, "Sechin's role in the case bolstered his reputation inside the ruling elite as a feared Kremlin en-
forcer who wields an increasing amount of power within a system
built up by Russian President Vladimir Putin."[46]

Whether or not Uliukaev is ultimately found guilty, his case, in
highlighting corruption within the ruling elite, could damage Putin,
especially given that his government openly stated not ago that it will
not be able to increase pensions to adjust to inflation. Prime Minister
Dmitrii Medvedev explained cheerily to a pensioner in Crimea in August 2016: "There just isn't any money now. You hang in there."[47] Ironically, Medvedev himself has now become the target of corruption
allegations. In early March 2017 Aleksei Navalny's Anti-Corruption
Foundation released a video showing that Medvedev has amassed
an empire of assets (including luxurious country estates, vineyards
and yachts) through deals concealed by a web of false charities.[48]
The video, watched on YouTube by an estimated 11 million viewers
in the first three weeks, was what inspired mass street protests on
March 26.

Navalny was among the more than 1,000 people in Moscow who
were detained during the protests. He was released after a fifteen-day
stint in jail, but has faced more obstacles. In early May an assailant
threw poisonous green dye in his face, causing serious damage to one
eye and forcing Navalny to go abroad for treatment. Navalny is not to
be deterred and has continued to insist that he will run for the Russian
presidency in 2018, despite the legal challenges to his candidacy. (He
was found guilty of corruption in February 2017 and given a five-year

suspended sentence. Though the charges were blatantly bogus, they apparently disqualify him by law from running.)

Even if he does not run, Navalny's growing public prominence, his obvious charisma and his ability to draw impressive crowds in opposition to the regime pose a huge threat to the Kremlin. And Putin and his colleagues are obviously struggling to decide how to respond. When asked recently by a British journalist how he could be doing what he is doing and still be alive, Navalny said this: "'Why haven't they killed you, why haven't they locked you up?' People are always asking me this. Look, I have no answer to that question. I suppose the most likely is that they didn't manage to lock me up when they could have done easily, and then after a certain point it became more difficult."[49] The tragic fate of other Kremlin opponents cannot be far from Navalny's mind, but he apparently chooses to focus on one goal—the downfall of the Putin regime.

AFTERWORD

Putin is a serial killer. . . . Western leaders should be aware that when they shake hands with Putin, they shake hands with a murderer.

—Leonid Martynyuk, Russian filmmaker and opposition democrat, speaking at the National Endowment for Democracy, October 2016

Before he took office Donald Trump vowed that during his presidency America's relations with Russia would improve and he and President Putin would become good friends. Now that Trump and his advisers must grapple with the reality of Russia pursuing its aggressive political and military agenda abroad, that goal probably seems challinging. The Kremlin has continued to insist that its 2014 invasion and occupation of Crimea was legitimate because Crimea historically belonged to Russia. Russia has maintained its military presence in Eastern Ukraine, supporting Ukrainian separatists and pursuing efforts to destabilize the government in Kiev. Moscow persists in backing the brutal regime of Bashar al-Assad in Syria, where casualties mount daily as a result of constant missile fire by both Assad and Russian forces, and the humanitarian crisis has reached epic proportions. In Afghanistan, Russia has been providing military aid to the Taliban, claiming the threat from ISIS there legitimizes its collusion with a group that is intent on overthrowing the U.S.-backed government. Also, in defiance of a 1987 treaty between Russia and the United States that bans testing of land-based intermediate-range missiles, Russia has recently deployed a new cruise missile, which could increase threats to NATO member and alter the strategic balance significantly.[1]

These developments, at the very least, should have dampened Trump's expectations that Putin is a man he and his western allies can do business with. To be sure, a warming of relations between Washington and Moscow would, theoretically, be useful in furthering the West's agenda. But the Trump administration faces a major obstacle in this regard—the fact that the Kremlin's political legitimacy is largely based on its ability to stir up fear of external enemies among its people. Portraying the West as a hostile force that is bent on undermining Russia's interests is a key element of Kremlin policy. Moreover, Putin and his colleagues, operating in a political vacuum with little input from those they govern, seem to believe what they say about the threat to Russia from the West.

Authoritarian states make for difficult negotiating partners, and Putin, for the moment, seems firmly entrenched in power, despite the courageous efforts of those who oppose him, including Aleksei Navalny, Vladimir Kara-Murza and other democratic activists and journalists. Putin's approval ratings in opinion polls continue to be over 80 percent. But all this could change. In fact, some argue that because Russians are often fearful of stating their political views openly, there may be hidden discontent with Putin that is not expressed to pollsters. Also, Russians traditionally look up to their rulers just because they are in power, as they did in tsarist times. As Olga Bychkova of *Ekho Moskvy* put it: "The approval rating we see is not for Putin, it is for the tsar, and if tomorrow they replace him with a different leader, who will soon have the same approval rating, the majority will vote for the tsar appointed to sit on the throne."[2] Although Putin's party, United Russia, received over 70 percent of the seats in the September 2016 Duma elections, the turnout was below 50 percent, which suggests that a significant element of the population may be disenchanted with the current political regime, or at the very least indifferent.

Many of those Russians who protested on the streets in surprisingly large numbers this spring came out, not only against government corruption, but also against the stagnant economy. Although the Russian economy is on the upturn after a deep recession, it remains in serious trouble. According to Stratfor's *Market Watch*, "Russia is a mess:" the average monthly wage dropped 8 percent in 2016, while the poverty rate reached close to 15 percent. And only ten of Russia's eighty-five regions are financially stable.[3] It is important to note that, even if oil prices rise further and the Kremlin can tackle its domestic and foreign debt, it still has the long-range problem of an economic infrastructure that is crumbling. Putin's policy has been for the economy to rely on oil and gas resources, which has stifled technological innovation and efficiency in other areas of industry. At some point, the Kremlin will face a day of reckoning. Recall that Putin's Soviet predecessors had the same approach and that economic stagnation was a major factor in the collapse of the Soviet Union.[4]

When Trump assumed the presidency, Moscow had good reason to be optimistic about its relations with Washington. Trump had earlier suggested flexibility on the issue of Crimea and Ukraine and questioned the viability of NATO. He had also expressed doubts that Russia had hacked the Democratic National Committee and dismissed the idea that Putin was a murderer. But congressional and FBI investigations of Russia's interference in U.S. elections were a constraint on Trump in reaching out to Moscow. And the deadly chemical bombing attack in Syria on April 4 by Assad forces seemed to motivate Trump to take a stronger stance against Putin because it was clear that Russia was complicit in the strike. Trump told *The New York Times* the day after the attack: "I think it's a very sad day for Russia because they're aligned [with Assad]."[5] Secretary of state Rex Tillerson a few days later said in no uncertain terms that the Assad era was "coming to an end," warning Russia about continuing to support the Syrian leader.[6] This was a sharp departure from the earlier position of the Trump administration, which was that it was inevitable that Assad would remain in power.

On May 2, Trump and Putin had their first telephone call since the Syrian bombing and it was reported to be productive, if not eventful. Both sides agreed that they should do all they could to end the violence in Syria, but, in contrast to his offers of hospitality to other world leaders, Trump did not invite Putin to visit the White House. Earlier that day German Chancellor Angel Merkel paid a personal visit to Putin in Sochi, her first in over two years. In contrast to Trump— and to Tillerson, who declined to meet with Russian opposition leaders on his first visit to Moscow as secretary of state—Merkel did not shy away from bringing up the issue of human rights. Indeed, she pressed Putin on the arrests of protesters in Russia, its recent ban on Jehovah's Witnesses, and the persecution of gays in Chechnya. She also hardened Germany's position on the implementation of the Minsk agreement, which is meant to end the conflict in Ukraine, and made it clear that sanctions against Russia would remain in place.[7]

Unfortunately, during his first meeting with NATO members later in May, Trump seemed to downplay the strategic importance of the NATO alliance, arousing deep concern among his European counterparts. Washington is still committed to maintaining sanctions against Moscow until it meets Western demands about Ukraine—at least for the time being. But Trump declined to specifically endorse the NATO mutual defense treaty, which has been the cornerstone of the alliance in protecting member countries from Russian aggression, and he scolded fellow NATO allies about their financial contributions to the alliance. Trump's stance prompted Merkel to say that Europe should concentrate on its own interests and "take our fate in our own hands."[8]

Merkel, who has been German chancellor since 2005, has years of experience with Putin and, as de-facto leader of the European allies, she speaks and acts with authority in dealing with Russia. Trump and his advisers would do well to look to Merkel as an example in their own relations with the Russian leader, especially given how important it is that the United States presents a united front with its European counterparts in shaping policy toward Russia. In a number of recent European elections, most recently in France, voters have come out forcefully against right-wing nationalist candidates (who were often favored by Putin). This suggests that Trump will have to stand shoulder-to-shoulder with Europe, even if his instinct, or some part of his nationalist base, would have him do otherwise.

What should western policy toward Russia be? First and foremost for America and Europe alike, there should be no expectation of a breakthrough with Russia on the urgent problems that plague the international order. As the authors of a recent study for the Carnegie Foundation put it: "the focus should be on managing a volatile relationship with an increasingly emboldened and unpredictable Russian leadership."[9] Russia's brazen interference in Western electoral processes through cyber attacks is a case in point. This new, aggressive form of geopolitical warfare is testing vulnerable democracies everywhere. According to a U.S. intelligence officer: "It's not that the Russians are doing something others can't do. It's that Russian hackers are willing to go there, to experiment and carry out attacks that others countries would back away from."[10] The challenge of Russia's cyber attacks and its increasing use of disinformation and fake news to discredit political figures in the West calls for a forceful and concerted response. The West needs a comprehensive strategy to protect its telecommunications infrastructure and coordinate punitive measures in retaliation for these attacks.

Secondly, the West should not cave in to the idea that it shares common cause with Russia in the struggle against terrorism. (Ironically, Trump is borrowing from Putin as he cites the threat of terrorism to justify what many see as his undemocratic policies toward Muslims and other ethnic minorities.) The Kremlin has used the fight against terrorism as an excuse for its military presence in Syria and its collusion with the Taliban in Afghanistan, whereas in reality its aim is to extend its sphere of political and military influence.

Russia is deeply entrenched in Syria for several reasons. It has a history of close ties with Syria that go back to the early Cold War and since 1971 has had a naval base in Syria at Tartus on the Mediterranean that is of major strategic importance. Syria provides Russia with a crucial foothold in the Middle East, and the Assad regime is seen by Moscow as essential for maintaining it. The Kremlin recently came up with an initiative to create four separate "deescalation" zones in Syria, where civilians could supposedly move freely and get aid relief without the threat of bombs. The plan was supported by Iran, Turkey and Assad. But observers have criticized it because the first priority of the plan was to protect the Assad regime from rebel forces and to have the rebels fight ISIS instead. The West, short of introducing ground troops in Syria, needs to insist to Russia that the murderous al-Assad regime has to go and that the bombing campaign that is directed against rebels who oppose Assad has to stop.

As for the situation with Ukraine, Russia is deeply invested in holding on to Crimea, in large part for domestic reasons. Putin has used the annexation of Crimea to portray it as a symbol of Great Russia, a return to the glorious days of the Russian empire. Immediately after the annexation, Putin's ratings, bolstered by Russians' feelings of national pride, soared to ninety percent. The Kremlin is no doubt convinced that any capitulation on the Crimea issue would have a negative effect on Putin's image as a defender of Russian national interests as he puts himself forth for re-election in the spring of 2018. The continuation of Western sanctions against Russia is highly unlikely to convince the Kremlin to give up Crimea. So perhaps Western allies should consider using recognition of Crimea as part of Russia to extract concessions from Moscow on other issues, in particular the resolution of the conflict in Eastern Ukraine.

The Minsk II agreement, brokered in 2015 to end the fighting in Ukraine, has been largely a failure, given Moscow's refusal to enforce the cease-fire and remove its heavy weapons from Eastern Ukraine. The sticking point is the status of the Donetsk and Lugansk regions and how much autonomy they would have from Kiev. Also, Kiev is demanding that it get full control over its eastern border with Russia. Apart from wresting concessions from Russia, the West, and the U.S. in particular, should continue its political and diplomatic engagement in Ukraine as it restores its economy and addresses the problem of rampant government corruption.

In early May of this year, before he was dismissed by Trump, FBI Director James Comey testified before the United States Senate and called Russia the greatest threat to democracy "of any nation on earth." Comey was evidently referring in part to Russia's interference in the U.S. electoral process. (The Trump administration, significantly, was quick to dissociate itself from the statement, stressing that this was the view of the FBI.) But if one goes beyond this reference and considers the murders of political opponents and journalists by the Putin regime, as well as its sinister role in the terrorist attacks discussed here, it becomes even more clear that Russia is a dangerous and unpredictable adversary. The U.S. and its allies need to present a forceful front against the Kremlin, and that should include a strong demand that the Kremlin observe the canons of human rights set forth by the community of nations in the UN as well as by the Helsinki

Accords. These rights include citizens' protection from politically-motivated extrajudicial killing.

As I did research and writing for this book, I realized that its implications went beyond the story of a criminal, dictatorial regime and how it operates. The book has a broader, more universal message about the phenomenon of political murder and what it means for our world today. This message is best conveyed in the words of Franklin Ford, who I drew upon in my introduction: "History has repeatedly demonstrated that assassination . . . has tended to ignore man's hard-won regard for due process and to defeat the highest purposes of political life. If governments and their declared opponents were to act (or, sometimes better still, refrain from acting) in the light of that knowledge, a world facing a host of other problems would have at least one good reason to rejoice."[11]

Hopefully, the courageous efforts of the men and women I describe here, who died for "the highest purposes of political life," have contributed to a democratic future for Russia and a better world.

ACKNOWLEDGMENTS

My first thanks are to my literary agent, Philip Turner, for his encouragement of my book project from the beginning and his invaluable help, including editing, in moving the manuscript through to publication. I also want to thank my editor at Thomas Dunne, Stephens Power, for his enthusiasm for my book and his excellent editing. Thanks are also due to Thomas Dunne for taking on my book and for his valuable suggestions on how to improve my manuscript.

There are several people who have provided me with indispensable help as I worked on the book. Galina Frid gave me much-needed assistance in my research, as did Jessica Landy. Rosa Cortez and Mike Krivetz were always on call for me when I needed them for my computer issues. I am also grateful to John Dunlop, David Satter, Peter Reddaway, Martin Dewhirst, Ed Lucas, Yevgenia Albats, Andrei Soldatov, David Law, Christian Caryl, Catherine Fitzpatrick, Vladimir Milov, Brain Gyln Williams, and Vadim and Kathryn Birstein for providing me with many sources of information, as well as advice. In addition, the late Robert Silvers and Hugh Eatkin at the *New*

York Review, in editing and publishing my writings on the subject of the book, helped me in formulating my ideas and expressing them. And Mike Wicksteed, communications officer for the Litvinenko Inquiry, graciously facilitated my attendance at the Inquiry hearings.

This book could not have been written without the cooperation of those who kindly allowed me to interview them: Nadezhda Azhgikhina, Akhmed Zakaev, Musa and Peter Klebnikov, Congressman William Keating, Tanya Lokshina, and Alex Goldfarb. Alex also kindly read my manuscript and gave me useful suggestions.

I am especially grateful to Marina Litvinenko, to whom this book is dedicated, for giving me so much of her valuable time for interviews and for inspiring me in writing the book. Thanks are also due to her son, Anatoly Litvinenko, for allowing me to interview him.

And finally I owe a debt to my daughter Molly Knight Raskin for encouraging my book project and for help in various stages of editing the manuscript.

NOTES

Introduction

1. Boris Nemtsov and Vladimir Milov, *Putin. Itogi. Nezavisimyi Ekspertnyi Doklad (Putin: The Results: An Independent Expert Report)* (Moscow: *Novaia gazeta*, 2008). My article, "The Truth about Putin and Medvedev," appeared in *The New York Review of Books*, 55, no. 8, May 15, 2008.

2. Franklin Ford, *Political Murder: From Tyrannicide to Terrorism* (Boston: Harvard University Press, 1985), 367.

3. Holman W. Jenkins, Jr., "The CIA Keeps Putin's Secrets," *The Wall Street Journal*, January 3, 2017, http://www.wsj.com/articles/the-cia-keeps-putins-secrets-1483488301.367.

4. "Poison in the System," *Buzzfeed*, June 12, 2017, https://www.buzzfeed.com/heidiblake/poison-in-the-system?utm_term=.qe6Bz8pqw#.gyaLzKRqX. This is one of an excellent four-part series investigating suspicious deaths of Russians in Britain.

5. Ford, *Political Murder*, 1.

1. Covert Violence as a Kremlin Tradition

1. Hélène Carrère d'Encausse, *The Russian Syndrome: One Thousand Years of Political Murder*, translated by Caroline Higgitt (New York: Holmes & Meier, 1992), 393.

2. James Cracraft, *The Revolution of Peter the Great* (Cambridge: Harvard University Press, 2003), 15–16.

3. Carrère d'Encausse, 156.

4. Ibid., 396.

5. Amy Knight, *Who Killed Kirov? The Kremlin's Greatest Mystery* (New York: Hill and Wang, 1999).

6. As quoted in Ishaan Tharoor, "Echoes of Stalin in the Murder of a Russian Foe," *The Washington Post*, March 4, 2015, https://www.washington post.com/news/worldviews/wp/2015/03/04/echoes-of-stalin-in-the -murder-of-a-putin-foe-in-moscow/.

7. "Boris Nemtsov: Liberal Martyr," the *Economist*, February 28, 2015, http://www.economist.com/news/europe/21645432-russias-rising -political-hatred-claims-victim-scrupulously-honest-reformist-leader -liberal-martyr.

8. Arkady Vaksberg, *The Murder of Maxim Gorky: A Secret Execution* (New York: Enigma Books, 2007), 328–329.

9. Ibid., 364.

10. See Vadim J. Birstein, *The Perversion of Knowledge: The True Story of Soviet Science* (Cambridge, MA: Westview Press, 2001).

11. Pavel Sudoplatov and Anatoli Sudoplatov, *Special Tasks: The Memoirs Of An Unwanted Witness—A Soviet Spymaster* (Boston: Little Brown, 1994), 80.

12. Svetlana Alliluyeva, *Only One Year*, translated by Paul Chavchavadze. (New York: Harper & Row, 1969), 154.

13. Paul Goldberg, *The Yid: A Novel* (New York: Picador, 2016), 5.

14. See Amy Knight, *Beria: Stalin's First Lieutenant* (Princeton: Princeton University Press, 1993).

15. See Amy Knight, "Pyotr Masherov and the Soviet Leadership: A Study in Kremlinology," *Survey: A Journal of East and West Studies*, Winter 1982, 26, no. 1 (114), 151–168.

16. *Pravda,* June 15, 1980.

17. Nikolai Khokhlov, *In the Name of Conscience*, (New York: David McKay, 1959), 363.

18. Kelly Hignett, "The Curious Case of the Poisoned Umbrella: The Murder of Georgi Markov," *The View East*, September 9, 2011, https:// thevieweast.wordpress.com/2011/09/09/the-curious-case-of-the

-poisoned-umbrella-the-murder-of-georgi-markov/. Also see Oleg Kalugin, *The First Directorate: My 32 Years in Intelligence and Espionage
Against the West* (New York: St. Martin's Press, 1994), 178–186.

19. Paul Klebnikov, *Godfather of the Kremlin: The Decline of Russia in the
Age of Gangster Capitalism* (Orlando: Harcourt, Inc., 2000), 144–169.

20. Boris Yeltsin, *Midnight Diaries*, translated by Catherine A. Fitzpatrick
(New York: Public Affairs, 2000), 222.

21. Karen Dawisha, *Putin's Kleptocracy: Who Owns Russia?* (New York:
Simon & Schuster, 2014), 142–162.

22. Ibid., 172.

23. Yuri Felshtinsky and Vladimir Pribylovsky, *The Corporation: Russia and
the KGB in the Age of President Putin* (New York: Encounter Books,
2008), 118.

24. See Nemtsov's autobiography: *Ispoved' buntaria* (Confessions of a Rebel)
(Moscow: Partizan, 2007), 53.

25. http://news.bbc.co.uk/2/hi/world/monitoring/415278.stm.

26. Klebnikov, *Godfather*, 305.

2. How the System Works: Putin and his Security Services

1. Brian Taylor, *State Building in Putin's Russia* (Cambridge: Cambridge
University Press, 2011), 2.

2. Masha Lipman, "Putin's Halting Progress," the *Washington Post*,
April 24, 2002, https://www.washingtonpost.com/archive/opinions/2002
/04/24/putins-halting-progress/4f457fef-05f1-4450-8367-ddd97b270aed/
?utm_term=.99581670646d.

3. On Yeltsin and his security services, see my book *Spies Without Cloaks:
The KGB's Successors* (Princeton: Princeton University Press, 1996).

4. Ewen MacAskill, "Putin calls internet a 'CIA project' renewing fears of
web breakup," *The Guardian*, April 24, 2014, https://www.theguardian
.com/world/2014/apr/24/vladimir-putin-web-breakup-internet-cia.

5. Khristina Narizhnaya, "Russians Go West," *World Policy Journal*, Spring
2013, http://www.worldpolicy.org/journal/spring2013/russians-go-west.

6. http://cook.livejournal.com/11/9/2015. On Putin and his plagiarized
dissertation, see "Researchers Peg Putin as a Plagiarist over Thesis," the
Washington Times, March 24, 2006, http://www.washingtontimes.com
/news/2006/mar/24/20060324-104106-9971r/.

7. Andrei Soldatov and Irina Borogan, *The New Nobility: The Restoration of Russia's Security State* (New York: Public Affairs, 2010), 22.

8. Andrei Soldatov and Irina Borogan, *The Red Web: The Struggle Between Russia'a Digital Dictators and The New Online Revolutionaries* (New York: Public Affairs: 2015), ix.

9. Aliide Naylor, "How Russia is Trying to Rein in the Internet," Vocativ, May 19, 2017, http://www.vocativ.com/430843/russia-internet-government-social-media-censorship/, https://rns.online/internet/FSB-razoslala-rekomendatsii-po-borbe-s-virusom-vimogatelem-WannaCrypt-2017-05-13/.

10. Vladimir Putin, *First Person: An Astonishingly Frank Self-Portrait*, translated by Catherine A. Fitzpatrick (New York: Public Affairs, 2000), 144;201.

11. "Neofitsial'naia bibliografiia N. Patrusheva," Internet-biblioteka "Antikompromat," http://www.anticompromat.org/patrushev/patrushbio.html.

12. "Ochen' nezametnyi Patrushev," *Sobesednik*, June 25, 2007, http://sobesednik.ru/publications/sobesednik/2007/06/24/patruchev-career.

13. Soldatov and Borogan, *The New Nobility*, 22.

14. Ibid.,153.

15. Victor Yasmann, "Putin Orders New Counterterrorism Committee," RadioFreeEurope/RadioLiberty, February 17, 2006, http://www.rferl.org/content/article/1065889.html.

16. See: *The Litvinenko Inquiry. Report into the Death of Alexander Litvinenko,* by Sir Robert Owen, London, January 2016 [hereafter cited as *The Owen Report* and available at www.litvinenkoinquiry.org], 91.

17. Viktor Cherkesov, "Nel'zia dopustit', chtoby voiny prevatilis' v torgovtsev," *Kommersant*, October 9, 2007.

18. Irina Shcherbak, "Fond Naval'nogo: glava Sovbeza Nikolai Patrushev vladeet osobniakom, na kotoryi pri dokhodakh ego sem'i prishlos' by kopit 3666 let," *Znak,* December 9, 2014, https://www.znak.com/2014-12-09/fond_navalnogo_glava_sovbeza_nikolay_patrushev_vladeet_osobnyakom_na_kotoryy_pri_dohodah_ego_semi_pr.

19. https://lenta.ru/lib/14160892/full.htm; http://www.rumafia.com/ru/news.php?id=738.

20. Kirill Mel'nikov and Elena Kiseleva, "Andrei Patrushev osvoit 'Sakha-

lin-3,'" *Kommersant*, September 27, 2013, http://www.kommersant.ru /doc/2305845.

21. "Vysshie chinovniki uvodiat den'gi na zapad," the *New Times*, May 21, 2007.

22. David Kramer, "U.S. invites a Russian Fox into the Chicken Coop," the *Washington Post*, February 19, 2015.

23. On the Magnitsky case, see Bill Browder, *Red Notice: A True Story of High Finance, Murder, and One Man's Fight for Justice* (New York: Simon & Schuster, 2015).

24. Taylor, *State Building Under Putin's Regime*, 46.

25. Aleksandr Khinshtein, "Shofer eks-glavyi MVD Nurgalieva razoblachen kak glavar' prestupnoi gruppirovki," *MKRU*, May 23, 2013, http://www .mk.ru/politics/2013/05/23/858761-shofer-eksglavyi-mvd-nurgalieva -razoblachen-kak-glavar-prestupnoy-gruppirovki.html.

26. Pavel Chikov, "Nasledstvo Rashida Nurgalieva,"*Forbes*, May 16, 2012, http://www.forbes.ru/sobytiya-column/vlast/82231-nasledstvo-rashida -nurgalieva.

27. Brian Whitmore, "Russia: Powerful New Investigative Body Begins Work," *RadioFreeEurope/RadioLiberty*, September 10, 2007, http:// www.rferl.org/content/article/1078611.html.

28. See the committee's website: http://sledcom.ru/sk_russia.

29. Aleksandr Khinshtein, "Bogemskoe pravo," *Moskovskii komsomolets*, July 1, 2008, http://www.mk.ru/editions/daily/article/2008/07/01/33710 -bogemskoe-pravo.html.

30. Robert Coalson, "Russia's Top Investigator, Aleksandr Bastrykin, In Hot Water Again," *RadioFreeEurope/RadioLiberty*, July 30, 2012, http://www .rferl.org/content/russia-aleksandr-bastrykin-profile/24658719.html.

31. As quoted by Andrew Kramer in *The New York Times,* July 26, 2012.

32. Roman Anin, "Kvartirnyi vopros," *Novaia gazeta*, September 18, 2012, https://www.novayagazeta.ru/articles/2012/09/19/51504-kvartirnyyvopros.

33. http://www.interpretermag.com/russia-update-september-28-2016/.

34. http://cook.livejournal.com/246676.html.

35. The English version of the film, "Chaika: An Investigative Documentary by the Anti-Corruption Fund," appeared on YouTube on January 26, 2016: https://www.youtube.com/watch?v=3eO8ZHfV4fk.

36. Mark Galeotti, "THE FSO: praetorians, protectors, political force," *In Moscow's Shadows*, October 24, 2013, https://inmoscowsshadows .wordpress.com/2013/10/24/the-fso-praetorians-protectors-political -force/.

37. Yekaterina Sinelschikova, "'Putin's people': The mysterious agency that guards the president's life," *Russia Beyond the Headlines*, June 1, 2016, http://rbth.com/politics_and_society/2016/06/01/putins-people-the -mysterious-agency-that-guards-the-presidents-life_599181.

38. "Pered uvol'neniem glava FSO Murov zavladel nedvizhimost'iu 2 mlrd," *Sobesednik*, May 26, 2016, http://sobesednik.ru/rassledovanie/20160526 -pered-uvolneniem-glava-fso-murov-zavladel-nedvizhimostyu-na.

39. On Kochnev, See Mark Galeotti, "Why the Departure of Putin's Chief bodyguard Actually Matters," European Council on Foreign Relations, May 26, 2016, http://www.ecfr.eu/article/commentary_why_the_depar ture_of_putins_chief_bodyguard_actually_7032.

40. Sinelschikova, "Putin's People."

41. See Dawisha, *Putin's Kleptocracy*, 74–80.

42. As quoted in Ibid., 309–310.

43. Mark Galeotti, "Putin's New National Guard—what does it say when you need your own personal army?" *In Moscow's Shadows*, April 5, 2016, https://inmoscowsshadows.wordpress.com/2016/04/05/putins-new -national-guard-what-does-it-say-when-you-need-your-own-personal -army/#more-3346.

44. See the Russian website agentura.ru, of Andrei Soldatov and Irina Boro- gan, a crucial source of information on the security services, http:// www.agentura.ru/dossier/russia/fskn/.

45. "'Drug lords danced with joy, when US blacklisted me'-Russian anti- drug chief," *RT*, March 20, 2015, https://www.rt.com/politics/official -word/242485-viktor-ivanov-rt-interview/.

46. Mikhail Fishman, "Putin Closes Drug Agency, Casts Aside Longtime Supporter Ivanov," the *Moscow Times*, 5/19/2016, https://crimerussia.ru /gover/viktor-ivanov-prigrel-narkotorgovtsa/.

47. "Ivanov nazval slukhi o likvidatsii fskn preuvelichennymi," *Forbes.ru*, February 17, 2015, http://www.forbes.ru/news/280475-ivanov-nazval -slukhi-o-likvidatsii-fskn-preuvelichennymi.

48. http://www.agentura.ru/dossier/russia/svr/specnaz/.

49. Leon Neyfakh, "The Craziest Black Market in Russia," *Slate*, May 22, 2016, http://www.slate.com/articles/news_and_politics/cover_story/2016/05/the_thriving_russian_black_market_in_dissertations_and_the_crusaders_fighting.html.

3. Galina Starovoitova: Putin's First Victim?

1. https://www.unodc.org/tldb/pdf/Russian_Federation/CPC_2001_EN.pdf.

2. http://www.aparchive.com/metadata/youtube/f3fdcaaf9392117283647654a419a905.

3. See my article on the murder: "Crime, but No Punishment: Crimes Frightening Effects on Russian Democracy," *Washington Post Outlook*, December 6, 1998.

4. Tatiana Vol'tskaia, "Oni ubivaiut tekh, kogo slushaiut liudi," *Svoboda.org*, May 17, 2016, http://www.svoboda.org/a/27740352.html.

5. Galina Starovoitova, "Sovereignty After Empire. Self-determination Movements in the Former Soviet Union," U.S. Institute of Peace, November 1997, http://www.usip.org/sites/default/files/pwks19.pdf.

6. Boris Bruk, "She Has Stepped Into Eternity. In Memory of Galina Starovoitova," *Institute of Modern Russia*, May 16, 2013, http://imrussia.org/en/politics/460-she-has-stepped-into-eternity-in-memory-of-galina-starovoitova.

7. Ibid. Also see the Russian website, Starovoitova.ru.

8. Vladimir Kara-Murza, "Ubiistvo Galiny Starovoitovoi raskryto? *Svoboda.org*, August 28, 2015, http://www.svoboda.org/a/27214454.html.

9. See a February 4, 1994 interview with Starovoitova in English: "Yeltsin Misread the Elections," *Demokratizatsiya*, 2, no. 2, 1994, https://www.gwu.edu/~ieresgwu/assets/docs/demokratizatsiya%20archive/02-2_Starovoitova.pdf.

10. Dawisha, *Putin's Kleptocracy*, 106-127; Masha Gessen, *The Man Without a Face: The Unlikely Rise of Vladimir Putin* (New York: Riverhead Books, 2012), 120–129.

11. Dawisha, *Putin's Kleptocracy*, 126–141.

12. Ibid.

13. Andrew Meier, *Black Earth: A Journey Through Russia After the Fall* (New York: W.W. Norton, 2003), 344.

14. Anastasiia Mikhailova, "Tri versii ubiistva Starovoitovoi," RBK telekanal, August 20, 2015, http://www.rbc.ru/politics/20/08/2015/55d5b36e9a 7947ad179c701c.

15. See the detailed and meticulously researched account of these murders on the blog of Blikol Osinov, http://osinov.livejournal.com/4801.html.

16. Ibid.

17. Ibid.; Dawisha, *Putin's Kleptocracy*, 177–178; Anton B-Samarin, "Sud ne poveril deputatskomu rassledovaniiu," *Kommersant*, March 14, 2005, http://www.kommersant.ru/doc/554196; Anastasiia Kirilenko, "Putin, Shutov, 'Ozero' i 'Belyi lebed' " *Svoboda.org*, December 21, 2014, http:// www.svoboda.org/a/26755073.html

18. http://osinov.livejournal.com/4801.html.

19. Interview with Olga Starovoitova, *Ekho Moskvy*, November 22, 2013, http://echo.msk.ru/programs/year2013/1202491-echo/.

20. Irina Tumakova, "Advokaty ishchut protivorechiia v pokazaniakh Ruslana Lin'kova," *Izvestiia*, October 23, 2004, http://izvestia.ru/news /295671.

21. Dmitrii Gordienko, "Ruslan Lin'kov opoznal v sude odnogo iz streliavshikh v Galinu Starovoitovu," *Fontanka.ru*.—29 июня 2004, http:// starovoitova.ru/rus/main.php?i=9&s=153.

22. Oksana Yablokova, "Suspect Detained in Starovoitova Murder," the *Moscow Times*, February 5, 2000, http://old.themoscowtimes.com/sitemap /free/2000/2/article/suspect-detained-in-starovoitova-murder/267084 .html.

23. *Ekho Moskvy*, November 22, 2013.

24. http://osinov.livejournal.com/4185.html.

25. *Ekho Moskvy*, November 22, 2013.

26. Meier, *Black Earth*, 345–348.

27. Ibid., 348.

28. Starovoitova.ru: novosti i khod sledstviia, http://www.starovoitova.ru /rus/main.php?i=9&s=4.

29. Ibid.

30. The official indictments and final sentences are available at Starovoi tova.ru.

31. Viktor Kosiukovskii, "Ubiistvo Starovoitovoi: Sledy spetssluzhb?"

Russkii Kur'er, March 14, 2005, http://rusk.ru/st.php?idar=10535; Mikhailova, "Tri versii ubiistva Starovoitovoi."

32. Konstantin Shmelev, "V ubiistve Galiny Starovoitovoi nashli organiza-tora," *Fontanka.ru*, November 7, 2013, http://www.fontanka.ru/2013/11 /07/068/.

33. https://wikileaks.org/gifiles/docs/54/5410884_re-insight-russia-head-of -major-criminal-group-arrested.html.

34. The interview was published on March 25, 2016 on the website of *Open Russia*: https://openrussia.org/post/view/13831/.

35. Aleksandr Litvinenko, with Aleks Goldfarb, *LPG-Lubianskaia prestup-naia gruppirovka* (New York: Grani, 2002), 82, http://royallib.com/read /litvinenko_aleksandr/lubyanskaya_prestupnaya_gruppirovka.html#0.

36. Interview with Shenderovich on the website *Open Russia*, December 25, 2015, https://openrussia.org/post/view/11565/.

37. Vol'tskaia, "Oni ubivaiut."

38. Interview with *Radio Svoboda*, August 28, 2015, http://www.svoboda .org/content/transcript/27214454.html.

39. Initially, according to one source, Linkov was suspected by local inves-tigators of being involved in the murder. See Brian Whitmore, "The Strange Investigation of Galina Starovoitova's Murder, *Prism*, 5, issue 2, January 29, 1999.

40. Ruslan Linkov, *Zapiski nedobitka*, (St. Petersburg: AMFORA, 2007).

41. See an interview Linkov had with Radio Liberty about the book: http:// www.svoboda.org/content/transcript/410813.html; and Anna Narinskaia, "Vodila Vladimirovich," *Kommersant.ru*, September 27, 2007, http:// kommersant.ru/doc/807006?themeid=960.

4. Terror in Russia: September 1999

1. Gregory L. White, "Boris Nemtsov's Career Traces Arch of Russia's Dimmed Hopes for Democracy," *The Wall Street Journal*, February 28, 2015; http://www.wsj.com/articles/boris-nemtsovs-career-traces-arc-of -russias-dimmed-hopes-for-democracy-1425168024.

2. See Sergei Kovalev, "Putin's War," *The New York Review of Books*, 47, no. 2, February 10, 2000, http://www.nybooks.com/articles/2000/02/10 /putins-war/.

3. Vladimir Vedrashko, "Na vse to Volia..ch'ia?" *Radio Svoboda*, September 8, 2009, http://www.svoboda.org/content/article/1818078.html.

4. Ibid.

5. John B. Dunlop, *The Moscow Bombings of September 1999. Examinations of Russian Terrorist Attacks at the Onset of Vladimir Putin's Rule*, with a Foreword by Amy Knight (Stuttgart: Ibidem-Verlag, 2012), 85-89. Also see my review of the book: Amy Knight, "Finally We Know About the Moscow Bombings," *The New York Review of Books*, 59, no. 18, November 22, 2012, http://www.nybooks.com/articles/2012/11 /22/finally-we-know-about-moscow-bombings/; and David Satter, *Darkness at Dawn: The Rise of the Russian Criminal State* (New Haven & London: Yale University Press), 63-71.

6. Dunlop, *The Moscow Bombings*, 9.

7. The words of Sergei Mingalev in the documentary film "Disbelief," produced by Alexander Nekrasov in 2004, https://archive.org/details /Disbelief2004.

8. Grigory Pasko, "Is Mikhail Trepashkin's Life in Danger?" December 13, 2006, http://robertamsterdam.com/grigory_pasko_is_mikhail _trepashkins_life_in_danger/.

9. *Ekho Moskvy*, September 1, 2015, http://echo.msk.ru/blog/echomsk /1614184-echo/.

10. As quoted in Dunlop, *The Moscow Bombings*, 59.

11. Andrei Pointkovsky, "Svidetel' Gol'dfarb," *Grani.ru*, October 13, 2009, http://graniru.org/Politics/Russia/m.160589.html.

12. Alex Goldfarb with Marina Litvinenko, *Death of a Dissident: The Poisoning of Litvinenko and the Return of the KGB* (New York: Free Press, 2007), 191.

13. See the transcript of a round-table discussion: "Vzryvy domov v 99-m: komu vygodno," *Radio Svoboda*, September 8, 2015, http://www .svoboda.org/content/transcript/27233566.html.

14. Ibid.

15. Dunlop, *The Moscow Bombings*, 236.

16. Ibid., 139.

17. Reuven Paz, "Al-Khattab: From Afghanistan to Dagestan," International Policy Institute for Counter-Terrorism, September 20, 1999, http://web .archive.org/web/20001217021000/http://www.ict.org.il/articles /articledet.cfm?articleid=94.

18. Alexander Litvinenko and Yuri Felshtinsky, *Blowing up Russia: The Secret Plot to Bring Back KGB Terror* (New York: Encounter Books, 2007), 130. The book was first published in Russian as *FSB vzryvaet Rossiiu*. (See note 33, below.)

19. Dunlop, *The Moscow Bombings*, 161–162.

20. Greg Myre, "Warlord Becoming Most Feared Man in Russia," AP, September 15, 1999, http://community.seattletimes.nwsource.com/archive/?date=19990915&slug=2983256.

21. Muhammad al-'Ubaydi, "Khattab (1962-2002)," Combating Terrorism Center at West Point, February, 2015, https://web.archive.org/web/20150814143452/https://www.ctc.usma.edu/v2/wp-content/uploads/2015/03/CTC_Khattab-Jihadi-Bio-February2015-3.pdf.

22. Satter, *Darkness at Dawn*, 66.

23. Dunlop, *The Moscow Bombings*, 158–159.

24. See the blog of Roman Dobrokhotov on Live Journal, September 9, 2009, http://dobrokhotov.livejournal.com/383212.html; Dunlop, *The Moscow Bombings*, 248–251.

25. On this incident, see Litvinenko and Felshtinsky, *Blowing up Russia*, 54–99; Dunlop, *The Moscow Bombings*, 167–215; Satter, *Darkness At Dawn*, 25–33.

26. Litvinenko and Felshtinsky, *Blowing Up Russia*, 56–57.

27. Ibid., 62–66.

28. Ibid., 72.

29. Dunlop, *The Moscow Bombings*, 210.

30. Litvinenko and Feldshtinsky, *Blowing Up Russia*, 77.

31. Pavel Voloshin, "Geksogen. FSB. Ryazan," *Novaia gazeta*, March 13, 2000.

32. Satter, *Darkness at Dawn*, 32.

33. Aleksandr Litvinenko, Yurii Fel'shtinskii, *FSB vzryvaet Rossiyu* (New York: Liberty Publishing House, 2002).

34. https://www.youtube.com/watch?v=9sx2YmSXDy8.

35. Dunlop, *The Moscow Bombings*, 203–208. The Arifdzhanov article appeared in *Sovershenno sekretno*, no. 6, 2002.

36. Dmitrii Sokolv, "Riazan', sentiabr' 1999: ucheniia ili terakt?" *Politkom.ru*, September 11, 2002, http://old.sakharov-center.ru/news/2007/0918/spravka.php.

37. Ibid.

38. Ibid.

39. Dunlop, *The Moscow Bombings*, 211. Also see *grani.ru*, May 30, 2003, http://graniru.org/Events/Terror/m.34083.html.

40. Dunlop, *The Moscow Bombings*, 120–121.

41. Sokolov, "Riazan'."

42. "Zhertvy terakta. Kak zhivut volgodontsy, postradavshie ot vzryva v 1999 godu," *Argumenty i fakty*, September 11, 2014, http://www.rostov .aif.ru/society/persona/1336299 (9/11/2014).

43. "Volgodonsk residents commemorate victims of 1999 terrorist act," *Caucasian Knot*, September 16, 2013, http://eng.kavkaz-uzel.ru/articles/18393/.

44. Sergei Kovalev,"Why Putin Wins," *The New York Review of Books*, 54, no. 18, November 22, 2007, http://www.nybooks.com/articles/2007/11 /22/why-putin-wins/.

5. Silencing Critics

1. Elena Pokalova, *Chechnya's Terrorism Network: The Evolution of Terrorism in Russia's North Caucasus* (Santa Barbara, CA: Praeger, 2015), 122.

2. Memorandum of telephone conversation between Clinton and Blair, February 8, 2000. National Security Council and Records Management Office, "Declassified documents concerning Tony Blair," *Clinton Digital Library*, accessed June 3, 2017, https://clinton.presidentiallibraries .us/items/show/48779.

3. Caroline Wyatt, "Bush and Putin: Best of Friends," BBC News, June 16, 2001, http://news.bbc.co.uk/2/hi/europe/1392791.stm.

4. http://www.edition.cnn.com/2002/WORLD/europe/09/10/ar911.russia .putin/index.html.

5. Polakova, *Chechnya's Terrorist Network*, 122.

6. Ibid., 124.

7. Goldfarb, *Death of a Dissident*, 248.

8. Prague Watchdog, September 24, 2003, http://www.watchdog.cz/ ?show=000000-000003-000002-000037&lang=1; CPJ/Committee to Protect Journalists, https://cpj.org/killed/europe/russia/.

9. Anna Politkovskaya, *A Small Corner of Hell: Dispatches From Chechnya* (Chicago and London: University of Chicago Press, 2003), 26–27.

10. See a report by the International Federation of Journalists: https://www.ifex.org/russia/2009/06/23/ifj_partial_justice_report.pdf.

11. Viacheslav Izmailov, "Kto ubil Igoria Domnikova?" *Novaia gazeta*, July 14, 2005, http://2005.novayagazeta.ru/nomer/2005/50n/n50n-s00.shtml.

12. Sergei Sokolov, Vera Chelishcheva, "Nazvan zakazchik ubiistva zhurnalista Igoria Domnikova, *Novaia gazeta*, March 10, 2015, http://www.novayagazeta.ru/inquests/67568.html.

13. Vera Chelishcheva, "Sud prikratel delo protiv zakazchika ubiistva zhurnalista Igoria Domnikova," *Novaia gazeta*, May 13, 2015, http://www.novayagazeta.ru/news/1693743.html.

14. Newsru.com, April 17, 2003, http://www.newsru.com/russia/17apr2003/killed.html.

15. As cited in Mavra Kosichkina, "Gibel' Sergeia Iushenkova: kto eto sdelal, lordyi?" *Politruk*, April 23, 2003, http://www.wps.ru/en/pp/politruk/2003/04/23.html.

16. Vladimir Korsunskii, "Putin vinoven v ubiistve Iushenkov," *Grani.ru*, March 22, 2004, Grani.ru/Politics/Russia/m.64562.html. That Iushenkov and Berezovsky reconciled was confirmed by Alex Goldfarb. See Goldfarb, *Death of a Dissident*, 278.

17. Korsunskii, "Putin vinoven;" Mariia-Liuiza Tirmaste, Sergei Diunin, Siuzanna Farizova, "Ubiistvo na ulitse Svobody," *Kommersant.ru*, April 18, 2004, http://www.compromat.ru/page_13012.htm.

18. "Genri Resnik: Kodaneva ogovorili," *grani.ru*, March 17, 2004, http://grani.ru/Politics/Russia/m.63911.html.

19. Rashid Alimov and Bellona Web, "FSB Threatened Sergey Yushenkov," *Pravda.ru*, April 24, 2003, http://www.pravdareport.com/hotspots/crimes/24-04-2003/2654-pasko-0/.

20. Nabi Abdullaev, "Berezovsky's Man Held in Yushenkov's Murder, the *Moscow Times*, June 27, 2003, http://old.themoscowtimes.com/sitemap/free/2003/6/article/berezovskys-man-held-in-yushenkovs-murder/237530.html.

21. Goldfarb, *Death of a Dissident*, 259.

22. Ibid., 258.

23. See John B. Dunlop, *The 2002 Dubrovka and 2004 Beslan Hostage Crises. A Critique of Russian Counter-terrorism* (Stuttgart: ibidem-Verlag,

2006). Also see my review of the book: Amy Knight, "The Kremlin Cover," *The Times Literary Supplement*, May 19, 2006.

24. Goldfarb, *Death of a Dissident*, 274–276. For more on Politkovskaya and Terkibaev, see chapter 6.

25. Ibid., 277.

26. "Shchekochikhin, Iurii," *Lenta.ru*, https://lenta.ru/lib/14170685/.

27. Virginie Coulloudon, "Yuri Shchekochikhin: How Long Can One Write About the Same Thing?" *RFERL Russian Report*, July 16, 2003, http://www.rferl.org/content/article/1344361.html; "Iurii Shchekochikhin: Smert' Zhurnalista," video, *Sovershenno Sekretno*, 2008. https://www.youtube.com/watch?v=EoGcb7cdY6A.

28. Victor Yasmann, "Corruption Scandal Could Shake Kremlin," *RFERL Russian Report*, September 26, 2006, http://www.rferl.org/content/article/1071621.html.

29. "Kak Shchekochikhin 'sdal' Adamova FBR," *Kompromat.ru*, http://www.compromat.ru/page_19030.htm.

30. Author interview with Nadezda Azhgikhina, November 9, 2016. She observed of her husband, "he was not a politician, but a romanticist."

31. "Agent Neizvesten," *Novaia gazeta*, October 30, 2006, http://2006.novayagazeta.ru/nomer/2006/82n/n82n-s05.shtml.

32. Sergei Sokolov, "10 let nazad umer Iurii Shchekochikhin," *Novaia gazeta*, July 2, 2013, https://www.novayagazeta.ru/articles/2013/07/03/55342-my-stavim-tochku.

33. Author interview with Nadezda Azhgikhina.

34. Richard Behar, "Did Boris Berezovsky Kill Himself? More Compelling, Did He Kill Forbes Editor Paul Klebnikov?" *Forbes*, March 24, 2013, http://www.forbes.com/sites/richardbehar/2013/03/24/did-boris-berezovsky-kill-himself-more-compelling-did-he-kill-forbes-editor-paul-klebnikov/2/#56a349e7123a.

35. Ironically, Klebnikov wrote his PhD dissertation at the London School of Economics on Petr Stolypin, the reformist Russian prime minister who was assassinated by Russian radical revolutionaries in 1911.

36. http://www.forbes.ru/forbes/issue/2004-05.

37. Musa Klebnikov, testimony to Helsinki Commission, June 23, 2009, https://www.csce.gov/sites/helsinkicommission.house.gov/files/TESTIMONY.Klebnikov.pdf.

38. The book, *Razgovor s varvarom*, is available on the website *Kompromat.ru*: http://www.compromat.ru/page_17052.htm.

39. "Pola Khlebnikova ubil varvar," *Izvestiia*, June 17, 2005, http://www.compromat.ru/page_16927.htm.

40. Anna Politkovskaya, *A Russian Diary* (London: Vintage Books, 2007), 128.

41. See Timothy Wittig, *Understanding Terrorist Finance* (London Palgrove Macmillan, 2011), 9.

42. Freelance Bureau, June 27, 2001, http://www.compromat.ru/page_10901.htm.

43. "Nukhaev, Khozh-Akhmed," *Lenta.ru*, October 31, 2016, https://lenta.ru/lib/14160692/full.htm#18.

44. As quoted in Ellen Barry, "Murder Highlights Russian System's Flaws," *The New York Times*, July 11, 2009, http://www.nytimes.com/2009/07/12/world/europe/12klebnikov.html?pagewanted=all.

45. *Newsru.com*, September 19, 2013, http://www.newsru.com/russia/19sep2013/pavl.html.

46. "Po delam Politkovskoi i Khlebnikova smenilsia sledovatel'," *Rosbalt*, May 30, 2015, http://www.rosbalt.ru/moscow/2015/05/30/1403329.html.

47. Klebnikov, *Godfather of the Kremlin*. Also see Pavel Sedakov, "Taina sledstviia: kto mog zakazat' ubiitsvo Pola Khlebnikova," *Forbes*, July 8, 2013, http://www.forbes.ru/sobytiya/obshchestvo/240893-taina-sledstviya-kto-mog-zakazat-ubiistvo-pola-hlebnikova.

48. Sedakov, "Taina sledstviia."

49. Author interview with Musa and Peter Klebnikov, New York City, July 19, 2016.

50. Sedakov, "Taina sledstviia."

51. "Dela Khlebnikova i Politkovskoi snova vmestve," *Rosbalt*, February 17, 2016, www.rosbalt.ru/moscow/2016/02/17/1490917.html.

52. Author interview with Musa and Peter Klebnikov.

6. Mafia-Style Killings in Moscow: Kozlov and Politkovskaya

1. https://georgewbush-whitehouse.archives.gov/news/releases/2002/05/20020524-10.html.

2. https://georgewbush-whitehouse.archives.gov/news/releases/2003/06/20030601-2.html.

3. https://www.congress.gov/108/bills/sres258/BILLS-108sres258ats.pdf.

4. *Congressional Record-House*, July 19, 2004, 16113.

5. *Congressional Record-Senate*, March 17, 2005, 5286.

6. "Memoria. Andrei Kozlov," *Polit.ru*, January 6, 2015, http://polit.ru /news/2015/01/06/kozlov/.

7. Valerii Kalabugin, "Kto vedet strannovatuiu deiatel'nost' Andreia Kozlova?" *Nezavizimaia gazeta*, June 1, 2004, http://www.ng.ru/ideas /2004-06-01/11_kozlov.html.

8. "Za chto ubili Andreia Kozlova?" *banki.ru*, September 15, 2006, http://www.banki.ru/news/daytheme/?id=206133.

9. Walter Kego and Alexander Georgieff, "The Threat of Russian Criminal Money: Reassessing EU Anti-Money Laundering Policy," Stockholm: Institute For Security and Development Policy, 2013.

10. Mikhail Zakharov, "Za banki otvechu," *Profil'*, June 15, 2004, http:// www.compromat.ru/page_15067.htm.

11. Roman Bessonov, "A Child of Two Augusts: Russian Kozlov Assassinated," *Executive Intelligence Review*, 13, no. 37, October 6, 2006, http:// www.larouchepub.com/eiw/public/2006/2006_40-49/2006_40-49/2006 -40/pdf/60-63_640_wetworks.pdf.

12. Ibid.

13. Ibid.

14. Jeffrey Donovan, "Russia: Contract Killings Once Again on the Rise," RadioLiberty/RadioFreeEurope, October 12, 2006, http://www.rferl .org/a/1071990.html.

15. "Avstriiskaia politsiia mozhet vozbudit' delo protiv kliuchevykh chinovnikov kremlia, utverzhaet *New Times*," *Newsru.com*, May 23, 2007, http://www.newsru.com/world/23may2007/otmyv.html; "Memoria. Andrei Kozlov."

16. Ibid.

17. Adam Federman, "Moscow's New Rules," *Columbia Journalism Review*, January-February, 2010, http://www.cjr.org/feature/moscows_new _rules.php?page=all.

18. "VIP-zakaz Alekseia Frenkelia," *Gazeta.ru*, January 12, 2007, http:// www.compromat.ru/page_19974.htm. For a detailed analysis of the Kozlov murder see the website http://www.topa.ru/frenkel/mission .php, which is sponsored by supporters of Frenkel.

19. "Za chto ubili Andreia Kozlova?;" Frenkel website.

20. Kazim Baibanov, "B 'delo Frenkelia' vziali bank 'Diskont,'" *Gazeta.Ru*, April 3, 2008, http://www.compromat.ru/page_22302.htm.

21. Lina Panchenko, "Kozlova 'dostali generaly iz FSB,'" *Moskovskii komsomolets*, March 21, 2008, http://www.mk.ru/editions/daily/article /2008/03/21/49114-kozlova-dostali-generalyi-iz-fsb.html.

22. Francesca Mereu, "Frenkel Gets Nineteen Years in Kozlov's Murder," *The Moscow Times*, November 14, 2008.

23. As quoted in *Wikipedia*, Politkovskaya, Anna Stepanova. Russian version.

24. See "Letter to Anna. The Story of Journalist Politkovskaya's Death," a film directed by Eric Bergkraut, with English narration by Susan Sarandon. Also my review of the film: Amy Knight, "Who Killed Anna Politkovskaya?" *The New York Review of Books*, 55, no. 17, November 6, 2008, http://www.nybooks.com/articles/2008/11/06/who-killed-anna -politkovskaya/.

25. "6 sil'nykh tsitat Anny Politkovskoi o Vladimire Putine," *Obozrevatel'*, July 10, 2014, http://life.obozrevatel.com/boiling/97263-6-silnyih-tsitat -annyi-politkovskoj-o-vladimire-putine.htm.

26. Knight, "Who Killed Anna Politkovskaya."

27. Dunlop, *The 2002 Dubrovka and 2004 Beslan Hostage Crises*; Anna Politkovskaya; "Tsena razgovorov," *Novaia gazeta*, October 27, 2002, https://www.novayagazeta.ru/articles/2002/10/28/13289-tsena -razgovorov.

28. Anna Politkovskaya, "Odin iz gruppy terroristov utselel, my ego nashli," *Novaia gazeta*, April 28, 2003, http://politkovskaya.novayagazeta.ru/pub /2003/2003-035.shtml.

29. As quoted in Dunlop, *The 2002 Dubrovka and 2004 Beslan Hostage Crises*, 59-60.

30. *The New York Times*, April 14, 2017, A7.

31. Knight, "Who Killed Anna Politkovskaya?"

32. Ibid.

33. Interview with Sokolov by Vladimir Kara-Murza, *Radio Svoboda*, June 9, 2014, http://memohrc.org/monitorings/ubiycy-nazvany-zakazchik -neizvesten.

34. "Ubiista Politkovskoi arestovan," *Newsru.com*, August 28, 2007, http:// www.newsru.com/russia/27aug2007/politkovskaya.html.

35. Aleksei Sokovnin, "Delo Politkovskoi," *Kommersant*, May 2, 2009, http://www.rospres.com/specserv/3537/.

36. Yulia Vishevetskaya and Markian Ostaptschuk, "Questions Remain Despite Politkovskaya Murder Convictions," *Deutsche Welle*, June 9, 2014, http://www.dw.com/en/questions-remain-despite-politkovskaya -murder-convictions/a-17693848.

37. Elena Rykotseva, interview with Vera Politkovskaya, *Radio Svoboda*, October 7, 2009. http://www.svoboda.org/content/transcript/1846894 .html.

38. "Samoe glavnoe-eto zakazchik ubiistva Politkovskoi, a zakazchik esche ne naiden," *Kommersant.ru*, June 9, 2014, http://www.kommersant.ru /doc/2489813.

39. Ibid; Vishnevetskaya and Ostaptschuk, "Questions remain despite Polit- kovskaya murder convictions."

40. Mar'ianka Torocheshnikova, "Deviat' let bez Anny," *Radio Svoboda*, Oc- tober 7, 2015, http://www.svoboda.org/content/transcript/27293369.html.

41. Vladimir Kara-Murza, "Ubiitsy nazvany, zakazchik neizvesten," *Radio Svoboda*, June 9, 2014, http://www.svoboda.org/a/25415762.html.

42. Anna Stroganova, "Vera Politkovskaya, 'zakazchik ubiistva Mamy ne budet nazvan do smeny vlasti V Rossii," *RFI*, October 5, 2012, http://ru .rfi.fr/rossiya/20121005-vera-politkovskaya-zakazchik-ubiistva-moei -mamy-ne-budet-nazvan-do-smeny-vlasti-v-r.

43. Mar'iana Torocheshnikova, "V Rossiii mozhno ubivat' neugodnykh," *Radio Svoboda*, January 10, 2016, http://www.svoboda.org/content /article/27474113.html.

44. Ibid.

45. Knight, "Who Killed Anna Politkovskaya?"

46. Ibid.

47. Sergei Diulin, interview with Petros Garibian, *Izvestiia*, November 9, 2012, http://www.rospres.com/crime/11399/.

48. Knight, "Who Killed Anna Politkovskaya?"

49. Kara-Murza, "Ubiitsy nazvany."

50. Aleks Gol'dfarb, *Sasha, Volodia, Boris . . . Istoriia ubiistva* (New York: AGC/Grani, 2010), 308.

7. The Litvinenko Story

1. *The Owen Report*, 104.

2. Gold'farb, *Sasha, Volodia, Boris*, 308–309.

3. Litvinenko Inquiry hearings, testimony of Daniel Quirke, February 16, 2015, 65, http://webarchive.nationalarchives.gov.uk/20160613090305 /https://www.litvinenkoinquiry.org/files/2015/10/lit160215-Redacted.pdf.

4. Litvinenko Inquiry hearings, Evidence of Marina Litvinenko, February 2, 2015, 145-6 http://webarchive.nationalarchives.gov.uk/201606 13090305/https://www.litvinenkoinquiry.org/files/2015/02/lit020215 .pdf; February 3, 2015 http://webarchive.nationalarchives.gov.uk/201606 13090305/https://www.litvinenkoinquiry.org/files/2015/02/lit030215 .pdf; evidence: video of Litvinenko's presentation. https://www.litvinen koinquiry.org/files/2015/02/Alexandr-Litvinenko-at-the-Frontline -Club-October-19-20061.mp4.

5. This author attended the Inquiry hearings in February 2015 and was present on January 21, 2016, when Sir Robert issued his report at a so-called lock-in for journalists. See Amy Knight, "Fatal Poison in London: The Report," *The New York Review of Books*, 63, no. 7, April 21, 2016, http://www.nybooks.com/articles/2016/04/21/fatal-russian-poison-in -london-the-report/.

6. *The Owen Report*, 13–15.

7. Pavel Evdokimov, "Mister Polonii," *Spetsnaz Rossii*, January 31, 2007; February 28, 2007. http://www.specnaz.ru/articles/125/3/533.htm; http:// www.specnaz.ru/articles/126/3/550.htm.

8. See Vladimir J. Birstein, *SMERSH: Stalin's Secret Weapon. Soviet Military Counterintelligence in WWII* (London: Biteback Publishing, 2011); Amy Knight, "The Special Departments in the Soviet Armed Forces," *ORBIS*, Summer 1984, 257-80.

9. Litvinenko, *Lubianskaia prestupnaia gruppirovka*, http://royallib .com/read/litvinenko_aleksandr/lubyanskaya_prestupnaya _gruppirovka.html#20480.

10. Author interview with Alex Goldfarb, June 29, 2016.

11. Marina Litvinenko, witness statement, March 27, 2013, Litvinenko Inquiry evidence, https://www.litvinenkoinquiry.org/files/2015/04/INQ01 7734wb.pdf.

12. Litvinenko Inquiry evidence, statement of Alexander Litvinenko, February 2, 2012, https://www.litvinenkoinquiry.org/files/2015/04/COM00 010001wb.pdf.

13. Marina Litvinenko witness statement.

14. Litvinenko Inquiry evidence, Boris Berezovsky witness statement, January 22, 2009. https://www.litvinenkoinquiry.org/files/2015/04/BER00 0011wb.pdf.

15. Goldfarb, *Death of a Dissident*, 121.

16. Berezovsky witness statement, January 22, 2009.

17. As quoted in *the Owen Report*, 22.

18. Berezovsky witness statement, January 22, 2009.

19. Author interview with Marina Litvinenko, April 26, 2014.

20. Litvinenko Inquiry hearings, testimony of Yuri Felshtinsky, March 11, 2015. https://www.litvinenkoinquiry.org/files/2015/03/lit110315.pdf.

21. Ibid.; Goldfarb, *Death of a Dissident*, 221–225.

22. Litvinenko Inquiry hearings, testimony of Marina Litvinenko, February 2, 2015, 100. https://www.litvinenkoinquiry.org/files/2015/02/lit020 215.pdf.

23. Goldfarb, *Death of a Dissident*, 3–19.

24. Ibid., 12.

25. Ibid., 333.

26. *The Owen Report*, 52–54. For a copy of the training video, with Litvinenko's photograph being fired at, see https://www.litvinenkoinquiry .org/files/2015/04/INQ017680wb.mp4.

27. Litvinenko Inquiry hearings, testimony of Alex Goldfarb, February 4, 2015, 128-9,. https://www.litvinenkoinquiry.org/files/2015/02/lit040215 .pdf.

28. Iuliia Latynina, "Kod dostupa" *Ekho Moskvy*, January 23, 2016, http:// echo.msk.ru/programs/code/1698982-echo/.

29. *The Owen Report*, 100–103.

30. Ibid., 68–71.

31. Litvinenko Inquiry evidence, https://www.litvinenkoinquiry.org/files /2015/03/BLK000049.pdf; https://www.litvinenkoinquiry.org/files/2015 /03/INQ015639.pdf.

32. Litvinenko Inquiry hearings, testimony of Alex Goldfarb, February 4, 2015, 106–107.

33. Litvinenko Inquiry evidence: https://www.litvinenkoinquiry.org/files/2015/03/lit180315.pdf.

34. Litvinenko Inquiry hearings, testimony of Alex Goldfarb, March 18, 2015, 119, https://www.litvinenkoinquiry.org/files/2015/03/lit180315.pdf

35. *The Owen Report*, 86–88.

36. Ibid.

37. Ibid., 80–81. Also see an interview with Lugovoy on *Ekho Moskvy*, October 10, 2016, http://echo.msk.ru/programs/razbor_poleta/1852746-echo/.

38. Litvinenko Inquiry evidence, witness statements of Andrei Lugovoy, https://www.litvinenkoinquiry.org/files/2015/04/INQ001788wb.pdf; https://www.litvinenkoinquiry.org/files/2015/08/INQ001842.pdf.

39. Litvinenko Inquiry evidence INQ017595, Interview with Berezovsky, March 30, 2007.

40. *The Owen Report*, 81.

41. Luke Harding, *A Very Expensive Poison: The Definitive Story of the Murder of Litvinenko and Russia's War with the West* (London: Guardian Books, 2016), 231.

42. Litvinenko Inquiry hearings, testimony of Dean Attew, February 23, 2015, 85–86. https://www.litvinenkoinquiry.org/files/2015/10/lit230215-Redacted.pdf.

43. Litvinenko Inquiry hearings, testimony of Tim Reilly, February 12, 2015, 69. https://www.litvinenkoinquiry.org/files/2015/02/lit120215.pdf.

44. Ibid., 35.

45. *The Owen Report*, 113–116; Harding, *A Very Expensive Poison*, 101–107.

46. Ibid, pp. 72-73; Alex Goldfarb and Anastasia Kirilenko, "Fresh evidence suggests Litvinenko was killed to keep him quiet," *The Guardian*, January 12, 2016, https://www.theguardian.com/world/2016/jan/12/alexander-litvinenko-russia-murder.

47. Litvinenko Inquiry Evidence, translation from a *Novaia gazeta* article, May 24, 2007, https://www.litvinenkoinquiry.org/files/2015/04/INQ015674wb.pdf.

48. Litvinenko Inquiry hearings, testimony of Yuri Shvets, March 12, 2015, 81–83, http://webarchive.nationalarchives.gov.uk/20160613090305/https://www.litvinenkoinquiry.org/hearings.

49. Harding, *A Very Expensive Poison*, 231.

8. The Poisoning

1. Litvinenko Inquiry hearings, testimony of Spencer Scott, February 11, 2015, 37–48, https://www.litvinenkoinquiry.org/files/2015/10/lit110215 -Redacted.pdf.

2. Ibid., pp. 49–50.

3. Litvinenko Inquiry hearings, opening statements, January 27, 2015, 71–73. https://www.litvinenkoinquiry.org/files/2015/10/lit270115-Reda cted.pdf

4. Litvinenko Inquiry hearings, testimony of Tim Reilly, February 12, 2015, 90–94, https://www.litvinenkoinquiry.org/files/2015/02/lit120215.pdf.

5. *The Owen Report*, 132–133.

6. Ibid., 146.

7. Ibid., 142–144.

8. Ibid., 115.

9. Litvinenko Inquiry hearings, testimony of Michael Jolly, July 28, 2015, 74, https://www.litvinenkoinquiry.org/files/2015/07/lit280715.pdf.

10. *The Owen Report*, 152.

11. Ibid., 162.

12. Ibid., 152–163.

13. Litvinenko Inquiry, Witness Statement of Dmitrii Kovtun, June 6, 2015, https://www.litvinenkoinquiry.org/files/2015/07/INQ021208.pdf.

14. *The Owen Report*, 216–225.

15. Litvinenko Inquiry evidence: https://www.litvinenkoinquiry.org/files /2015/04/HMG000358wb.pdf.

16. See the Russian website Agentura.ru for details.

17. Oleg Bukharin, "The FSB and the U.S.-Russian Nuclear Security Partnership, *Nonproliferation Review*, Spring 2003, p. 140, https://www .nonproliferation.org/wp-content/uploads/npr/101buka.pdf.

18. Don Murray, "The Sadistic Poisoning of Alexander Litvinenko," CBC News, December 19, 2006, https://web.archive.org/web/20070103223932 /http://www.cbc.ca/news/reportsfromabroad/murray/20061219.html.

19. Litvinenko Inquiry hearings, Attew witness statement November 23, 2006, https://www.litvinenkoinquiry.org/files/2015/04/INQ005970wb .pdf.

20. *The Owen Report*, 169; Litvinenko Inquiry Hearings, Scaramella testimony, February 25, 2015, 133–135, http://webarchive.nationalarchives

.gov.uk/20160613090305/https://www.litvinenkoinquiry.org/files/2015/02/lit250215.pdf.

21. Litvinenko Inquiry, January 27, 2015, opening statements, 84–86, https://www.litvinenkoinquiry.org/files/2015/10/lit270115-Redacted.pdf.

22. Litvinenko Inquiry hearings, testimony of Craig Mascall, February 26, 2015, 160–170. https://www.litvinenkoinquiry.org/files/2015/10/lit260215-Redacted.pdf; also see evidence for the Inquiry: https://www.litvinenkoinquiry.org/files/2015/04/INQ012408wb.pdf; https://www.litvinenkoinquiry.org/files/2015/04/INQ018199wb.pdf.

23. Litvinenko Inquiry evidence, http://webarchive.nationalarchives.gov.uk/20160613090305/https://www.litvinenkoinquiry.org/files/2015/04/INQ012404wb.pdf.

24. *The Owen Report*, 195; Litvinenko Inquiry hearings, February 25, 2015, testimony of Norbeto Andrade, 120-124, http://webarchive.national archives.gov.uk/20160613090305/https://www.litvinenkoinquiry.org/files/2015/10/lit260215-Redacted.pdf.

25. Litvinenko Inquiry hearings, read testimony of Berezovsky, March 16, 2015, 16. https://www.litvinenkoinquiry.org/files/2015/03/lit160315.pdf.

26. Litvinenko Inquiry hearings, testimony of yaragi Abdul, February 27, 2015, 87-104, http://webarchive.nationalarchives.gov.uk/20160613090305/https://www.litvinenkoinquiry.org/files/2015/10/lit270215-Redacted.pdf; author interview with Akhmed Zakaev, London, February 5, 2015.

27. Interview with Akhmed Zakaev, February 5, 2015.

28. Litvinenko Inquiry Hearings, testimony of Alex Goldfarb, February 4, 2015, 132–159, https://www.litvinenkoinquiry.org/files/2015/02/lit040215.pdf.

29. Ibid.

30. Author's interview with Marina Litvinenko, April 26, 2014.

31. Litvinenko Inquiry hearings, testimony of John Harrison, March 3, 2015, 81-98; evidence, Lugovoy witness statement, October 26, 2011, http://webarchive.nationalarchives.gov.uk/20160613090305/https://www.litvinenkoinquiry.org/files/2015/08/INQ001842.pdf.

32. Litvinenko Inquiry hearings, opening statements, January 27, 2015, 132, https://www.litvinenkoinquiry.org/files/2015/10/lit270115-Redacted.pdf.

33. *The Owen Report*, 180; Interfax, transcript of press conference of A.

Lugovoy and D. Kovtun, May 31, 2007, Inquiry evidence, https://www
.litvinenkoinquiry.org/files/2015/08/INQ001886.pdf.

34. Litvinenko Inquiry, evidence from Marina Wall, July 28, 2015, 63,
https://www.litvinenkoinquiry.org/files/2015/07/lit280715.pdf.

35. Litvinenko Inquiry hearings, testimony of Craig Mascall, February 27,
2015, 76, http://webarchive.nationalarchives.gov.uk/20160613090305
/https://www.litvinenkoinquiry.org/files/2015/10/lit270215-Redacted
.pdf.

36. Litvinenko Inquiry Hearings, Patarkatsishvili evidence read, February 17,
2015, 59, http://webarchive.nationalarchives.gov.uk/20160613090305
/https://www.litvinenkoinquiry.org/files/2015/10/lit170215-Redacted.pdf.

37. Litvinenko Inquiry hearings, Reilly testimony, February 12, 2015, 130.

38. Litvinenko Inquiry evidence, Berezovsky interview with police, March 30,
2007, tape 4, 11, https://www.litvinenkoinquiry.org/files/2015/04/INQ01
7631wb.pdf; tape 5, 11–12, March 30, 2007, https://www.litvinenkoinquiry
.org/files/2015/04/INQ017647wb.pdf.

39. http://en.kremlin.ru/events/president/transcripts/24026.

40. Litvinenko Inquiry evidence, Interfax, transcript of press conference of
A. Lugovoy and D. Kovtun, May 31, 2007, https://www.litvinenkoinquiry
.org/files/2015/08/INQ001886.pdf.

41. Ibid.

42. Litvinenko Inquiry evidence, Lugovoy interview with *El Pais,* https://
www.litvinenkoinquiry.org/files/2015/04/INQ017684wb.pdf.

43. Litvinenko Inquiry evidence, U.S. Embassy Cable, Moscow, September 18, 2007 (confidential), https://www.litvinenkoinquiry.org/files/2015
/07/BLK000057.pdf.

44. https://www.youtube.com/watch?v=WrjUFWnrDy0.

45. See Kseniia Lugovaia's website: http://ksenialugovaya.ru/novosti/.

46. http://www.bbc.com/news/world-europe-16859830.

47. Litvinenko Inquiry evidence, statements from Valter Litvinenko, https://
www.litvinenkoinquiry.org/files/2015/03/INQ014629.pdf; https://www
.litvinenkoinquiry.org/files/2015/03/COM00011004.pdf; https://www
.litvinenkoinquiry.org/files/2015/03/COM00011011.pdf.

48. Litvinenko Inquiry hearings, testimony of Alex Goldfarb, March 17,
2015, 13, https://www.litvinenkoinquiry.org/files/2015/03/lit170315.pdf;
Harding, *A Very Expensive Poison,* 294–298.

49. Litvinenko Inquiry hearings, testimony of Marina Litvinenko, February 2, 2015, 21–22, https://www.litvinenkoinquiry.org/files/2015/02/lit020215.pdf.

50. *The Owen Report*, 246.

51. Knight, "Fatal Poison in London."

52. Jonathan Strong, "Heavy-handed Putin, the *American Thinker*, June 18, 2009.

53. Knight, "Fatal Poison in London."

9. Continued Onslaught Against Kremlin Challengers

1. https://www.congress.gov/bill/110th-congress/house-concurrent-resolution/154/text.

2. https://www.congress.gov/bill/110th-congress/house-concurrent-resolution/151/text.

3. Ray Finch, "Snapshot of a War Crime: The Case of Russian Colonel Yuri Budanov," *PIPSS, The Journal of Power Institutions in Post-Soviet Societies*, Issue 12, 2011, https://pipss.revues.org/3840.

4. As quoted in Luke Harding, *Expelled: A Journalist's Descent into the Russian Mafia State*, (New York: St. Martin's Press, 2012), 86.

5. Finch, "Snapshot of a War Crime."

6. Ibid.

7. Fatima Tlis, "Markelov Assassination Tied to Release of Budanov?" *North Caucasian Weekly*, January 23, 2009, http://www.jamestown.org/programs/nc/single/?tx_ttnews%5Btt_news%5D=34401&cHash=7ae3981d38.

8. *Kavkazskii uzel*, January 20, 2015, http://www.kavkaz-uzel.eu/articles/218822/.

9. Reporters without Borders: May 2, 2011, https://rsf.org/en/news/do-guilty-verdicts-double-murder-mark-beginning-end-impunity.

10. Ibid.

11. RIA Novosti, January 19, 2014: http://ria.ru/spravka/20140119/989790241.html.

12. Olga Malysh, "Why Was Stanislav Markelov Killed," *The Other Russia*, January 23, 2009.

13. Harding, *Expelled*, 89.

14. Ibid., 90.

15. Ibid., 94.

16. Estemirova, Natal'ia, *Lenta.ru*, https://lenta.ru/lib/14199221/.

17. Ibid.

18. Shura Burtin, "Za chto ubili Natashu Estemirovu?" Burtin.livejournal
    .com, July 20, 2009.

19. See the documentary "Kto Ubil Natal'iu Estemirovu," posted on You-
    Tube, May 29, 2015, https://www.youtube.com/watch?v=ly5IbS_uwXY.

20. http://www.waynakh.com/eng/2009/07/all-world-give-reaction-for
    -murder-of-estemirova/.

21. Harding, *Expelled*, 101.

22. https://pen.org/book/salman-rushdie-reads-wild-garlic-gatherers-by
    -natalia-estemirova.

23. Burtin, "Za chto ubili Natashu Estemirovu?"; Danila Gal'perovich,
    "Natal'ia Estemirova: chetyre goda posle ubiistova," Russian Service of
    Voice of America, July 15, 2013, http://www.golos-ameriki.ru/content/dg
    -estemirova/1701906.html.

24. http://hro.rightsinrussia.info/archive/human-rights-defenders/oleg
    -orlov/trial-continues.

25. Gal'perovich, "Natal'ia Estemirova."

26. "On The Killing of Natalia Estemirova," Memorial Website, July 17,
    2009, http://memo.ru/eng/news/index.htm.

27. Burtin, "Za chto ubili Natashu Estemirovu." Also see the website of Me-
    morial for a report on the telephone conversation: http://www.memo.ru
    /2009/07/20/2007095.htm.

28. See Medvedev's telegram to Memorial, July 18, 2009: http://www.memo
    .ru/2009/07/20/2007092.htm; Luke Harding, "Dmitry Medvedev Rejects
    Claim Chechen Leader Ordered Killing," *The Guardian*, July 16, 2009,
    https://www.theguardian.com/world/2009/jul/16/natalia-estemirova
    -killing-russia-chechnya.

29. "Bearing Witness in Chechnya: The Legacy of Natalia Estemirov," Pen
    Center New York, October 23, 2009, https://pen.org/book/conversation
    -elena-milashina-tanya-lokshina.

30. RIA Novosti, April 28, 2011, http://ria.ru/justice/20110428/369088920
    .html.

31. Elena Milashina, "Pokazatel'naia rasprava," *Novaia gazeta*, July 16,
    2012, http://www.novayagazeta.ru/inquests/53550.html.

32. Memorial, *Novaia gazeta* and FIDH (International Federation for Human Rights), "Two Years After the Murder of Natalia Estemirova: The Investigation Continues Along a False Path," September, 2011, http://www .memo.ru/2011/10/19/nesten.pdf. My following discussion draws on this report.

33. Ibid., 10.

34. Ibid., 12.

35. Ibid., 22–23.

36. As quoted in *The Guardian*, July 7, 2009. The reset was officially started in March, 2009, when Secretary of State Hillary Clinton presented Russian Foreign Minister Sergei Lavrov with a prop "reset" button. That the word "reset" was misspelled in Russian may have been a harbinger of the ultimate failure of the new U.S. policy toward Russia.

37. As quoted in *The New York Times*, July 8, 2009.

38. Peter Baker, "Obama Resets Ties With Russia, But Work Remains," *The New York Times*, July 7, 2009, http://www.nytimes.com/2009/07/08 /world/europe/08prexy.html.

39. Mikhail Zygar, "The Reset That Never Was," *Foreign Policy*, December 9, 2016, http://foreignpolicy.com/2016/12/09/the-russian-reset-that -never-was-putin-obama-medvedev-libya-mikhail-zygar-all-the -kremlin-men/.

40. Jan Hornat, "Obama's 'Reset' with Russia: Failure or Lost Opportunity," *Post*, March 15, 2013, http://postnito.cz/obamas-reset-with-russia -failure-or-lost-opportunity/.

41. http://www.heritage.org/research/testimony/2011/07/rethinking-reset -re-examining-the-obama-administration-russia-policy.

42. "Bearing Witness in Chechnya: The Legacy of Natalia Estemirova."

43. "Russia: Bring Natalia Estemirova's Murderers to Justice," Human Rights Watch, July 13, 2012, https://www.hrw.org/news/2012/07/13/russia-bring -natalia-estemirovas-murderers-justice.

44. "Case History: Natalia Estemirova," Frontline Defenders.org, https:// www.frontlinedefenders.org/en/case/case-history-natalia-estemirova #case-update-id-2226.

45. Ali Feruz, "Vse v tom zhe pekle," *Pravozashchita*, July 15, 2016, http:// old.memo.ru/d/267661.html.

10. Boris Berezovsky: Suicide or Murder?

1. Litvinenko Inquiry, witness statement of Michael Cotlick, July 20, 2010, https://www.litvinenkoinquiry.org/files/2015/04/INQ016762wb.pdf.

2. Robert Coalson, "Berezovsky and Putin: The Real Tandem of Putinism?," *RadioFreeEuropeRadioLiberty*, March 24, 2013. http://www.rferl.org/content/russia-berezovsky-death-legacy-analysis-putin/24937601.html.

3. Michael Freedman, "Dark Force," *Forbes*, May 11, 2007, http://www.forbes.com/global/2007/0521/046.html.

4. Nemtsov, *Ispoved' buntarya*, 59–60.

5. Celestine Bohlen, "Russian Security Agencies Raid Media Empire's Offices," *The New York Times*, May 12, 2000, http://www.nytimes.com/2000/05/12/world/russian-security-agencies-raid-media-empire-s-offices.html.

6. Ibid.

7. *Kommersant*, no. 96, May 31, 2000, http://www.kommersant.ru/doc/149293.

8. Ibid.

9. Amy Knight, "The Curse of the *Kursk*," *The Globe and Mail*, August 28, 2000, http://www.theglobeandmail.com/opinion/the-curse-of-the-kursk/article769470/. I should add that I visited Murmansk, the home of the Russian Northern Fleet, in the summer of 2015. Many of the crew from the *Kursk* were from this city. Everyone who I spoke to still has deep resentment toward Putin.

10. Ian Traynor, "Putin Aims *Kursk* Fury at Media," *The Guardian*, August 24, 2000, https://www.theguardian.com/world/2000/aug/25/kursk.russia2. Putin's reaction is similar to that of Donald Trump and his diatribes about "Fake News."

11. http://pandoraopen.ru/2016-01-18/zhyostkaya-kritika-putina-po-povodu-apl-kursk-poslednyaya-peredcha-dorenko-na-ort/.

12. "Berezovsky, Putin, and an Absence of Respect," *The Moscow Times*, March 23, 2013, https://themoscowtimes.com/news/berezovsky-putin-and-an-absence-of-respect-22633.

13. *Kommersant*, November 15, 2000, http://www.kommersant.ru/doc/163303.

14. *Death of a Dissident*, 233.

15. Ibid., 236–238.

16. Ibid., 238–239.

17. Ibid.

18. RIA Novosti, 2/14/2011, http://ria.ru/spravka/20110214/334228053.html.

19. Ibid.

20. *Death of a Dissident*, 248.

21. http://www.compromat.ru/page_18101.htm.

22. Berezovsky interview, *Ekho Moskvy*, January 25, 2006, http://echo .msk.ru/news/302921.html?=last.

23. Litvinenko Inquiry evidence, https://www.litvinenkoinquiry.org/files /2015/08/INQ001875.pdf.

24. http://rumafia.com/en/dosje/38.

25. News.ru.com, February 13, 2008, http://www.newsru.com/world/13feb 2008/badri_umer.html.

26. Masha Gessen, "Comrades-In-Arms," *Vanity Fair*, November 13, 2012, http://www.vanityfair.com/news/politics/2012/11/roman-abramovich -boris-berezovsky-feud-russia.

27. Approved Judgment, Mrs. Justice Gloster, DBE, in the case of Berezovsky vs. Abramovich, August 31, 2012, http://cisarbitration.com/wp -content/uploads/2013/07/Decision-Abramovich-vs.-Berezovsky.pdf.

28. Ibid.; OPUS 2 International, Official Court Reporters, Berezovsky v. Abramovich, Transcript, Day 4, October 6, 2011: http://pravo.ru/store /interdoc/doc/298/Day_4.pdf.

29. http://www.compromat.ru/page_31831.htm.

30. Ian Cobain, "Boris Berezovsky Was 'Depressed After Court Battle With Abramovich,'" *The Guardian*, March 26, 2013, https://www .theguardian.com/world/2014/mar/26/boris-berezovsky-inquest-spoke -suicide-roman-abramovich.

31. Il'ia Zhegulev, "Poslednee inter'viu Borisa Berezovkogo: Ia ne vizhu smysla zhizni," *Forbes*, March 23, 2013, https://web.archive.org/web /20130601170326/http://m.forbes.ru/article.php?id=236176.

32. Ian Cobain, "Boris Berezovsky Inquest Returns Open Verdict on Death," *The Guardian*, March 27, 2014, https://www.theguardian.com/world /2014/mar/27/boris-berezovsky-inquest-open-verdict-death.

33. Claire Duffin, "Billionaire critic of Putin may have been murdered, rules coroner," *The Telegraph*, March 28, 2014, http://www.telegraph .co.uk/news/uknews/10728908/Billionaire-critic-of-Putin-may-have -been-murdered-rules-coroner.html.

34. BBC News, March 27, 2014, http://www.bbc.com/news/uk-england -berkshire-26778866.

35. Mariia Mishina, interview with Sabirova, *Novoe vremia*, March 25, 2013, http://newtimes.ru/stati/novosti/54a0b26a712c900a9594f01abc6f aff6-on-govorul-mne-ochen-ploho.html.

36. Ibid.

37. Author interview with Marina and Anatoly Litvinenko, London April 23, 2014.

38. Patrick Sawer and Tom Parfitt, "Boris Berezovsky: 'My friend Boris would not have taken his own life,'" *The Telegraph*, March 31, 2013, http://www.telegraph.co.uk/news/uknews/9962460/Boris-Berezovsky -My-friend-Boris-would-not-have-taken-his-own-life.html.

39. http://www.vedomosti.ru/finance/articles/2016/07/26/650538 -londonskii-suanachka.

40. As quoted in vesti.ru, May 12, 2013: http://www.vesti.ru/doc.html?id =1083667.

41. Interview with Alex Goldfarb, February 27, 2017.

42. For a complete expose on Stepanova, her husband, and Kliuev, including details of their massive real estate and financial holdings, see the following website: http://russian-untouchables.com/eng/olga-stepanova/. Also see Browder, *Red Notice*, 318–326; 347–353.

43. As quoted in Luke Harding, "Russian with Links to Whistleblower Left UK Day After Death, Court Told," *The Guardian*, May 10, 2016. Also see Robert Mendich, "Russian Lawyer Accused of Being 'Candidate' in Murder of Whistle Blower," *The Telegraph*, May 19, 2016.

44. Tom Parfitt, "Lawyer Denies He Could Have Killed Banker," the *Sunday Times*, May 23, 2016.

45. Luke Harding and Shaun Walker, "'Poisoned' Russian Whistleblower Was Fatalistic over Death Threats," *The Guardian*, May 19, 2015, https://www.theguardian.com/uk-news/2015/may/19/poisoned-russian -whistleblower-was-fatalistic-over-death-threats.

46. John Keenan, "The Strange Death of Alexander Perepilichnny," *Prospect*, September 12, 2016, http://www.prospectmagazine.co.uk/world/the-strange-death-of-alexander-perepilichnny.

47. His Honour Judge Nicholas Hilliard QC, "Inquest into the death of Alexander Perepilichnyy," May 22, 2017, https://www.judiciary.gov.uk/wp-content/uploads/2017/04/perepilichnyy-ruling-on-public-interest-immunity-and-related-issues-20170523.pdf.

11. The Boston Marathon Bombings: Russia's Footprint

1. Eric Schmitt and Michael S. Schmidt, "Two U.S. Agencies Added Boston Bomb Suspect to Watch List," *The New York Times*, April 24, 2013, http://www.nytimes.com/2013/04/25/us/tamerlan-tsarnaev-bomb-suspect-was-on-watch-lists.html?ref=us.

2. House Homeland Security Committee Report, *Preventing Another Boston Marathon Bombing*, April 2015, https://homeland.house.gov/press/homeland-security-committee-releases-follow-report-boston-marathon-bombings/, 11; *The Road to Boston: Counterterrorism Challenges and Lessons From the Marathon Bombings*, House Homeland Security Committee Report, March 2014, https://homeland.house.gov/files/documents/Boston-Bombings-Report.pdf.

3. Masha Gessen, *The Brothers: The Road To An American Tragedy* (New York: Riverhead Books, 2015). Also see Sally Jacobs, David Filipov, and Patricia Wen, "The Fall of the House Tsarnaev," *The Boston Globe*, December 15, 2013, http://www.bostonglobe.com/Page/Boston/2011-2020/WebGraphics/Metro/BostonGlobe.com/2013/12/15tsarnaev/tsarnaev.html.

4. Gessen, *The Brothers*, 63.

5. Ibid., 79–81.

6. Scott Helman and Jenna Russell, *Long Mile Home: Boston Under Attack, the City's Courageous Recovery and the Epic Hunt for Justice* (New York: Dutton, 2014), 35–36.

7. Ibid., 46.

8. U.S. v. Tsarnaev, Jury Trial—Day 51, April 28, 2015, http://thebostonmarathonbombings.weebly.com/uploads/2/4/2/6/24264849/day_51_trial_day_april_28_2015_transcript-defense-witnesses-51.pdf.

9. Ibid.

10. A good example is the network of ten Russians who were residing on the U.S. East Coast and were exposed by the FBI as "sleeper agents" for the SVR in June 2010.

11. Mairbek Vatchagaev, "Why Tamerlan Tsarnaev is Outside of Chechen Mentality," *Eurasia Daily Monitor*, vol. 10, issue 83, May 2, 2013, http://www.jamestown.org/programs/edm/single/?tx_ttnews%5Btt_news%5D=40825&cHash=d5aa5ba44b8d9b178e232d854d1ddde7#.V7s5SbV7fBI.

12. http://www.cnn.com/2013/04/24/us/boston-brainwash/.

13. Transcript of the Tsarnaevs' news conference, April 26, 2013, from *The New York Times*.

14. United States v. Dzhokhar Tsarnaev, Jury Trial—Day 54, May 4, 2015: http://thebostonmarathonbombings.weebly.com/uploads/2/4/2/6/24264849/day_54_trial_day_may_4_2015_transcript.pdf, 72–73.

15. United States v. Dzhokhar Tsarnaev, Jury Trial—Day 56, May 6, 2015, http://thebostonmarathonbombings.weebly.com/uploads/2/4/2/6/24264849/1393_trial_day_56_may_6_2015_transcript.pdf.

16. Christian Caryl, "The Bombers' World," *The New York Review of Books*, 60, no. 19, June 6, 2013, http://www.nybooks.com/articles/2013/06/06/bombers-world/. See also Caryl's interview with Greta Van Susteren, April 29, 2013, http://www.foxnews.com/on-air/on-the-record/index.html#http://video.foxnews.com/v/2338904976001/boston-terror-probe-who-is-the-mysterious-misha/?playlist_id=86925.

17. Irina Gordienko, "Bostonskii vzryvatel' byl davno zariazhen," *Novaia gazeta*, April 27, 2013, http://www.novayagazeta.ru/inquests/57925.html. It is important to note that Gordienko's source was an employee of Dagestan's anti-terrorism center, which is run by the FSB and often leaks misinformation.

18. http://www.fbi.gov/news/pressrel/press-releases/2011-request-for-information-on-tamerlan-tsarnaev-from-foreign-government.

19. Telephone interview with Congressman William Keating, January 16, 2014.

20. *The Road to Boston*, 11.

21. Curiously, during his testimony in June 2013 before the House Judiciary Committee, FBI chief Robert Mueller let it be known that Tamerlan had

come to the FBI's attention on at least two occasions prior to March 2011. In response to a question by Representative Steve King, Mueller allowed that "his name came up in two other cases." He then added that these cases involved two other persons and were later closed. King then asked "So it's reasonable that the letter of March 4, 2011 refocused the FBI on Tamerlan?" Mueller responded: "Absolutely." James Henry, "Missing Evidence of Prior FBI Relationship with Boston Bomber," whowhatwherewhy.org, June 6, 2015, http://whowhatwhy.org/2015/06/06/missing -evidence-of-prior-fbi-relationship-with-boston-bomber-2/.

22. http://www.fbi.gov/news/pressrel/press-releases/2011-request-for -information-on-tamerlan-tsarnaev-from-foreign-government.

23. http://www.masslive.com/news/index.ssf/2017/04/fbi_releases_report _detailing.html.

24. Unclassified Summary of Information Handling and Sharing, Inspector General's report issued April 10, 2014, https://www.oig.dhs.gov /assets/Mgmt/2014/OIG_Bos_Marathon_Bom_Rev_Apr14.pdf.

25. Ibid.

26. "Keating to FBI: We Need Answers on Boston Bombings," press release from Bill Keating, July 31, 2013, https://keating.house.gov/media -center/press-releases/keating-fbi-we-need-answers-boston-bombings.

27. Alan Cullison, "After Murder Suspect's Death, Probe Is Decried, Defended," *The Wall Street Journal*, May 23, 2013, http://www.wsj.com /articles/SB10001424127887323475304578500883785930480.

28. Follow-up interview with Congressman William Keating, June 5, 2015.

29. Transcript of the Tsarnaevs' news conference, April 26, 2013, from *The New York Times*.

30. Tom Balmforth, "Mystery Swirls around Boston Bombing Suspect's Trip to Daghestan," RadioFreeEurope/RadioLiberty, April 22, 2013, http://www.rferl.org/content/tsarnaev-boston-bombings-trip-to -daghestan/24965405.html.

31. Ibid.

32. Zakaev telephone interview from London, June 4, 2015.

33. Gessen, *The Brothers*, 108.

34. U.S. v. Tsarnaev-Jury Trial—Day 52, 26–39, http://thebostonmarathon bombings.weebly.com/uploads/2/4/2/6/24264849/1362_trial_day_52 _april_29_2015_transcript.pdf.

35. U.S. v. Tsarnaev-Jury Trial—Day 52. Also see Simon Shuster, "Exclusive: Dagestani Relative of Tamerlan Tsarnaev is a Prominent Islamist," *Time.com*, May 8, 2013, http://world.time.com/2013/05/08/exclusive -cousin-who-became-close-to-tamerlan-tsarnaev-in-dagestan-is-a -prominent-islamist/.

36. Brian Glyn Williams, *Inferno in Chechnya: The Russian-Chechen Wars, the Alqaeda Myth, and the Boston Marathon Bombings* (Lebanon, NH: University Press of New England, 2015), 250. Terrorism specialist Elena Pokalova concurs: "The spectrum of terrorist attacks perpetrated by the Caucasian Emirate indicates that the threat remains local and targeted against Russia." Pokalova, *Chechnya's Terrorist Network*, 166.

37. Gordienko, "Bostonskii vzryvatel' byl davno zariazhen." Also see Williams, *Inferno in Chechnya*, 247–248.

38. Mairbek Vatchagaev, "Hot Issue—A Profile of Mahmud Mansur Nidal: The Alleged Dagestani Connection to Boston Bomber Tamerlan Tsarnaev," Jamestown Foundation, May 3, 2013, http://www.jamestown.org /single/?tx_ttnews%5Btt_news%5D=40828&no_cache=1#.V8l66rV7fBI.

39. Vatchagaev, "Why Tamerlan Tsarnaev is Outside of Chechen Mentality."

40. "Ziauddin Sardar Explains the Long History of Violence Behind Hizh ut-Tahrir," the *New Statesman*, November 14, 2005, http://web.archive .org/web/20080511175612/http://www.newstatesman.com /200511140010.

41. Jury Trial of Dzhokhar Tsarnaev—Day 50, April 27, 2015, 112–113, http://thebostonmarathonbombings.weebly.com/uploads/2/4/2/6 /24264849/day_50_trial_day_april_27_2015_transcript_defense _witnesses_50.pdf.

42. Williams, *Inferno in Chechnya*, 252.

43. Scott Shane, "Agents Pore Over Suspect's Trip to Russia," *The New York Times*, April 28, 2013, http://www.nytimes.com/2013/04/29/us /tamerlan-tsarnaevs-contacts-on-russian-trip-draw-scrutiny.html?_r=0.

44. Vatchagaev, "Why Tamerlan Tsarnaev is Outside of Chechen Mentality."

45. Tracy Jan, "Suspect returned from Russia 'with a willingness to kill people,' Kerry says," *The Boston Globe*, April 24, 2013, https://www .bostonglobe.com/news/politics/2013/04/24/secretary-state-john-kerry -says-tamerlan-tsarnaev-returned-from-russia-with-willingness-kill -people/59mtQpCSKTKk38udnyybSI/story.html.

46. Janet Reitman, "Jahar's World," *Rolling Stone*, July 17, 2013, http://www.rollingstone.com/culture/news/jahars-world-20130717.

47. Jury Trial of Dzhokar Tsarnaev—Day 50, 92–94.

48. Jury Trial of Dzhokar Tsarnaev—Day 51, April 28, 2015, 135.

49. House Homeland Security Report, March 2014, 15–16.

50. http://www.cnn.com/2015/03/05/us/boston-marathon-bombing-trial-help/.

51. House Homeland Security Report, March 2014, 7.

52. See a video of Putin's comments: http://rt.com/news/putin-boston-bombing-terrorists-381/.

53. See Amy Knight, "Playing Moscow's Game," *NYR Daily*, June 1, 2013, http://www.nybooks.com/daily/2013/06/01/syria-terrorism-playing-moscows-game/.

54. Valery Dzutsati, "Russian Security Services Offer Surprising Revelations about Boston Bombings," *Eurasian Daily Monitor*, 10, no. 80, April 29, 2013, https://jamestown.org/program/russian-security-services-offer-surprising-revelations-about-boston-bombings-2/.

55. "Foreign Fighters: An Updated Assessment of the Flow of Foreign Fighters into Syria and Iraq," The Soufran Group, December 2015, http://soufangroup.com/wp-content/uploads/2015/12/TSG_ForeignFightersUpdate3.pdf.

56. Paul A. Goble, "Number of Russian Citizens Fighting for ISIS in Syria Up Dramatically Last Year," Euromaidan Press, April 21, 2017, http://euromaidanpress.com/2017/04/21/number-of-russian-citizens-fighting-for-isis-in-syria-up-dramatically-in-last-year-euromaidan-press/#arvlbdata.

57. Michael Weiss, "Russia's Playing a Double Game with Islamic Terror," *Daily Beast*, August 23, 2015, https://counterjihadreport.com/2015/08/25/russias-playing-a-double-game-with-islamic-terror/.

58. Ibid.

12. Another Democrat Falls Victim: The Nemtsov Murder and Its Aftermath

1. See Amy Knight, "Russia: Another Dead Democrat," *NYR Daily*, March 2, 2015, http://www.nybooks.com/daily/2015/03/02/russia-another-dead-democrat/.

2. See the 2015 film "My Friend Boris Nemtsov," by Zosia Rodevich, https://www.google.com/search?q=zosia+rodevich+my+friend+boris+YouTube&ie=utf-8&oe=utf-8#q=zosia+rodevich+my+friend+boris+nemtsov.

3. https://www.rt.com/news/236387-reaction-provocation-nemtsov-murder/.

4. See "Boris Nemtsov's Mother: 'This is Unbearably Hard for Me," RFERL, February 26, 2016, http://www.rferl.org/content/boris-nemtsov-mother-this-is-unbearably-hard-for-me/27575931.html; and "My Friend Boris Nemtsov."

5. Yelena Dikun, "Profile of Boris Nemtsov: Russia's newest first deputy premier," *PRISM* (The Jamestown Foundation), 3, Issue 5, April 18, 1997, https://web.archive.org/web/20070930191549/http://www.jamestown.org/publications_details.php?search=1&volume_id=4&issue_id=189&article_id=2244.

6. Ibid. Obituary of Boris Nemtsov, *The Guardian*, March 1, 2015, https://www.theguardian.com/world/2015/mar/01/boris-nemtsov.

7. Nemtsov, *Ispoved' buntarya*, 52.

8. Ibid., p. 62.

9. *Putin. Itogi.*

10. See Knight, "The Truth About Putin and Medvedev."

11. *Zimnyaya Olimpiada v Subtropikakh. Nezavisimyi Ekspertnyi Doklad [Winter Olympics in the Subtropics: An Independent Expert Report]* by Boris Nemstov and Leonid Martynyuk, Moscow, May 2013. See my piece on the report, "Putin's Downhill Race," *The New York Review of Books,* 60, no. 14, September 26, 2013, http://www.nybooks.com/articles/2013/09/26/putins-downhill-race/.

12. http://www.foreign.senate.gov/imo/media/doc/Nemtsov_Testimony.pdf.

13. See an interview with Prokhorov by Ksenia Novikova on *Democracy.net*, April 27, 2017, https://www.opendemocracy.net/od-russia/ksenia-novikova/it-s-deeply-personal-matter-interview-with-vadim-prokhorov-boris-nemtsov-s.

14. As quoted in Andrew Kramer, "Fear Envelops Russia after Killing of Putin Critic Boris Nemtsov," *The New York Times*, February 28, 2015, http://www.nytimes.com/2015/03/01/world/europe/killing-of-boris-nemtsov-putin-critic-breeds-fear-in-russia.html.

15. The complete interview is published in Russian on Nemtsov's website, nemtsov.ru.

16. See Milov's detailed analysis of the murder on his Live Journal page on March 2, 2015: http://v-milov.livejournal.com/404358.html. Also, see Amy Knight, "A Kremlin Conspiracy Gone Wrong?'" *NYR Daily*, March 15, 2015.

17. Catherine A. Fitzpatrick, "Putin's Usual Suspects: The Bullshit Chechen-Charlie Hebdo Connection," *Daily Beast*, March 9, 2015, http://www.thedailybeast.com/articles /2015/03/09/putin-s-usual-suspects-the-bull shit-chechen-charlie-hebdo-connection.html.

18. See the 2016 film on the murder by Leonid Martynyuk and Andrei Pointkovsky, "That Doesn't Mean You Have to Kill Him," available on YouTube: https://www.youtube.com/watch?v=uT7QmSbM4A8.

19. Milov on LiveJournal.

20. Interview on NPR's *Morning Edition,* March 5, 2015: http://www.npr .org/sections/parallels/2015/03/05/390754346/boris-nemtsov-he -directed-his-words-against-putin-himself.

21. http://www.interpretermag.com/alexey-navalny-on-the-murder-of -boris-nemtsov/.

22. Ibid.

23. Fitzpatrick, "Putin's Usual Suspects."

24. https://life.ru/t/новости/150539?from=lifenews.ru; *https://life.ru/t /новости/150563.*

25. Sergei Mashkin, "Svidetel' ne uznal ubiitsu Borisa Nemtsova," *Kommersant*, March 27, 2015, http://www.kommersant.ru/doc/2695010. Evgenii was later identified as Evgenii Molodykh and testified at the trial that the shooter resembled the accused triggerman, Zaur Dadaev.

26. Grigorii Tumanov, "Oppozitsiia seichas perezhivaet ne luchshie vre-mena," *Kommersant*, November 27, 2015, http://www.kommersant.ru /doc/2865042.

27. Sergei Mashin, "V ubiistve Borisa Nemtsova poiavilis' gashish i geroin," *Kommersant*, November 13, 2105, http://kommersant.ru/doc /2852232.

28. Telephone interview with Zakaev, March 13, 2015; Knight, "A Kremlin Conspiracy Gone Wrong."

29. Film "That Doesn't Mean You Have to Kill Him."

30. Shaun Walker, "Putin Makes First Appearance in 11 days: 'It Would Be Boring Without Gossip,'" *The Guardian*, March 16, 2015, https://www.theguardian.com/world/2015/mar/16/vladimir-putin-makes-first-public-appearance-amid-health-speculations.

31. https://openrussia.org/post/view/3463/.

32. http://www.cnn.com/2015/10/09/world/nemtsova-russia-putin-amanpour/.

33. http://www.newsru.com/russia/31oct2015/most.html.

34. http://en.news-4-u.ru/fso-responded-to-the-request-gudkov-on-the-protection-of-the-moskvoretsky-bridge-and-he-concluded-the-kremlin-is-in-danger.html.

35. Mariya Bondarenko, "Chubais rasskazal o svoikh sovetakh docheri Nemtsova naschet doprosa Kadyrova," RBC, September 1, 2015, http://www.rbc.ru/politics/01/09/2015/55e5c59d9a79476e89986c47.

36. "Gosobvineniye na sude ob ubiistve Nemtsova usileno," Interfax, August 18, 2016. http://www.interfax.ru/russia/524205.

37. Catherine A. Fitzpatrick, "Russia's Investigative Committee Asked Gen. Zolotov to Probe Violations by Sever Battalion Linked to Nemtsov Murder Suspects," the *Interpreter*, May 18, 2016, http://www.interpretermag.com/russia-update-may-16-2016-2/.

38. The *Insider: rassledovanie reportazhi analitika*, February 3, 2017, http://theins.ru/opinions/43609.

39. Egor Skovoroda, "Sud zavershil rassledovanie ubiistva Borisa Nemtsova. Kakovy ego (neuteshitel'nye) itogi?," *Meduza*, May 31, 2017, https://meduza.io/feature/2017/05/31/sud-zavershil-rassledovanie-ubiystva-borisa-nemtsova-kakovy-ego-neuteshitelnye-itogi; Igor' Murzin, "Vernemsia k teme o role v ubiistve Nemtsova modeli Anny Duritskoi," *Kasparov.ru,* May 30, 2017.

40. Interview with Prokhorov.

41. See Knight, "A Kremlin Conspiracy Gone Wrong."

42. https://humanrightscommission.house.gov/events/hearings/worldwide-threats-media-freedom.

43. See Kara-Murza's interview with Voice of America (in Russian), April 30, 2015, http://www.golos-ameriki.ru/a/karamurza-on-nemtsov-list/2743596.html; "Kongressu predstavili 'spisok Nemtsova, " *Kommersant,*

April 24, 2015. https://web.archive.org/web/20150424050051/http://
kommersant.ru/doc/2715191.

44. See the blog by Vadim Birstein, Russian Retropective, "Kara-Murza's
Brave Fight," http://www.vbirstein.com/karamurza/. Also see Masha
Gessen, "'Total Catastrophie of the Body: A Russian Story," *NYR Daily*,
February 21, 2017, http://www.nybooks.com/daily/2017/02/21/total
-catastrophe-of-the-body-kara-murza-poisoning/.

45. Ibid.

46. http://video.foxnews.com/v/5311416183001/?#sp=show-clips.

47. https://www.mccain.senate.gov/public/index.cfm/floor-statements?ID
=D0AAD5B4-2827-484A-B0CD-088C1536DCAD.

48. http://abcnews.go.com/International/putin-friend-poisoned-russian
-activists-wife-tells-trump/story?id=45310449.

13. Kadyrov, Putin, and Power in the Kremlin

1. Fitzpatrick, "Putin's Usual Suspects."

2. See Amy Knight, "The Kremlin's Chechen Dragon," *NYR Daily*,
May 27, 2010, http://www.nybooks.com/daily/2010/05/27/kremlins
-chechen-dragon/.

3. Nemtsov, *Ispoved'*, 129–130.

4. Ilya Yashin, "A Threat To National Security: An Independent Expert
Report," Moscow, Februrary 2016, http://www.4freerussia.org/wp
-content/uploads/2016/03/A-Threat-to-National-Security.pdf.

5. As quoted in Yashin, "A Threat to National Security."

6. *North Caucasus Weekly*, no. 45, vol. 7, November 2006., https://
jamestown.org/program/movladi-baisarov-killed-in-moscow-2/.

7. Knight, "The Kremlin's Chechen Dragon."

8. Joshua Yaffa, "Putin's Dragon," *The New Yorker*, February 8 and 15,
2016. That Aliyev became a shameless apologist for the Kadyrov regime,
after a career as an independent journalist, is clear from an interview he
gave to *Prague Watchdog* on May 8, 2008. When asked about the testi-
monies of victims of Kadyrov on widespread torture and summary executions that were collected by human-rights activists, he responded: "The
people who said there was torture and killing did not present me with any
evidence," http://www.watchdog.cz/?show=000000-000004-000001
-000226&lang=1.

9. "The Family: A Film about Ramzan Kadyrov, Whom Putin Calls a Son," Open Russia, May 25, 2015, http://www.khodorkovsky.com/the-family-a-film-about-ramzan-kadyrov/.

10. "Counter-terrorism in the North Caucasus: A Human Rights Perspective. 2014–first half of 2016." Report by the Memorial Human Rights Centre, Moscow, 2016. http://memohrc.org/sites/default/files/doklad_severnyy_kavkaz_-_angl.pdf, 76.

11. Ibid., 21–24.

12. "Like Walking A Minefield: Vicious Crackdown on Critics in Russia's Chechen Republic," Human Rights Watch, August 30, 2016, https://www.hrw.org/report/2016/08/30/walking-minefield/vicious-crackdown-critics-russias-chechen-republic.

13. Elena Milashina, "Ubiistvo chesti" *Novaia gazeta*, April 3, 2017, https://www.novayagazeta.ru/articles/2017/04/01/71983-ubiystvo-chesti; Andrew Kramer, "'They Starve You. They Shock You.' Inside the Anti-Gay Program in Chechnya," *The New York Times*, April 21, 2017.

14. Elena Milashine, V Chechne idut profilakticheskie raboty," *Novaia gazeta*, April 24, 2017, https://www.novayagazeta.ru/articles/2017/04/24/72263-v-chechne-idut-profilakticheskie-raboty. Also see Amy Knight, "Putin's Monster," *NYR Daily*, May 19, 2017, http://www.nybooks.com/daily/2017/05/19/putins-monster-ramzan-kadyrov/.

15. "The Family."

16. Brian Whitmore, "Ramzan Kadyrov: The Kremlin's Id," *RadioLiberty/RadioFreeEurope*, January 19, 2016. http://www.rferl.org/content/the-kremlins-id/27497053.html.

17. Yashin, "A Threat to National Security," 20.

18. "The Family."

19. Ibid.

20. Yashin, "A Threat to National Security," 24.

21. Ibid., 25.

22. Paul Bond, "Chechen Leader Asks Hilary Swank for Proof of Charitable Donation," the *Hollywood Reporter*, February 16, 2012, http://www.hollywoodreporter.com/news/hilary-swank-ramzan-kadyrov-chechen-prime-minister-292049.

23. http://memohrc.org/sites/default/files/doklad_severnyy_kavkaz_-_angl.pdf, 34–35.

24. Tanya Lokshina, "Public Humiliation: Chechen Leader's Simple Strategy to Control Social Media," *The Guardian*, October 10, 2016, https://www.theguardian.com/world/2016/oct/10/public-humiliation-chechen-leader-ramzan-kadyrov-strategy-control-social-media.

25. Yashin, "A Threat to National Security," 12.

26. Thomas Grove, "The Strongman of Instagram," the *Wall Street Journal*, August 26, 2016, http://www.wsj.com/articles/the-strongman-of-instagram-1472221224; "Like Walking a Minefield."

27. Neil MacFarquhar, "A Warlord's Cuddly Makeover, With a Nod to Donald Trump," *The New York Times,* November 22, 2016, http://www.nytimes.com/2016/11/22/world/europe/chechnya-ramzan-kadyrov-donald-trump.html.

28. https://www.instagram.com/p/BApvJo8tBVe/.

29. BBC News, February 1, 2016, http://www.bbc.com/news/world-europe-35459613.

30. *The Moscow Times*, February 1, 2016.

31. Ramzan Kadyrov, "Shakaly budut nakazany po zakonu Rossiiskoi Federatsii, " *Izvestiia*, January 18, 2016, http://izvestia.ru/news/601935.

32. Anna Nemtsova, "Putin's Out-of-Control Creature in Chechnya," *Politico,* February 2, 2016, http://www.politico.com/magazine/story/2016/02/how-putin-created-a-monster-in-chechnya-213583.

33. Whitmore, "Ramzan Kadyrov."

34. *Komsomol'skaia pravda*, May 6, 2013, http://www.kp.ru/online/news/1432736/.

35. Instagram.com, May 17, 2015, https://www.instagram.com/p/2xw_OjCRsw/.

36. https://lenta.ru/news/2015/03/13/kadyrov_dadaev/.

37. Elena Milashina, "Prokliatie Ichkerii. Doklad Novoi Gazety," *Novaia gazeta*, October 3, 2016, https://www.novayagazeta.ru/articles/2016/10/03/70025-proklyatie-ichkerii-doklad-novoy-gazety.

38. Ibid.

39. Ibid.

40. Catherine A. Fitzpatrick, "What Has Kadyrov Been Up To?" the *Interpreter*, August 26, 2016, http://www.interpretermag.com/what-has-kadyrov-been-up-to-quietly-cultivating-regional-and-kremlin-officials-now-a-meeting-with-putin/#14930.

41. Ibid.

42. MacFarquhar, "A Warlord's Cuddly Makeover."

43. Ekaterina Sokrianskaia, "Chechnya's Anti-Gay Program," *The New York Times*, May 3, 2017, https://www.nytimes.com/2017/05/03/opinion/chechnyas-anti-gay-pogrom.html?_r=0.

44. Neil MacFarquhar, "Putin Dismisses Sergei Ivanov, a Longtime Ally, as Chief of Staff, *New York Times*, August 12, 2016, http://www.nytimes.com/2016/08/13/world/europe/sergei-ivanov-putin-russia.html?_r=0.

45. Andrei Sukhotin, "Istochnik: Uliukaev Ne Bral Deneg V Ruki," *Novaia gazeta*, November 15, 2016, https://www.novayagazeta.ru/news/2016/11/15/126584-istochnik-ulyukaev-ne-bral-deneg-v-ruki; http://carnegie.ru/commentary/?fa=66244.

46. http://www.upstreamonline.com/live/1211633/sechin-took-part-in-ulyukayev-sting.

47. MacFarquhar, "Putin Dismisses Sergei Ivanov."

48. https://www.youtube.com/watch?v=qrwlk7_GF9g&t=441s.

49. Shaun Walker, "Alexei Navalny on Putin's Russia: 'All autocractic regimes come to an end,'" *The Guardian*, April 29, 2017, https://www.theguardian.com/world/2017/apr/29/alexei-navalny-on-putins-russia-all-autocratic-regimes-come-to-an-end.

Afterword

1. Michael Gordon, "Russia Deploys Missile, Violating Treaty and Challenging Trump," *The New York Times,* February 14, 2017, https://www.nytimes.com/2017/02/14/world/europe/russia-cruise-missile-arms-control-treaty.html?_r=0.

2. Anna Nemtsova, "Is Putin as Popular as Trump Says?" the *Daily Beast*, September 9, 2016, http://www.thedailybeast.com/articles/2016/09/09/is-putin-as-popular-as-trump-says.

3. *Stratfor Market Watch*, January 31, 2017, http://www.marketwatch.com/story/russia-is-a-mess-the-poverty-rate-is-soaring-and-only-10-of-85-regions-are-financially-stable-2017-01-31.

4. See Amy Knight, "Why is Putin So Popular?" *Prospect*, December 2014, http://www.prospectmagazine.co.uk/magazine/why-is-putin-so-popular.

5. Transcript of interview with Trump, *The New York Times*, April 5, 2017, https://www.nytimes.com/2017/04/05/us/politics/donald-trump-interview-new-york-times-transcript.html

6. Gardiner Harris, "Tillerson Warns Russia on Syria, Saying Assad Era is 'Coming to an End,'" *The New York Times*, April 11, 2017, https://www.nytimes.com/2017/04/11/world/europe/russia-syria-rex-tillerson.html

7. Neil MacFarquhar and Alison Smale, "Angela Merkel Presses Vladimir Putin on Treatment of Gays and Jehovah's Witnesses," *The New York Times*, May 2, 2017, https://www.nytimes.com/2017/05/02/world/europe/merkel-putin-russia.html?_r=0.

8. Alison Smale and Steven Erlanger, "Merkel, After Discordant G-7 Meeting, Is Looking Past Trump," *The New York Times,* May 28, 2017, https://www.nytimes.com/2017/05/28/world/europe/angela-merkel-trump-alliances-g7-leaders.html.

9. "Illusions vs Reality: Twenty-Five Years of U.S. Policy Toward Russia, Ukraine and Eurasia," Carnegie Endowment for International Peace, February 9, 2017, http://carnegieendowment.org/2017/02/09/illusions-vs-reality-twenty-five-years-of-u.s.-policy-toward-russia-ukraine-and-eurasia-pub-67859.

10. Sheera Frenkel, "The New Handbook for Cyberwarfare is Being Written By Russia," *BuzzFeed*, March 19, 2017, https://www.buzzfeed.com/sheerafrenkel/the-new-handbook-for-cyberwar-is-being-written-by-russia?utm_term=.vuBNLxo4w#.vfLgLKeDz.

11. Ford, *Political Murder*, 388.

INDEX